The Matrix and Meaning

"Finally, a Jungian book on character that links sensitive clinical insights to the mythopoetic imagination and to the developmental dynamism of the archetypal psyche. Nancy Dougherty and Jacqueline West have written an original and deeply significant book that brings together the best insights of contemporary analysis and is a virtual map of the soul. A must-read for clinicians and scholars of all persuasions, this is a book on character that has character, and one destined to become a classic in the field."

Stanton Marlan, Ph.D., is a Jungian analyst and adjunct Professor of Clinical Psychology at Duquesne University. The author of *The Black Sun: The Alchemy and Art of Darkness*, Dr. Marlan is also the prior editor of the *Journal of Jungian Theory and Practice*, and editor of two previous books on alchemy.

"This book manages to weave together threads of the archetypal and the clinical into a sophisticated and poetic exploration of spirit and soul. It presents a unique model of character disorders that reveals the relationships between diagnostic categories and is a must-read for therapists drawn to the clinical acumen of Nancy McWilliam's *Psychoanalytic Diagnosis*. Grounded in practical examples, the authors masterfully guide the reader, through a rich integration of images and clinical wisdom, to understanding that 'we transform through our character structures, not in spite of them.'"

Thomas Kelly, M.S.W. is a senior training analyst and prior President of the Inter-Regional Society of Jungian Analysts, now serves on the Executive Board of the IAAP (the International Association of Analytic Psychology), and is the current President of the Council of North American Societies of Jungian Analysts (CNASJA). He has a private practice in Montreal and teaches and lectures widely.

"Too much psychotherapy emphasizes description, category, treatment plan, and ignores the dynamism of each human soul. In *The Matrix and Meaning of Character*, Jungian analysts Dougherty and West revivify our understanding and our language around the many ways psyche organizes itself in response to early traumata. They remind us that psyche is a dynamic energy system, not a set of clinical categories, and they provide case studies and archetypal stories which illustrate this shape-shifting drama playing through that fragile field and form we call character."

James Hollis, Ph.D., Jungian Analyst, and Director of Jung Center of Houston, TX, has authored numerous books, including *Under Saturn's Shadow: The Wounding and Healing of Men*; *The Middle Passage: From Misery to Meaning in Midlife*; *Creating a Life: Finding Your Individual Life*; and *Mythologems: Incarnations of the Invisible World*.

"The clinical world has long been divided between those who depend on diagnosis as a guide, and those who find diagnosis unacceptably restrictive and lifeless. In this wonderfully useful book, the authors provide us with a diagnostic system that is instructive, comprehensive, and, at last, illuminated by the poetry of archetype. I expect that this book will, for years to come, provide clinicians with a way of not only understanding one's choice of defensive strategy, but also seeing the rich beauty of character."

Michael Kahn, Ph.D., author of *Basic Freud: Psychoanalytic Thought for the 21st Century*, has also written *Between Therapist and Client* and *The Tao of Conversation* and is a clinical psychologist in private practice. Professor Emeritus at the University of California, Santa Cruz, Dr. Kahn is presently director of a counseling center at the California Institute of Integral Studies where he trains psychotherapists.

"At last! An original new work that puts 'character' rather than 'neurosis' at the heart of our psychic realities and wounds, that pours the fresh water of living language over those arid diagnostic categories, and does it with imagination, intelligence, sensitivity, and the power of story. Read it. Just do it."

Lyn Cowan, Ph.D., a senior training analyst and prior President of the Inter-Regional Society of Jungian Analysts is the author of *Portrait of the Blue Lady: The Character of Melancholy*; *Tracking the White Rabbit: A Subversive View of Modern Culture*; and *Masochism, A Jungian View*.

"This is a book for which those of us who practice the everyday clinical work of depth psychology have been waiting a long time. While honoring the archetypal mode of diagnosis, it bridges the gap between Freudian memory and Jung's vision of the intentionality of the psyche, between the developmental and symbolic ways of seeing personality. The thrust of the book is a bold analytic reimagination, correcting Freud's view of personality limitation and Jung's fantasy of personality transcendence. Instead the authors see within the confines of character a destiny enlivened by spirit, a world of wholeness emerging from within the grain of character. They do so by presenting us with an original developmental model, which they then animate with images from myth and fairy tale. The result is an original and valuable container for the main streams of depth psychology."

Ronald Schenk, Ph.D., President of the Inter-Regional Society of Jungian Analysts, has authored several books, including *The Soul of Beauty: Toward a Psychology of Appearance*; *Dark Light: The Appearance of Death in Everyday Life*; and *The Sunken Fish, the Wasted Fisher, the Pregnant Fish: Postmodern Reflections on Depth Psychology*. He has a private practice in both Dallas and Houston, TX and lectures widely.

"This original Matrix of archetypal and developmental concepts will be useful for the seasoned practitioner and student alike, and is likely to become a much-used reference. The work's capacity to orient the clinician amidst diagnostic considerations and movements within analysis is immensely practical and inspiring."

Catharine J. Jones, M. Div., LCSW, current President and former Director of Training at the C. G. Jung Institute of Chicago, lectures both nationally and internationally.

"For the most illuminating view of Character as the *source* of healing and transformation, this book is the book to read. While, 'character' is most often referred to as disorder, diagnosis absent paradox is absent meaning. It cannot point the way to the wellspring, the source, of healing – one's own character and one's own soul. Jacqueline West and Nancy Dougherty have cleared a path to that paradox and show us how to hold the resulting tension. They have done so in a well articulated and poetic way."

Jerome S. Bernstein, M.A., is the author of *Living in the Borderland: The Evolution of Consciousness and the Challenge of Healing Trauma*, as well as *Power and Politics: The Psychology of Soviet-American Partnership*. Prior President of the C. G. Jung Institute of Santa Fe, Mr. Bernstein is in private practice in Santa Fe, New Mexico.

Character structures underlie everyone's personality. When rigidly defended, they limit us; yet as they become more flexible, they can reveal sources of animation, renewal and authenticity.

The Matrix and Meaning of Character guides the reader into an awareness of the archetypal depths that underlie character structures, presenting an original developmental model in which current analytic theories are synthesized. The authors examine nine character structures, animating them with fairy tales, mythic images and case material, creating a bridge between the traditional language of psychopathology and the universal realm of image and symbol.

This book will appeal to all analytical psychologists, psychoanalysts and psychotherapists who want to strengthen their clinical expertise. It will help clinicians to extend their clinical insights beyond a strictly behavioural, medical or cognitive approach, revealing the potential of the human spirit.

Nancy J. Dougherty, M.S.W., is senior training analyst in the InterRegional Society of Jungian Analysts and the C. G. Jung Institute of Chicago. She is coordinator of training in the Florida Association of Jungian Analysts Seminar and is in private practice in Naples, Florida.

Jacqueline J. West, Ph.D., is President and Training Director of the C. G. Jung Institute of Santa Fe, a senior training analyst in the InterRegional Society of Jungian Analysts and Jung Institute in Santa Fe. She is in private practice in Sante Fe, New Mexico.

The Matrix and Meaning of Character

An Archetypal and Developmental Approach

Nancy J. Dougherty &
Jacqueline J. West

 Routledge
Taylor & Francis Group

LONDON AND NEW YORK

First published 2007 by Routledge
27 Church Road, Hove, East Sussex, BN3 2FA

Simultaneously published in the USA and Canada
by Taylor & Francis Inc
270 Madison Avenue, New York, NY 10016

Routledge is an imprint of the Taylor & Francis Group, an informa business

© 2007 Nancy J. Dougherty & Jacqueline J. West

Typeset in Times by Garfield Morgan, Swansea, West Glamorgan
Printed and bound in Great Britain by T J International Ltd, Padstow,
Cornwall
Paperback cover design by Anú Design

This publication has been produced with paper manufactured to strict
environmental standards and with pulp derived from sustainable forests.

British Library Cataloguing in Publication Data
A catalogue record for this book is available from the British Library

Library of Congress Cataloging in Publication Data
Dougherty, Nancy J.
  The matrix and meaning of character : an archetypal and developmental
approach / Nancy J. Dougherty & Jacqueline J. West.
      p. cm.
  Includes bibliographical references and index.
  ISBN 0-415-40301-4 (hbk) – ISBN 0-415-40300-6 (pbk) 1. Character. 2.
Personality. 3. Archetype (Psychology) I. West, Jacqueline J. II. Title.
  BF818.D68 2007
  155.2–dc22
                                                              2006021638

ISBN 978-0-415-40301-6 hbk
ISBN 978-0-415-40300-9 pbk

Contents

Acknowledgements

More people have contributed to the publication of our book than we can possibly name. Teachers, mentors, analysts, friends, colleagues, candidates and most particularly our patients have all informed and enriched our hearts and minds.

From among these many, we would like jointly to name a number of individuals who have contributed to our moving this work into the world: Jerome Bernstein, Gus Cwik, Kate Hawes at Routledge, Catharine Jones, Tom Kelly, Claudette Kilkarney, Stan Marlan, Clarissa Pinkola Estés, Ron Schenck, and Murray Stein.

In addition, I (ND) would like to express my appreciation to Lois Khan, Lueva Lerner, Harriet Gordon Machtiger, Laura McGrew, Sharon Smith, and Bill Walker for their generous support and personal warmth and kindness. And I (JJW) would like to thank Joan Buresh, Jim Boggs, Daniel Bordeleau, Joan Hertzberg, Michael and Virginia Kahn, Deanne Neumann, Meredith Oenning, and Tim Sanderson for their steadfast belief in me and their invaluable friendship.

We would like to recognize our Jungian institutes as essential training and collegial vessels: The Inter-Regional Society of Jungian Analysts, the C. G. Jung Institute of Chicago, and the C. G. Jung Institute of Santa Fe.

We each offer an enthusiastic round of thanks to our ever-present families. We treasure and are grateful for the life affirming gifts of those of you who grew up around us as we wrote. For JJW: Joshua and Devorah. For ND: Randy, Alex and Jayme, and now Margaret, Suzanne and Jackson Randall.

We also each wholeheartedly thank our husbands whose daily presence and love in our lives has provided essential support and optimal challenge. I (JJW) would like to celebrate you, Geoffrey, for how your remarkably robust love, your stimulating companionship, and your persistent individuality grace and enliven my life. I (ND) would like to express my deepest appreciation of Sandy, whose capacity for play, steady presence and attention to our daily lives is sustaining and whose dreams of sailing warm waters has created the home and the family we are today.

Most centrally, we would like to express gratitude to each other, to our friendship, camaraderie, and the resilient sense of meaning and purpose that we share about this work. Faced with our undeniable differences, we turned towards curiosity about each other. Supported by tenacity and love, we learned through dialogue about the intricacies of our personal character differences. These dialogues not only led us into an appreciation of how character structures can serve to both defend and inspirit relationship and individuation, but they also directed us towards the differentiation of the various character structures that are the subject of this book. This process has nurtured us deeply, not only personally but professionally. We each feel remarkably honored to have such a fine companion in this journey.

Finally, we thank the wellsprings of spirit that have so generously nourished us along the way.

Introduction

The Matrix from which character emerges

The breath of Isis

One of the guiding inspirations for this book has been the magnificent Egyptian myth of Isis and Osiris. This great story has always touched our hearts, particularly the moment when the breath of Isis brings the fragmented body of Osiris back to life.[1] In the myth:

> Isis and Osiris ruled over the beloved kingdom of the ancient Egyptians. In the midst of great harmony and wholeness, Osiris' evil brother Set began to gather power. Set captured his envied brother and hacked his body into thirteen pieces, which he scattered and hid along the Nile. In tremendous grief, Isis roamed the banks of the Nile, carrying a winnowing basket, collecting the pieces of Osiris. She traveled into the underworld, where she assembled the pieces of her husband upon an altar. She flew over his re-membered body and breathed into his mouth. His desire for her was awakened, and he inseminated her. This union created the divine child Horus, the harbinger of the new world.

Our aim in this book is to enliven the body of knowledge about character structures by re-membering the mythological themes that underlie human development. As clinicians we have learned a vocabulary for describing patterns of character structures. This diagnostic language is a highly developed and remarkably rich resource. Yet, when it is used routinely and

inattentively, it loses meaning and value. In the field, concretized and reduced, it can be used in ways that are neither respectful to patients nor conducive to creative treatment. Many therapists are therefore reluctant to use this vocabulary. Indeed, our progressively differentiated clinical language can become like the fragmented body of Osiris; it becomes broken into discrete and relatively lifeless bits. In that process, we lose sight of the living meaning within these deadened words. For example, "narcissism" is a term pregnant with meaning that can inform wholeness. Archetypal breath can awaken this meaning and thus enliven the spirit hidden within such a term. Enlivened diagnostic language can then be used to sharpen and simultaneously deepen and even direct clinical work.

Before we proceed any further, we would like to encourage you to explore your present conceptualizations about character structures. Let us ask several questions: Are you comfortable with using the language of psychopathology? Do you tend to avoid using it? If you use it, do you differentiate among your patients between neuroses and character disorders? Do these distinctions affect your interventions? If you use diagnostic terms, do you think of them as something your patients have, or are they patterns of psyche that are part of the human condition?

We have concluded that identifiable character structures underlie everyone's reality. These structures are described in classical diagnostic language as character disorders. However, we imagine that character exists along a continuum for all of us: from character structure to character disorder, just as a continuum exists from personality to personality disorder. Mixtures of archetypal reality and personal history, numinous energy and early personal wounds are met with defenses employed by the psyche in an attempt to create safety, cohesion, and consistency. The interactions of these factors evolve into identifiable character structures. Thus, one's character structure is an individual portrait that embodies archetypal themes and personal wounds, as well as achievements and developmental defenses.

Etymologically "character" is derived from the Greek *charakter*, to engrave, and contains the Latin root, archetypum, which means original or distinct. Referring to a distinctive quality or an aggregate of distinctive qualities, "character" denotes an individual's pattern of behavior or personality, his traits or qualities (*Webster's Dictionary* 1983: 304). The rich roots of this word inform us that our character is a distinct series of marks on our personality. While we may develop increasingly flexible and fluent ego structures, our individuality is engraved in our character.

Each character structure holds at its core a paradox: it is a defensive structure, as well as an adaptive and prospective profile, informed archetypally and developmentally. Thus, our woundedness, our individuality, and our gifts are directly related. Within one's character structure is the essence of what is needed for transformation and individuation. Indeed, in our own analyses and in our work with patients, we have observed consistently that transformation happens through our character structures, not in spite of them. It is through our woundedness, with its archetypal background, that we can access our deepest healing and creative energies and awaken the process of individuation.

When we were training to become analysts, as we studied together for our comprehensive exams and as we each continued in our analyses, we found that our conversations were enlivened when we began to see diagnostic terms in archetypal language. This was all the more true when we brought ourselves into the picture. We each began to encounter and describe our own personalities, the landscapes of our own psyches, imaged diagnostically and archetypally. Together, we began to see how the patterns within our character structures pervaded our analyses and our lives, and we began to examine how they affected our relationships, with each other, with our families and friends, as well as with our patients.

We describe our experience because we want to encourage you to consider your own underlying character structure. We encourage you, the reader, to consider which character pattern most closely describes your own experience. Do you see yourself as having an underlying pattern most akin to narcissism? borderline dynamics? schizoid reality? This is not an easy question to ask, since this vocabulary is frequently employed to categorize what is abnormal. Used this way, it implicitly separates the therapist and the patient: it is applicable to the patient, while it is not applicable to the therapist. In contrast, we are proposing that the patterns this vocabulary so carefully delineates are applicable to one and all, however difficult they are to recognize and own in ourselves. When we allow ourselves to see these structures as patterns that underlie our own character, we find that we work with patients in a field of mutuality, in contrast to a field of hierarchical distance in which there is the knower and the known. Therefore, we invite you to ask how you see yourself in these terms as we proceed. Feel through and try on the various descriptions of character. When you get a sense of which pattern best describes your underlying character structure, consider how this underlying pattern affects your interactions with others.

When we understand the developmental and archetypal realities of character structure, we can participate in a more informed intersubjective field in which we can engage with another with increased creativity and integrity. Clinically, we can be more discriminating about our patients' needs, including increasing our attunement regarding the impact of our personality upon theirs. Schizoid, borderline, and narcissistic dynamics, for example, have a moment-to-moment impact in an analysis. Recognizing these dynamic states is vital since these powerful processes can eclipse or illumine a therapeutic relationship. Meanwhile these dynamics are, of course, at play in the world at large as well and their exploration can open the doors of our hearts and our imaginations to the depths of human experience and the meaning of our lives.

You might want to jump ahead into the next chapters at this point. Do you respond more intensely to the story about the wicked queen or a frozen child? Would you give anything for love, or are you conservative in all manner of things? Are you more drawn to someone who is witty than another who is wise? For some of you, the following theoretical section in this Introduction is essential before proceeding; for others, diving headlong into the well will suit your fancy better.

An archetypal and developmental Matrix of character structures

Clinical language itself is a system of images, and the phenomena that it imagines are also portrayed in other symbolic systems, e.g. in fairy tales and myths. In clinical language, we talk of people as obsessive-compulsive, borderline, etc. Archetypally, we talk of people as being inspired by Dionysus, living in a glass coffin, entrapped by a tar-baby, serving like Cinderella, etc. Understanding when and how each of these languages are symbolic representations of the same underlying realities has guided us in our descriptions of character structures.

Employing archetypal themes and images as well as clinical knowledge of psychopathology as warp and woof for weaving archetypal and clinical threads into one fabric, we have identified nine interrelated character structures. Our model of pre-Oedipal character structures integrates contemporary psychoanalytic thinking about character with Jungian concepts about the nature and dynamics of the psyche. These nine character structures are not a typological system; they are diagnostic and archetypal images synthesized into a mythopoetic model. We recognize that other categories could always be employed but we offer this model as one useful way that images of character can be ordered.[2] We have culled our clinical vocabulary from a number of sources, but have repeatedly referenced McWilliams (1994) who so adeptly synthesized years of work by Jung, Freud, Kernberg, Millon, Kohut, Stern, Bowlby, Fairbairn, Winnicott, Guntrip, and numerous others in the psychoanalytic and psychological literature.

You can see in our Matrix (p. 6) that the nine character structures are related to each other developmentally and archetypally. Developmentally, every individual passes through three early but distinguishable phases as the ego emerges from the collective unconscious. We have chosen to refer to these phases as the primal phase, the narcissistic phase, and the pre-neurotic phase. Additionally, any one individual may adopt a particular relational pattern: withdrawing, seeking, or antagonistic. The relational pattern that informs a person's life emerges from a matrix of factors including archetypal forces, biological predispositions, and developmental realities, as well as the element of randomness or chance – the mysteries of life. The three character structures within any particular relational pattern are portrayed in thematically related though endlessly different images, stories, and life profiles.

The individual chapters of this book are devoted to these nine character structures in turn. Amplifications from fairy tales, mythology, art, poetry, and literature, along with theoretical reviews and case descriptions, will weave a portrait of each structure. To set the stage for these chapters, a few more introductory explorations are in order. First, we will review the nature of the developmental phases and then turn to how each relational pattern appears in each phase.

The developmental phases

We imagine as do many psychological, as well as theological theorists (Fairbairn 1954; Neumann 1954; Jung 1956a; Edinger 1972; Fordham 1974; Eigen 1986) that human development begins in a state of unity. This state has been referred to symbolically as the uroboric unity, psychic core, pristine unitary ego, holy of holies, unnamable creator – the Self. Classic analytical psychology was primarily concerned with how the ego develops in relationship to the Self, consciousness out of the unconscious. Edinger extended this basic premise, positing that as consciousness differentiates itself from unconsciousness, the constant tension between the ego and the Self leads to the development of an ego–Self axis (Edinger 1972). Contemporary Jungian theory has supplemented these ideas with more detailed considerations about how this relationship between ego and Self is developed in the context of interactions between the child and her environment, most essentially her caretakers.[3] We have integrated these perspectives and delineated, as noted above, three developmental phases.

We see these phases as narratives about common patterns that emerge within a complex system. Acquaintance with complexity theory and non-linear dynamics encourages us to hold the tension between assigning a causal reality to either an innate patterning or to the effects of the environment, including interactions with others. With an eye on this tension, not its resolution, we are freed to describe configurations of development that narrate a story about a child's reality at an approximate age. A developmental phase overlaps with a relational pattern in an emergent character structure. The character structure is portrayed in its thematically consistent images and logical structures; we frequently refer to this portrait as the landscape of the character structure. Thus, we consider the developmental phases to be one aspect of an "arrangement that is more kaleidoscopic than linear and monolithic" (Harris 2005: 8).

Before we describe each of these phases, let us clarify what we mean when we speak of an archetype and of the ego–Self axis. We use these words as evocative descriptions of psychic experience, not reified ideas that

An archetypal and developmental Matrix of character structure

The Relational Patterns

	Seeking Pattern	Antagonistic Pattern	Withdrawing Pattern
Pre-Neurotic Phase	Hysteria	Passive-Aggressive	Obsessive-Compulsive
Narcissistic Phase	Dependent-Narcissism	Alpha Narcissism	Counter-Dependent Narcissism
Primal Phase	Borderline	Psychopath	Schizoid
Dynamic Quality of the Relational Patterns	Enmeshed	Dominance	Encapsulated
Prevalent Expressions of the Collective Unconscious	Affect	Aggression	Mind and Imagination

← **Emerging Development of ego-Self axis**

have a distinct, even if "unknowable," reality that exerts a causal effect upon human development. We refer to an experience as archetypal when it embodies dimensions that are symbolized as eternal, numinous, frequently bipolar, and filled with awe and terror. Experiences of these dimensions have always been with us. In the psyche, they are recognizable in images, affects, or actions.

The ego–Self axis is a metaphor for the system that evolves out of the interaction between consciousness and the unconscious. Along with many Jungians (Shulman, Bernstein, Wilkinson, Knox, and Hogenson) we have been interested in integrating complex adaptive systems theory and its applications to the internal workings of the human psyche into our work. Viewed through the lens of complexity theory, the ego–Self axis is a self-organizing, complex adaptive system that displays emergent phenomena. The autopoietic dynamism (from the Greek: *auto* for self and *poiesis* for creation or production) of such a system is a unified network of processes that produce the destruction and transformation of its components (Maturana and Varela 1991). These interactions and transformations express a fundamental complementarity between structure and function, and continuously regenerate and realize the network of processes that produced them. In this sense, both the ego and the Self, as components of the whole system, are realized and transformed through the process of a functioning ego–Self axis. In effect, the differentiation of the ego from the Self, and the development of a dialogue between the two, is an expression of the destruction and transformation that is characteristic of a self-organizing system. The ego–Self axis continuously regenerates and realizes experiences that we have described above as archetypal. We understand this to be a describable though numinous process.

From a Jungian perspective, the psyche, akin to a self-organizing system, is the totality of conscious and unconscious processes. While the ego functions as the center of the conscious personality, the Self functions as the center of the psyche. We employ these words as metaphors for processes. We do not intend the Self to be understood as a reified structure, an identifiable other, a concrete, literal, divine figure that controls the world, but as an objective reality that weaves universal meaning into subjective, personal reality (Jung 1943: para. 32). As a process, the Self may be symbolized as a force, an unknowable presence, a wellspring, a god or goddess, etc. These symbolic expressions led Jung to consider the Self to be the archetype of wholeness that is the ordering and unifying center of the personality.

Born into a state of unity with *the All*, an infant's ego becomes progressively differentiated from the Self. The child learns to separate more fully from, yet remain dynamically engaged with the unconscious and hence with archetypal reality. Every infant must negotiate complicated and frequently frustrating experiences presented by archetypal reality, as well as by somatic, affective, and cognitive factors and by interactions with others.

When these experiences are threatening, the infant naturally employs defenses. Repeatedly used over time, these defenses can interfere with the relationship between the ego and the Self. They can rigidify the ego–Self axis rendering it inflexible and thus inhibiting the ability of the ego to gain access to the unconscious, and the Self to gain access to the ego. We imagine this as the defenses blocking the energy along the ego–Self axis, disrupting the emergence of a dialogic relationship. This defensive blockage effectively isolates the ego not only from the potentially overwhelming power of the Self but also from its numinosity, its richness, and wealth. The individual thus may find herself with little access to the wellspring of life, her own authenticity, and her instinctual spirit, soul, and body source. Overwhelmed by or cut off from the unconscious, she is effectively defended against the great mysteries of life.[4]

General discussion about the primal phase

The earliest of the developmental phases, the primal phase, reflects the way issues are activated and managed during the first 18 months of life. During this period, the newly born infant is barely other than "one with the universe." In this state of newly emerging consciousness, the infant tends to experience the world in fundamentally archetypal terms. Much like a fairy tale in which others are seen as larger than life, like a witch, a queen, a knight on a white horse, or a fearsome beast, the infant perceives reality in numinous, absolute terms. For example, she may experience her mother's frown as life-threatening wrath or her mother's momentary absence as an eternal "hell."

Given that the nascent ego is relatively undifferentiated from the unconscious, it remains easily repossessed by the archetypal realms. Thus, as the infant attempts to negotiate her very early, first differentiations (the baby from the mother, the ego from the Self), her psyche is hauntingly challenged by reabsorption into a lack of differentiation. In the face of stress that would initiate such a disintegrative regression, the infant employs a number of different defenses. These include the classic, primary defenses of splitting and projective identification (McWilliams 1994: 112).[5] These defenses are called primary not only because they are employed at such a young age, but also because they are relatively drastic and extreme. They effectively isolate sections of the psyche from interaction with other parts of the psyche and/or from interactions with others.[6] Jungian psychoanalysts describe additional, very early primary defenses of the Self (Stein 1967; Fordham 1974). These defenses are called into play before a coherent ego is formed and seem to be "'coordinated' by a deeper center in the personality than the ego" (Kalsched 1996: 1–3). Frequently personified as archetypal figures, these defenses serve to protect the mysterious inner core of the personality, the Self. In effect, the infant's psyche attempts to protect and isolate the Self from intolerable internal and/or external threats. We suggest that, in addition to the primary defenses and the defenses of the Self, an infant may employ a relational pattern defensively. Withdrawing, seeking and antagonism as patterns of interaction may serve as relational defenses. The coordination of these various defenses enables the nascent ego to maintain its hard-won differentiation and the Self to remain protected. A heavy reliance on one particular set of defensive strategies becomes cornerstone in the development of one's character structure.

If the infant's development proceeds optimally, her defenses will not become rigid and entrenched and she will develop the ability to hold her experience of reality flexibly; she will gradually learn that human life is multidimensional and ever-evolving. However, the more threatening an infant's intrapsychic or interpersonal reality is, the more she will experience her survival at stake and the more she will resort to an inflexible employment of these early defenses. McWilliams emphasizes that a defense begins as a healthy, creative adaptation and earns the term "defense" only when it is employed repetitively and inflexibly in the face of an unmanageable threat (1994: 97).

Current neuroscience researchers emphasize that the construction of early defensive structures interferes with the subsequent development of more complex neural networks. Schore elucidates how when an infant does not have the opportunity to interact with an emotionally responsive adult in an open dynamic system, its corticolimbic organization will be unprepared to handle the chaotic dynamics inherent in human relationships: "Such a system tends to become static and closed, and invested in defensive structures to guard against anticipated interactive assaults that potentially trigger disorganization and emotionally painful psychobiological states." Invested in defensive structures, the child then avoids novel situations and misses exposure to new learning experiences that are required for "the continuing experience-dependent growth of the right brain. This structural limitation, in turn, negatively impacts the future trajectory of self-organization" (Schore 1997: 624).

While defenses tend to exaggerate and entrench the infant's natural tendency to view the world in absolute terms, they simultaneously help to consolidate the ego's differentiation from the unconscious, protecting the infant from an overwhelming disorganization of personality and loss of its emerging contact with reality. Psychologically, the consolidation of differentiation is the principal task in the primal phase of development.

General discussion about the narcissistic phase

Narcissism, as a developmental step, involves the emergence of the dynamics of grandiosity, exhibitionism and omnipotence and the progressive development of a relationship between the ego and the Self. The character structures that emerge in this phase reflect the way a child negotiates the developmental tasks that arise primarily between 18 and 30 months of age.

During this phase, if the environment and fit between parent and child are good enough the progressive differentiation of the ego introduces an increasing amount of intrapsychic space that allows the initial development of reflective capacity. This intrapsychic development is paralleled in the outer world by a new experience of space between the child and his caretakers. This interpersonal space creates the opportunity for the child to seek and receive the parents' mirroring, as well as the possibility of experiencing an idealization of a valued other. Effective mirroring and idealizing enable a child to develop healthy narcissism that emerges as competence, coherence, resilience and the development of a creative dialogue between the ego and the Self.

However, if the environment and fit at this stage are relatively inadequate, i.e. if the child does not receive adequate or accurate mirroring or there is no person present that the child can idealize, she will begin to employ narcissistic dynamics defensively in order to maintain psychic integration. In this case, archetypal omnipotence and grandiosity inflate the nascent ego, creating a defensive ego–Self construct that precludes further differentiation of the ego from the Self and the creation of sufficient space for reflective consciousness (Schwartz-Salant 1982: 19). These defenses not only protect the child from the intolerable shaming and wounding situation in the moment but they also help her to avoid a fearful regression into the previous level of development, the primal phase.

General discussion about the pre-neurotic phase

The developmental challenges of the pre-neurotic phase follow the narcissistic phase. Character structures that develop at this point reflect the way a child masters the issues of the two-and-a-half to four year old. At this level of development, the child's psychic energy needs no longer be directed primarily towards the differentiation and initial development of the ego–Self axis. Now, the child is called upon to begin to negotiate his relationship to the larger world. Extracting himself from a primary concentration within a dyadic relationship, looking forward to the complications of a triadic relationship, he is in an in-between phase. He is no longer in the arms of the mother, and not yet fully engaged in the Oedipal struggle. As he proceeds to take on the challenges of triadic relatedness, he is confronted with desire, competition, and guilt.

Horner (1991) originally introduced the term "pre-neurotic" to signify a level of ego/object relations that is more mature than borderline personality organization and less mature than neurotic ego organization. McWilliams offers an extended account of mature defenses that become available at this point, noting that they include repression, rationalization, undoing, turning against one's self, compartmentalization, and displacement (1994: 117). As with the earlier primary defenses, each of these mature defenses is a normal aspect of psychological development, but it can interfere with development when it is relied upon repetitively and inflexibly. Employed defensively, these dynamics not only contribute to a constriction of the ego but they also render the ego further removed from a dynamic dialogue with the Self. In effect, these defenses create a break along the ego–Self axis, isolating consciousness from the unconscious. Bolstered by its newly won independence, the ego now has even more to fear from a disintegrative regression into the primal phase.

The relational patterns

Withdrawing, seeking, and antagonistic

The three developmental phases that we have just delineated interact with three distinguishable relational patterns. Two of these relational patterns we refer to as *withdrawing* and *seeking*. These classifications are an adaptation of the work of Frances Tustin who in her work with disturbed children differentiated between encapsulated and enmeshed dynamics (1990).[7] Tustin describes how one can observe an infant moving away from or towards her caretakers. In our Matrix, the movement away from others, in the face of inevitable frustrations and possible trauma, leads to the formation of an encapsulation that becomes manifest in a relational pattern of withdrawal. The movement towards her caretakers, in the face of inevitable frustrations and possible trauma, leads to the formation of enmeshments that become manifest in a relational pattern of seeking. In the face of significant frustration and more or less severe trauma, these patterns operate as interpersonal defenses, complementing the intrapsychic defenses characteristic of each phase of development.

We refer to a third relational pattern as *antagonistic*. This pattern resembles Horney's (1939) description of individuals "who move against others." Every child, at about nine months of age is called on to master "stranger anxiety." If the child is lacking a secure attachment and emotional ties, he may fall under the sway of a "stranger self-object" that is experienced as predatory (Grotstein 1982: 63). In Jungian terms this stranger self-object is *other*. It is inhuman and archetypal. Often personified as the dark side of the trickster, this archetypal other has the power to possess an undeveloped psyche. Jung referred to the phenomenon "when the ego is, so to speak, invaded by an archetypal figure" as possession (as cited in Hart 2001: 92).

Reviewing recent neuroscience research we can see how attachment failures invite this particular archetypal possession. Neural structures develop into neural networks through a sequential build-up of progressive attachment experiences between mother and infant that "light up" or activate connections between the brain stem and the limbic structures. However, when a robust infant meets threatening caretakers, necessary attachment bonds that are needed to contribute to emotional growth and subsequent neural maturity do not develop. The child misses this critical window of development and as a result of underuse, networks that could have developed to connect structures in the brain stem with the limbic system that generates and regulates emotional life, are *pruned*; unused they atrophy. The end result is that while activated brain stem structures have come *online* they remain to some degree unrelated to the limbic structures of the brain. Subsequently, further emotional development is severely impaired (Schore 2003a, 2003b).

With this severe lack of neural connectedness, related to the lack of sufficient interpersonal attachment, the child forms an identity with the dark side of the trickster and an antagonistic relational pattern develops. Possessed by the predatory trickster, the child becomes antagonistic towards all that is not himself: his caretakers and all others as well as his own inner life. Manipulation, domination and aggressive control are adopted as defensive maneuvers. Again, this interpersonal pattern will operate more or less rigidly depending on how severely the child's development was disrupted. And, as a defense, it will overlap with the intrapsychic defenses characteristic of each phase of development.

The archetypal landscapes of the patterns

As the relational defenses develop, we see the emergence not only of characteristic interpersonal dynamics but also characteristic archetypal landscapes. Ever so briefly: the person in the withdrawing pattern is inspired by the immensity of eternal, archetypal space. Drawing upon the resources of her mind and imagination she wanders in a landscape of echoic, frozen emptiness. The person in the seeking pattern, inspired by the ecstasy and depth of relationship, draws on the resource of archetypal affects and plunges into a landscape of chaotic, bombarding interactions. Meanwhile, the person in the antagonistic pattern, informed by the archetypal reality of predation, draws on his robust physical resources and lives in an archetypal landscape of dominance and submission. The consistent appearance of these archetypal themes within each of the relational patterns, woven into an interpersonal context during the different phases of development, differentiates and defines each character structure.

The character structures

Each character structure emerges as a "soft-assembly" (Harris 2005: 18) in the overlapping ground of a developmental phase and a relational pattern.

Each thus embodies a unique combination of intrapsychic defenses that arise at a particular phase and interpersonal defenses employed by a particular relational pattern. When these combined defenses are rigidified, the character structure itself becomes a defensive pattern.

Each relational pattern (withdrawing, seeking, and antagonistic) naturally manifests itself uniquely in each developmental phase. The essential characteristics of each relational pattern are most vividly portrayed in the primal phase, since this phase carries the rawest archetypal expressions of images, affects, and actions. In the withdrawing pattern, the person whose character structure is marked in this phase develops a schizoid character structure. In the seeking pattern, the person develops a borderline structure; in the antagonistic pattern, the person whose character structure is set in the primal phase develops a psychopathic structure.

As the developing child begins to employ narcissistic defenses, these defenses will be informed by her already established relational pattern with its underlying archetypal landscape. Thus, three distinguishable forms of narcissism emerge. In the withdrawing pattern, the person whose character structure is set in the narcissistic phase develops a counter-dependent character structure. In the seeking pattern, narcissism leads to the formation of the dependent narcissist, while in the antagonistic pattern, the person in the narcissistic phase becomes an alpha narcissist.[8] Each of the three character structures in the narcissistic phase employs narcissistic dynamics defensively and is informed by a defensive ego–Self conflation. However, these three characteristic patterns of relating are markedly different. In counter-dependent narcissism, archetypally empowered mind and imagination are employed by narcissistic defenses; in dependent narcissism the depths and heights of archetypal affect are employed; and in alpha narcissism the archetypal energy that moves one's body into manipulative and predatory acts is used defensively. We have found that differentiating between these forms of narcissism has clarified many of the riddles that pervade discussions about diagnosis and treatment of narcissism.

Finally, as the child moves into the pre-neurotic phase of development and develops ego defenses, she finds her character structure once again effected by her already established relational pattern with its underlying archetypal themes. We see that at this phase of development the child who has adopted a withdrawing pattern will tend to acquire an obsessive-compulsive character structure. In the seeking pattern, pre-neurotic defenses lead to the formation of an hysteric character structure, while in the antagonistic pattern, the person in the pre-neurotic phase develops a passive-aggressive character structure.

We are acutely mindful that a *person* does not fit into a category, nor does one category fully describe an individual. We encourage you to utilize these concepts symbolically, playfully even. Hold them lightly in your mind as you interact with others, or reflect upon yourself. We use them to illumine, not define. They may lead one to an energetic, awake recognition of an underlying character pattern that in its archetypal nature connects the person not only to her own source but to the source of universal meaning. Furthermore, although an individual develops one particular character structure that is her essential ground, she will naturally have some access to all of these dynamics and patterns. Indeed, the more individuated the person, the more each of these patterns will be at play in her life, supplementing her defining character structure. We have no intention of suggesting that these nine character structures even approximate an inclusive description of an individual.

Regression, shadow, and the intersubjective field

Regression

We have made several references to regression as we talked about the developmental patterns. Jung frequently emphasized the importance of a regression that proceeds into the "pre-natal" stage, the darkness of the unconscious where "slumbers the divine child patiently awaiting his conscious realization. This son is the germ of wholeness" (Jung 1956a: para. 508–10). This essential and creative process can be considered in terms of the developmental phases we have outlined. We noted that the child who is working on the consolidation of primary differentiations, or the adult whose character structure is informed by these dynamics, is challenged by reabsorption into a lack of differentiation in the unconscious. Similarly, the child who is working on the development of narcissistic resources is challenged by regression first to the primary phase, ultimately to a primitive lack of differentiation, as is the adult whose character structure is set at this phase. And the person in the pre-neurotic phase is analogously challenged by regression into these archetypal and undifferentiated realms.

For instance, when we are working with a person who has a dependent narcissistic structure, we can see that when she regresses, in analysis or in the face of disintegrative stress, she reenters a borderline-like state. She may begin to employ more primitive defenses, resorting to splitting and projective identification, and she may feel atypically at the mercy of raw, archetypal experiences of chaotic fragmentation. Similarly, when we are working with a hysterical patient, we might anticipate that, as she explores her early infantile memories and affects, she may regress into borderline areas. In order to facilitate the psyche's reorganization, the patient must not only enter into a working through of her defining character structure, but she must also reenter the earliest states that inform her structure.

The process of a creative regression, well held in the transference, can restructure the defenses and realign ego and Self. However, regression is naturally resisted, as these earlier states carry more potentially disintegrative and less functional dynamics than the developmentally later states. Indeed, this process of regression may be seen and experienced as a collapse, a treacherous descent, a terrifying defeat. The developmentally earlier states are inherently more difficult to bear; yet they are also the ground of our development. Thus, hard to bear or not, analytic exploration of these earlier patterns is a critical part of integrating the dynamic reserves of these earlier states which the later defenses are so rigidly set against. As these dynamics are brought into consciousness, the person gains more direct access to the vitality and authenticity that spring from the core of the psyche. When a person is released from the rigid grip of defenses and suffers a descent, she frequently encounters increasingly intense, even shattering and disorganizing confrontations with the Self. Jung observed that "the experience of the Self is always a defeat for the ego" (Jung 1955: 778). If she can tolerate the inherent defeat of her encounters with the Self, without ego disintegration, she may emerge with a renewed dialogue between ego and Self and be able to enter a life lived creatively and humbly, with a deeply anchored inner strength.

Shadow

As described, regression tends to occur within each relational pattern, reworking the relational pattern employed developmentally. But what about the relational patterns that are not one's own? For example, how does a person with a seeking relational pattern handle the dynamics that are characteristic of the other relational patterns? We understand the relationships between character structures of differing relational patterns as one way of imagining shadow dynamics. Since the challenges of each phase are met with the vocabulary of one's chosen relational pattern, the characteristics of the two relational patterns that are not informing one's own path remain distinctly *other*. For example, a person with a dependent narcissistic character structure has developed within the seeking relational pattern and will thus find people whose character structures lie within the withdrawing or the antagonistic patterns to be quite *other*. This otherness may be admired, envied, hated, ignored, rejected, etc., as is classically true of shadow elements. Yet, there will be aspects of this otherness that the person undoubtedly needs in order to develop her own wholeness.

From a Jungian perspective, we have long known about the contribution that confrontation with one's shadow can make towards healing and individuation. Recognition of the different character structures can enrich our capacity to see and encounter what is truly other. For example, while the dependent narcissist may find in analysis that she regresses into a borderline place, her shadow work will tend to lie in the withdrawing and the antagonistic patterns. This work may require an encounter with her shadowy forms of withdrawal as well as with her fascination with domination. Ultimately, these encounters may lead her toward the conscious development of these dynamics and thus towards individuation.

Traditionally, Jungians have been well trained to articulate and approach the shadow world. However, archetypal language alone has not sufficiently detailed many of the developmental particulars. Now, in the field of psychoanalysis, including the Jungian perspective, more focused observation and theoretical attention has been devoted to early infantile experience. This enables us to develop a more sophisticated vocabulary for developmentally early, archetypally imbued experience. We can now more clearly understand, feel, and describe the patterns that emerge within implicit memory, before language and explicit memory are developed. Weaving together new insights about development with archetypal amplifications, we can register the contrast between the intense emotional chaos of borderline reality; the eternally frozen, endless, and terrifying empty schizoid realms, and the never-ceasing, vigilant predatory fight for domination within the antagonistic pattern. With this increasing clarity we can truly appreciate what a shadow challenge each of these relational patterns presents to the others.

Combining a descent, a creative regression, with a reach for what is *other* enables a person to reconnect with both depth and wholeness and thus to develop a truly authentic connection to the Self. In the analytical treatment of rigid character structures, the dynamics of regression and the development and confrontation of shadow aspects of the personality assume essential roles. One of the important lessons of recent research in neuroscience is that the plasticity of the brain does respond to reparative relationship. As Wilkinson speculates: "it may be inferred that the analytic process . . . can develop new neural pathways in the brain . . . Such integration is facilitated as, through the transference, past is linked with present and emotional experience revisited and reworked" (Wilkinson 2005: 490). In terms of character structures, an insightful and well-attuned relationship can be seen to loosen rigid and restricting defensive structures and facilitate the emergence of a dynamic, energized, related life.[9]

Regression and shadow in the intersubjective field

An increasingly literate awareness of these paths of regression and these aspects of shadow work enables a therapist to increase her attunement not only to the patient's process but also, and essentially, to the intersubjective field between herself and her patient. This requires the analyst to be thoroughly familiar with her own character structure, including her regressive challenges and shadow dynamics. She will then be more able to understand how these dynamics interface with her patient. Working with a patient with a borderline character structure will be a very different experience for a therapist with an underlying dependent narcissistic structure than a therapist with, say, a counter-dependent structure. It seems essential to us that these differences are well recognized and explored since the intricate interactions of our multifaceted character structures are an extraordinarily valuable source of information and transformative energy.

Additional comments

The vision of Horus

At the beginning of this chapter, we told how the breath of Isis brought the fragmented body of Osiris back to life and how their reunion then created the divine child Horus, the harbinger of the new world. While the kingdom of Isis and Osiris gave rise to harmony, agriculture, music, and spirituality, the culture was split off from its own shadow elements. It was these disowned elements, carried by the evil brother Set, which ended their reign. The new king, Horus, whose name means "far-above-one," is represented as a hawk or sky falcon whose eyes are the sun and the moon. He introduces the development of perspective, a way to perceive a more encompassing view of life and gives birth to a new balance of powers in the world.

This myth of Isis and Osiris has inspired our intent to awaken the body of knowledge about character structures by drawing upon archetypal amplifications so that they may breathe life into the dismembered nomenclature of psychopathology. Mythologically, Isis' awakening of Osiris' remembered body leads to the birth of Horus. We liken Horus' perspective to the perspective provided by consciousness. The story thus presents us with an image of how an awakened clinical language can inspire the birth of a consciousness that liberates one's spirit.

Increased consciousness of character structures leads to the recognition of both their restraints and potentials. Formerly restricted by rigid defenses, one's character structure can be freed so that consciousness can become realigned with the Self and the potentials of one's spirit. This broadened perspective is supported by an integrated, archetypally enlivened use of the language of psychopathology. This enlivened language allows one to see one's own and another's character structure in a way that includes respect for the necessities of its development as well as an appreciation for the sources of transformation that lie within it. It may be a surprise to find that from the perspective of this model, rather than being considered a barrier to spiritual growth, our character structures are centrally involved in manifestations of the divine. Accordingly, spiritual practice becomes inseparable from introspective work on one's own psychological realities. Recognizing that our healing lies within our wounds and therefore within our character defenses moves the process of diagnosis from blaming to curiosity, exploration, and transformation. One then can truly appreciate character structure as an underground spring, a source of nourishment supporting a capacity to live a life of relatedness and compassion.

Calling out the names

> At the threshold of each hour
> To open the gates in the underworld
> One must know the names.
>   (Anonymous)

Murals and texts found in the ancient tombs of the Egyptians depict a long and dangerous journey as a path through the underworld. One who has died must find her way along this path in order to attain everlasting life. Frequently, the dead person, accompanied by various gods and goddesses, travels in a large barque or boat. The barque follows a path through the netherworld which is marked into various regions sometimes portrayed as hours, sometimes as chambers. The gateway to each region at times looks like a snake, at times like an actual doorway. The entrance to each hour, or chamber, is guarded by a fierce creature and attended by various divinities. As the barque approaches each threshold, the departed person must know the names of the guardians of the gateway in order to gain passage and proceed through the specific challenges of the terrain which lies before her. Successful and safe passage delivers her into the Hall of Judgment, where she may be seen to be sufficiently pure of heart to live eternally with Osiris.

The process of knowing the names for the gates is an evocative image for this book. We enter each chapter as one enters another hour, or chamber, in the netherworld. We call out "the names" which identify, honor, and contain each particular territory. In doing so, we aim to bring each of us into an increasingly deep and direct connection with the Self. *Naming* requires a full encounter: understanding, working through, feeling through, and truly digesting the essence of what is being named. In *The Matrix and Meaning of Character*, this form of naming entails calling out the names of the dynamics, the defenses, and the archetypal landscape that describe each character structure. This naming renders the ego progressively stronger and more flexible and therefore more capable of a dialogue with the Self. A defended, relatively weak and rigid ego can become possessed by unmediated archetypal energies or consistently restrict and distort the expression of the Self. In contrast, a dialogic relationship with the Self, imaged as "living an eternal life with Osiris," delivers one psychologically into a state of grace, into a state of living in harmony with *the All*, into the experience of the present moment as eternal peace. Thus, we will call out the names, inviting each of us to consider, to reflect, to ruminate, to encounter the divine and demonic forces of each hour, of each chapter.

Notes

1 Our adaptation of this myth is based on Faulkner, trans. (1969) *The Ancient Egyptian Pyramid Texts.*

2 There are a number of frequently named *disorders* that are noticeably absent from our Matrix. Several of these, e.g. panic disorder, dissociative identity disorder, and post-traumatic stress disorder are clinical syndromes that emerge from profound biological and environmental traumas (Van der Kolk et al. 1996). Early traumatic stresses so disrupt the early differentiations of the psyche that they can in essence derail the development of character. An in-depth exploration of clinical syndromes, i.e. Axis 1 diagnoses, lie outside the scope of this chapter. Further, it is our observation that a variety *of dynamic processes,* such as dissociation, sadism/masochism, and paranoia, arise in most of the nine character disorders we are describing.

3 In the field of infant observation research (Stern 1985), it has become increasingly clear that an infant has a number of choices and a degree of autonomy from the time of her birth. In terms of the development of character structure, we have chosen to emphasize the dynamics involved in the process of a child's development of both intrapsychic and interpersonal defenses.

4 We have decided for the sake of our own authenticity to alternate the use of "he" and "she" in *The Matrix and Meaning of Character.* Several colleagues have given us feedback that varying the use of gendered pronouns is either confusing/ distracting or implies a focus on women's pathology. Others have said how much they enjoy this equalization, how it serves "to wake them up." In the psyche and in life, living in a gendered reality is a challenge to be wrestled with. We regret any confusion or distress our choice about pronouns in this text may cause the reader.

5 McWilliams notes that while splitting is generally considered an ego defense, it does apparently operate in some cases at "a pre-object-constancy, pre-integrated-ego state" (McWilliams 1994: 112). It is this very early, pre-egoic use of splitting with which we are concerned.

6 It is the use of splitting and projective identification that led Melanie Klein to refer to an infant's repeated use of these defenses as the paranoid-schizoid position (Klein 1946: 2). She details in her terms how the projection into others of the undesired, split-off parts of the self or ego leads into a paranoid process, while the depleted regressed parts lead into a schizoid process (Hinshelwood 1989: 156).

7 Introduced by British analytic therapist Frances Tustin, encapsulation and entanglement are terms used to describe and differentiate the children she worked with who suffered from autism and childhood psychosis. Other analytic theorists have integrated and extended her concepts into their work with adult patients with various character issues (Bion, Grotstein, and Ogden). Other writers have postulated similar classifications. For example, Millon (1981) suggests that there are two basic continuums along which different personality styles are organized: the hysteric continuum, with individuals who are over-attached and thus tend to over-rely on others for rewards and comforts, and the schizoid continuum, with individuals who are under-attached and thus tend to over-rely on themselves for rewards and comforts.

8 The characteristics and intrapsychic dynamics of the alpha narcissist are essentially the same as the malignant or pathological narcissist described by Otto Kernberg (1975). We have chosen to use the descriptive term "alpha" in order to highlight the social role and predatory dynamics that this person embodies and feels entitled to assume with others.

9 It is important not to be reductionistic when considering biological or neurological research in terms of psychodynamic formulations. For example, research

indicating a biological substrate for a particular character structure does not establish this substrate as "the cause" of the development of a character structure. "The cause" is the result of the interactions of a complex set of variables over time: genetic, neurological, anatomical, interpersonal, psychological, developmental, and archetypal. We will proceed to explore issues concerning cause and effect in terms of mind and body throughout the text.

Part I

The withdrawing pattern

Chapter 1

Schizoid character structure

Encapsulated in ice

The Little Match Girl

It was dreadfully cold, snowing, and turning dark. It was the last
evening of the year, New Year's Eve. In this cold and darkness walked
a little girl. She was poor and both her head and feet were bare . . .
Now the little girl walked barefoot through the streets. Her feet were
swollen and red from the cold. She was carrying a little bundle of
matches in her hand and had more in her apron pocket. No one had
bought any all day, or given her so much as a penny. Cold and hungry,
she walked through the city; cowed by life, the poor thing!

(Andersen 1976: 306–8)

This is a portrait of a person lost, wandering, frozen, and unable to make contact. The Little Match Girl looks in the windows of the village houses at warm family feasts. Terrified to return to her own cold house and cruel father, she is also unable to ask for help. She resigns herself to sitting alone in the freezing snow. Having no warmth she can turn to, she withdraws into her own meager resources, she lights the few matches she has, and they lead her into the deadly embrace of her fantasy life.

It is important to note that the Match Girl has a cruel father and no mother. We can imagine clinically that this neglect of the most basic physical and emotional needs could leave a child frozen within herself. The isolation in her childhood becomes internalized into intrapsychic isolation. The schizoid patient experiences a terrifying emptiness, a nameless dread, an inner landscape unpopulated by human figures. She frequently turns to endless dreams and fantasies, which may be rich, symbolic, and mesmerizing. She may find solace in a well-developed intellect and develop an internal crystal palace in which she lives alone, safe but frozen. However, she may also find dangerous depths, unpredictability, and deadly horrors. Like the Little Match Girl, a schizoid child tends to be out of touch with her body and her affects, as well as her capacity to take action in the world. The schizoid person lacks a connection to her body as container, a bodily felt experience. It is as if the schizoid person lives in a body that is asleep, or a body that has not yet come alive. Her body tends to be well formed, yet stiff and unresponsive. She may have an aversion to touch. She may be alert to the point of hypervigilance, and easily overwhelmed.

Archetypally, people who regularly employ the withdrawing relational pattern have a great facility with mind and image. This realm can allow, invite, and even capture the withdrawing person into its imaginal richness and pull them out of participation in the challenging and complex realm of embodied, affectively charged human experience and relationships. People with a schizoid character structure are often at the mercy of their internal world. Possessed by the awesome power of the mental and imaginal aspect of the unconscious, the person has relatively little capacity to interact with others sensitively and intimately, as well as little capacity to stand up for themselves. As they attempt to maintain a protective personal space, they may appear aloof or removed. By resistance to social expectations and embracing eccentricity, they may cultivate an exaggerated uniqueness that further separates them from the world. At the same time internally, they may be rigorously self-critical and desperately alone.

It is not at all uncommon for patients with a schizoid profile to turn to a Jungian analyst. Their facility with the use of symbolically rich and prolific imaginal material and dreams presents the ripe possibility for a collusive analytic relationship. Our experience indicates that schizoid felt experience and defence structures are clinically underrecognized and even have a tendency to be idealized in one's patients. We imagine that this may be a result of these states remaining relatively unanalyzed and unworked in therapists themselves.

One such patient was a young professional woman who lived in her dreams. Never mind that she had a husband, three kids, and many acquaintances. What was compelling for her was her elaborate inner life. She would bring pages of meticulously recorded, elaborate archetypal dreams to every session. Flooding our space, these intense images rarely deigned to hand over a second for us to have human contact. Eventually, the seconds when we did connect began to accumulate. Over time, human warmth began to melt the ice. Around the same time, the quantity of her dreams decreased. Their content was at once less archetypal and more symbolic. They were related to her body and her life. And with this warmth, the landscape of emptiness could finally be seen for its bleakness, as well as its treasures. We will return to consider this case again later in this chapter (p. 43).

As a result of immersion in the imaginal aspect of the unconscious and subsequent easy contact with imaginal material, people with an underlying schizoid character style often seek vocations in philosophy, religion, psychoanalysis and poetry, mathematics and music. Once engaged in relationship, people with an underlying schizoid structure can be genuine and seemingly undefended. Yet traditional diagnostic criteria for personality disorders focus on defenses and limitations, not ego strengths and achievements. It is not unusual that people with this character structure possess a preference for image and abstract thought. With a more developed ego capacity in a person with an underlying schizoid structure, the capacity to use image and abstract thought may flower into the realms of art or science. Yet within the constraints of a character disorder, this creative facility may remain trapped and undeveloped in the unconscious.

Taking pleasure in solitude, appreciation of academic, philosophic, and spiritual pursuits are character traits that therapists often admire about our friends, our patients, and ourselves. People with schizoid sensitivity and intellectual resources not infrequently choose to become counselors and therapists where their acute capacity for observation can be utilized to assist others from a safe distance. For a therapist with schizoid issues, a particular kind of intimacy and sharing occurs in treatment, yet the power differential in the analytic relationship favors and works to protect the therapist. This therapist can have an experience of closeness, without the same stresses that make one-to-one relating so challenging for someone in this withdrawing relational pattern. Unworked and unanalyzed, however, schizoid encapsulation has a definite impact on the intersubjective field, on the development of a deep emotional connection, and on the potential for wounding one's patients unconsciously.

Not everyone is generously endowed with a life structure that supports the development of their imagination. Lest we romanticize the schizoid character, the pain and isolation involved in this structure can erupt into unexpected violence, perversity, and addiction. People with a schizoid personality structure have a wide array of adaptations. They range from a sheltered person whose periodic decompensations require hospitalizations, to a high functioning person with an academic career, to an artist whose originality makes them notable in their field. Common to all is their tendency for isolation. When one has little ego strength and minimal economic and cultural resources to draw upon, a desperate picture may emerge. A humiliated factory worker who accosts his wife, an isolated housewife who is unable to tolerate the outbursts of her children and spanks them black and blue, the alienated urban street chic artist who is deeply addicted to bondage and drugs, and the quiet adapted outsider who comes to school with a gun may all have a schizoid character structure.

Theoretical formulations

Moving from the world of fairy to the world of theory may seem like a huge step, yet the Match Girl's presence is symbolically present throughout theoretical considerations of a person who has a schizoid structure. Early psychological theorists often used the term schizoid to describe a person with a schizophrenic potential, who was not actively psychotic. August Hoch (1910) described a "shut in" personality as a reticent reclusive person who is stubborn in a passive manner. Kraepelin (1913) used the term "autistic personality" to characterize a detached passive adaptation, which stabilizes before reaching psychotic proportions. Eugene Bleuler first used the term "schizoidie" to describe a pattern of behavior of lesser severity, on a continuum with schizophrenia. He described his patients as suspicious, incapable of discussion, and comfortably dull (Bleuler 1922, 1929).

In Volume Three, *The Psychogenesis of Mental Disease*, Jung relates how consciousness in a schizoid personality is overwhelmed by archetypal content with more devastating results than in neurosis:

> These complexes are . . . unsystematic, apparently chaotic and random. They are further characterized, like certain dreams, by primitive or archaic associations closely akin to mythological motifs and combinations of ideas. These archaisms also occur in neurotics and normal people, but they are rarer.
>
> (Jung 1958: para. 563)

Jung's contribution is significant to this discussion as it emphasizes the extent to which archetypal reality can dominate a person's psyche and diminish or interfere with a person's experience of human reality. The mythic motifs that Jung refers to appear differently in the withdrawing pattern than they do in the seeking or antagonistic pattern. It is through the interesting lens of the mind and image that this child first experiences the world: it is also the foundation of her defensive structure. The inner world of a schizoid person is characterized by archaic and rich imagery; when she is threatened, she withdraws into her inner world of fantasy.

Reviewing archetypal imagery in the dreams, fantasies, and lives of people who have a schizoid structure, we repeatedly encounter words like isolation, emptiness, and meaninglessness used to describe the landscape of their woundedness. From a conscious or ego perspective, the unconscious itself is imaged and experienced as a *void*. This void is often experienced as a vast hollow space, an immense territory that is unpeopled and frequently uninhabited by any life form. This archetypal territory is encountered in the form of endless labyrinths, which have no centers and no exits, echoey haunted houses filled with demons, or cold prisons where they are held in isolation. It is essential to know this empty terrain in our patients' and our own psyches because it is by way of making a conscious passage through this landscape that the individuation process unfolds. Disconnected from ordinary life, fears of immersion into this vast underworld result in a chronic threat of psychic disintegration. As a result of this powerful unconscious force that draws one inwards, these patients may suffer pervasive bodily fears of disintegration; fears of vanishing into nothingness, coming apart into thin air, decaying into compost. As these fears of annihilation emerge, they wonder if they would be missed. Most often, with the fragile ties that they have with other people, they imagine that their absence would not be noted. One patient's fears of not being missed were confirmed. Withdrawn from the people around her and unable to reach out for help herself, she was caught immobilized in her apartment in a severe episode of psychic disintegration and paralysis. Alone for three days, neighbors only came looking for her after her hungry cats put out an angry call for help.

Schizoid origins in the primal phase of development

As we noted when we introduced our Matrix (p. 6), the schizoid character is situated in the overlapping ground of the withdrawing relational pattern and the primal phase. This phase reflects the way issues are activated and managed during the first 18 months of life. In the primal phase, the ego is relatively undifferentiated from and easily possessed by the unconscious. Captive in this cold and impersonal realm and subject to its titanic forces, schizoid struggle for survival as an individual is constant because of the threat of reabsorption back into the unconscious. Each of the three character styles rooted most deeply in the primal phase employ the most primitive defenses; relying primarily on withdrawal into fantasy, splitting, projective identification. Primary defenses are employed in a desperate and inflexible manner to prevent an overwhelming disorganization of personality and loss of contact with reality. The heavy reliance on one primary defense becomes a cornerstone in the development of one's character structure. As such, when a character can be distinguished by its use of one primary defense, we refer to it as the defining character structure.

While the woundedness that occurs in the narcissistic phase and pre-neurotic phase results in deep concerns about shame and guilt, respectively, character structures that are formed in all three relational patterns in the primal phase are centrally concerned with a basic struggle for survival. Just as people caught in borderline and psychopathic dynamics, the Little Match Girl does not suffer concerns about shame or guilt; she experiences her existence as constantly threatened. She is deeply withdrawn, paralyzed, and unable to reach out for help. Her lack of connection to others and withdrawal into fantasy cause her to succumb to the cold embrace of death.

In the schizoid experience described by Jung above, the archetypes themselves appear in a raw and unmediated form. This archetypal influx overwhelms the nascent ego and interferes with the accrual of images that comprise the personal layer of the complexes. Thus, the intrapsychic structures that would support the development of a personal life remain undeveloped and the person is left at the mercy of the archetypes. For the schizoid patient, when this powerful unmediated archetypal component overwhelms the emerging ego, the infant withdraws into defensive encapsulation in the unconscious in an attempt to defend the "vital heart of the self" (Guntrip 1969) or the "personal spirit" (Kalsched 1996). Standing in the snow, the Match Girl is alone in archetypal reality. No inspirited girl remains who could experience her freezing body and act on her own behalf.

In all three character structures in the primal phase, an underdeveloped ego and subsequent defended character structure impede the purposeful flow of psychic energy along the ego–Self axis. By definition, a functional ego–Self axis cannot exist without the development of an ego. When an ego is severely underdeveloped, the whole-making function of the psyche is inhibited from initiating and supporting an orderly development of the personality. As a consequence, intrapsychic structures remain undeveloped. For the schizoid, defensive encapsulation interferes with the fluent dialogue between individual consciousness and the Self, the source that could endow a life with meaning. When operational, the psychic energy which flows along the axis can inform the individuation process and connect us to the mysteries at the center of existence.

Harry Guntrip and the regressed heart of the self

Harry Guntrip, a member of the British school of object relations, writes sensitively and metaphorically about schizoid phenomena. Guntrip, an analysand of D. W. Winnicott, was a pastoral counselor and a person who sensitively describes these dynamics intrapsychically: "We have seen how too early and too intense fear and anxiety in an infant, who is faced with an environment that he cannot cope with, and does not feel nourished by, sets up a retreat from outer reality and distorts ego-growth by a powerful drive to withdrawal and passivity" (Guntrip 1969: 87). Guntrip imagines that the infant fearful of being toxically overwhelmed withdraws from the outer world in an attempt to recreate the safe environment that it experienced in utero. This withdrawal is not without grave dangers; for a living organism to regress to a pre-birth state is also to experience death. While the safety of hiding is sought, not infrequently, annihilation anxiety is experienced in this retreat from life. Depending on the amount of experienced threat and the degree of the encapsulation, this withdrawal and loss of sense of self is highly anxiety provoking and it is often felt by the patient as dying. While Guntrip observes that an experience of regression into the unconscious can be an experience of death for a person with a schizoid structure, this regression can ultimately carry the hope for rebirth within it.

Massive withdrawal from the outer world and subsequent schizoid encapsulation serves to deny the reality of existence and prevent the development of essential attachments. The infant turns against herself, suppresses natural feeling responses, and uses very primitive defenses to deal with a perceived hostile world. This psychic catastrophe is an experience of destruction by implosion. In order for the infant's annihilation anxiety to be managed, spontaneous expressions of the self are sacrificed in order that the organism can survive. Stated more dramatically by Johnson: "the organism essentially stops living in order to preserve its life" (1985: 56–7). Current neurobiological research informs us how these traumatic implosions set off profound relational and neurobiological cascades.[1]

Guntrip recounts a chilling dream shared by one of his patients that symbolizes the result of these phenomena in the unconscious. In the dream, she opened a steel drawer and inside was a tiny naked babe staring blankly with wide emotionless eyes. In the schizoid patient, an undeveloped capacity for emotional warmth and aliveness is locked away unevoked and isolated in the unconscious. It is as if their living heart has deeply withdrawn into the unconscious. Without access to this core source of feeling, loving ties cannot be developed with anyone, or with themselves. This deep retreat is experienced by the schizoid person as an experience of death. Schizoid patients report they feel unreal, not alive, a state sometimes self-described as zombie-like. We will further consider the dynamics of derealization and depersonalization in the schizoid personality in the case of Clark (p. 31).

The Match Girl is never able to reach out, her existence is confined to an eternal cold prison in which she is captive. In an adult schizoid person's life, we get glimpses of this state of being in their unresponsive emotional life and the lifelessness of their physical body. This deadened state is a defensive attempt to protect against further experiences of annihilation; it also keeps their own vulnerability unconscious. To this end, all interpersonal relatedness and experiences of attachment are guarded against: "This permanent damage to the immature ego, the structural headquarters of fear in their personality, is a basis for the danger of regressive breakdown in later life" (Guntrip 1969: 77).

Guntrip outlines a treatment process for schizoid patients, with which we concur, where a strong analytic container is created, within which encapsulation can open, a therapeutic alliance develop and a restorative symbiosis can be worked through. At this point, "the true self . . . hidden away in safe storage" can move towards the possibility of a rebirth. To use his metaphor, a successful analytic process can allow the person to access the encapsulated "heart of the self."

Schizoid defence of encapsulation

For all character structures in the withdrawing relational pattern, the dynamics and defenses related to encapsulation are central to the formation of the character structure. Schizoid defensive encapsulation is a matter of degree. Depending on the degree of an encapsulated defense, the cost to subsequent development can be enormous. In autistic children, their encapsulation may be so pervasive that any further character development is not possible. In neurotic people in this pattern, there can be intrapsychic encapsulated enclaves surrounded by hardened defenses.[2]

Defensive encapsulation works intrapsychically to create an illusion of a protective covering, a refuge. Yet when withdrawal into encapsulation goes too far into the unconscious, all sense of self and meaning is lost. In analytic language, this represents a withdrawal into objectlessness. Patients in the withdrawing pattern are all vulnerable to encapsulated retreats during stressful work in analysis. Flight into the unconscious draws one further and further out of life. When human consciousness attempts to live from within the unconscious, an important boundary between the conscious and the unconscious has been crossed. The consequences of a regressive encapsulation can crack a tenuous grip on the world and plunge the person into the underworld. In this dark place, one's individuality gets swallowed up and engulfed by the deep waters of the unconscious.

A conundrum of terminologies: schizoid, avoidant, and schizotypal

Schizoid character structure in our experience is underrecognized and underdiagnosed by clinicians for several reasons. The split that is suggested by the term schizoid has its roots in the words schism and schizo. This split has been theoretically considered in two distinct ways. Most frequently, the schizoid split that is referred to in psychoanalytic literature is the characteristic split in the schizoid person between the self and the outside world.

The confusing array of diagnostic categories that involve the term schizoid is another reason why schizoid character issues are underrecognized and underdiagnosed. Beginning with the publication of the *DSM III* in (American Psychiatric Association 1980), three discrete personality disorder diagnoses were created to distinguish the different behavioral manifestations that had previously been included in one schizoid continuum. These three categories are: schizoid personality (an asocial adaptation); the avoidant personality (a withdrawn adaptation); and the schizotypal personality (an eccentric adaptation). It is our experience that while these diagnostic differentiations indicate accurate behavioral distinctions, they contribute little to the recognition and understanding of schizoid developmental or treatment considerations. Further complicating the use of the word schizoid to refer to a personality disorder or character structure, in the *DSM IV* (American Psychiatric Association 1994), the psychotic levels of this character are included in the diagnoses of schizophrenia; schizophrenoform disorder and schizoaffective disorder. Setting these classifications aside, in this book we consider the schizoid continuum as one phenomenon of the nonpsychotic version of the schizoid character.

Finally, there is often confusion regarding the relationship between schizoid personality disorder and schizophrenia. It is accurate on the one hand to state that schizoid personality is the most frequent premorbid character diagnosis before the onset of schizophrenia. On the other, a person with a schizoid personality disorder or underlying structure has no more incidence of psychosis than any other character structure developed in the primal phase.

The last reason we want to consider that schizoid character structure or schizoid enclaves go undiagnosed is that it is the *intent* of the schizoid solution to "disappear." Withdrawal into the unconscious is a defense designed to minimize exposure to others and allow oneself to fade into the woodwork unnoticed.

In conclusion, it is our perspective that the confusing array of diagnostic terminology as well as the clinical association of schizoid issues with schizophrenia contribute to clinicians frequently assuming that schizoid character structures occur in only the most incapacitated individuals. As a result, these character issues remain underrecognized and underanalyzed in patients, in therapists, and in the world at large.

In this text, we will be using cases to ground and illustrate in more detail the dynamics we are describing. No real names are used, circumstances have been changed, and composites have been created.

Clark: accomplished, frozen, and alone in the midst of his family

Some schizoid patients present with an abundance of words, stories, dreams, and images. However, others present wordlessly; verbal silence pervades the hour. A young surgeon named Clark entered treatment. He was married and had three daughters. His initial sessions were filled with silence and physically apparent, but unstated terror. Mirroring this unconscious fear to him led us nowhere; he did not recognize this state in himself. So we sat together, hour after hour. Physically, he presented himself as a model professional, his persona was accurate but there was no life within it. His movements were exacting and stiff. In some ways, he appeared inanimate.

It took many nearly silent sessions before any trust was established. Only slowly did his story emerge. I learned that he had entered treatment because of his accumulated reviews at work that revealed a level of discord that he had ignored. These reviews spelled out his inability to relate to his coworkers. This first public naming of a limitation was a rude awakening; academic success and advancement had always come easily to him. It seemed that he truly had no experience that would enable him to address being challenged in the interpersonal realm. He told me that he was angry at the evaluative rebuff, but his anger was disembodied and intellectualized. As he understood social convention, anger was an appropriate response to confrontation in the workplace. While he could describe his anger, the words themselves were hollow. However, he did go on to explain how the relationship with his unit chief seemed "futile." Futility was an experience with which he was intimately familiar.

One year into analysis, he hesitantly told me that his wife had recently expressed dissatisfaction in the quality of their relationship. Clark was married to a woman who was on the boards of several charity organizations. Recently, she had attended a series of personal growth workshops and had begun to ask him for an emotional connection that she felt was lacking in their marriage. He was concerned: his marriage was important to him. When I asked him what he thought she meant, he speculated that it might have to do with their sex life. He went on to share that their sex life was regular, if perfunctory. He suspected that this was another incidence for which his emotional "shutdown" was responsible. His isolated adaptation carried with it a deep ambivalence about attachment.

It is invaluable to keep the focus of the analysis within the context of the therapeutic dyad. Since there is such a poverty of affect in working with schizoid patients, the prospect of changing the focus of treatment from the difficult interactions in the hour to the problems these patients encounter in their other relationships can be a temptation. While everyone in the withdrawing relational pattern has the same dependency needs as any other person, fears of engulfment and obliteration surface when they are faced with situations involving closeness or intimacy. While shifting the focus from the therapeutic relationship to a personal relationship outside the analytic container may seem to promise the therapist a sense of relief, it is important to remember that for these patients relationship difficulties are a result of the schizoid defense. This defense manifests in withdrawnness and impenetrability that needs to be directly addressed before the process of the emergence of psychic structures can proceed.

Although Clark was sometimes overly vigilant about my presence, at times I felt like a piece of furniture in the room. Working with children, British analyst Frances Tustin felt she was often "rendered non-existent" by the encapsulated children that she saw. When we are speaking to our patients and our words are being ignored, it is of immediate importance that we do not let the patient obliterate us. We need to find a way to make our presence known, to reclaim the patient's attention so the session is grounded in the reality of the therapeutic relationship, not only the contents of the patient's unconscious.

Continuing to keep the focus on the interactions in the room rather than shifting the focus to his marriage, Clark became more and more willing to tell me "about" his life. Yet whether his silence filled the room, or the empty relationships he spoke about filled the room, there was little room for me. He could be withdrawn from me when he was silent and withdrawn from me when he was talking. In this phase of treatment, I identified and named how he removed himself from our relationship. Then I interpreted this retreat as a defense. Often he showed apparent indifference to these comments. Often, it seemed to me that he was in a trance, his attention captive in the unconscious. As time went on, when he talked right past one of my comments, I stopped and asked him what he thought just happened between us. At first, he said that he didn't know. I kept asking him this question over a period of months. Often, he said he didn't even hear my words. Sometimes, he could admit to not caring about the topic; more and more, he got curious about what I said. We got into a pattern that when he talked over me, I'd touch, with measure, the arm of my chair with my fist and say, "Clark, there are two people in this room." For a while, these moments were tense; later, they grew more into a playful confrontation.

Within this process of challenge and connecting, his encapsulation seemed to loosen enough that we became more real to each other. His dream life began to come alive and he started to see how defended he was with others. Over time, he could identify how often he felt cut off from himself, shut down as a person, how often he operated as an "empty automaton." As Clark came to his sessions with more earnestness and intent, he noticed that he was becoming more vulnerable in the world. When he did feel wounded, he now could describe periods of time when he felt not real, or not alive. He was lost to the world and lost to himself. During extended states of derealization, he would dream that he got locked in a freezer in the hospital in pediatrics; he dreamed that his body was dispersed into the air in an underground cavern; he dreamed that he was locked out of his house and left in the alley. It was my experience that it took patient and careful attunement in our sessions to enable Clark to feel alive and connected to his sense of self again.

These intensified periods of derealization and depersonalization were painful and frightening to Clark. We worked to identify several stimuli which triggered these episodes. He traced some of these incidents to our sessions and others to occasions when he knew things were not going well at work. Our sessions were difficult, for he often had no memory of the interaction once his massive withdrawing had occurred. After much more exploration, he understood that periods of derealization occurred after he felt hurt.

He was most surprised, however, to discover that some of these periods of feeling numb occurred as a result of being close. He began to see how threatened he was by intimate contact, in his life and in his sessions with me. As he was able to identify his difficulty with close contact, we began to explore the source of his fears. He became able to identify that sometimes his withdrawn emotional behavior was a reaction to his fears of being engulfed by others. During this period of the therapy, dreams and fantasy images emerged of encroaching slimy tentacles, giant smothering breasts, and a subsequent loss of his body's boundaries.

The schizoid person feels their sense of individuality and basic security is constantly threatened by the outer world. Frequently experiencing others as demanding and intrusive, a schizoid person's withdrawal from interpersonal contact and flight into fantasy is employed when mature defenses are undeveloped and insufficient to keep the ego intact. The collapse of an unstable ego is real in the face of an experience of engulfment. Then a period of psychic disintegration may ensue. For a person with a schizoid disorder or an underlying schizoid character structure, abandonment is experienced as a lesser danger than engulfment.

Clark described his periods of a descent as "falling into a cold emptiness where there was no one, nothing mattered, nothing had any meaning." He could be in this state for weeks. When he became better about identifying that this was his condition, he could sometimes reach out for help and seek contact with me. Over the period of years that he was in treatment, the intervals of being lost shortened considerably. When a schizoid character defense dissolves, the archetypal threat to the patient is great. As the pattern of encapsulation begins to give way, unmediated archetypal affects begin to appear. Formerly unconscious primitive affects of rage, terror and despair can emerge in the analysis. At the same time that these raw affects arrive, so do an increased primal energy in and awareness of the body. Awakening to physical sensations, pain as well as pleasure, can complicate the life of a person who was formerly so encapsulated. Emergent sexuality, neglected health concerns, and the capacity to engage in destructive actions came to the forefront in my work with Clark. This experience of an enlivened body can be both threatening and promising.

Having weathered the experience of these affective and somatic storms together, our work progressed. Clark became aware that he valued his relationship with me. Lacking a cohesive sense of self, he began to project on to me his as-yet unawakened sense of wholeness and capacity to live a meaningful life. He experienced me as trustworthy. As I became more important to him, he also began to fear losing me. He dreamed that he came into my office only to find that I had moved out. In his dreams, his new analyst's office was in an empty basement. This therapist had long pointy nails and spiky hair.

Earlier in this chapter, we used the metaphor of "melting the ice" to allude to the process of working with the icy impenetrability of a schizoid defense. This defense is softened by the effect of the therapeutic relationship upon the patient. Learning to tolerate the emotional experience of needing and reaching out for another dismantles the rigidity of the schizoid defense. Clark began to show some interest in being involved in teaching interns at the hospital. Slowly, he became curious about himself; who he was and what he valued. He began to take some esthetic interest in his home. This interest surprised and pleased him. He had always left the duties of managing his home and relating to his children to his wife, but now he discovered that he had ideas about how their lives might become enriched by some changes. As he began to be able to tolerate experiencing his own feelings and sensations, he became able to tolerate more interactions with his family. His wife and daughters were pleased. Although still vulnerable to periods of derealization, he continued to take small steps into the world. In his venturing into the realm of home and hearth, his life began to yield treasures. As he brought these riches into the light, they could then be warmed by the sun.

Therapeutic reflections: encapsulation, preverbal terror, and patterns of defense

Calibrating relational rhythms with Clark was a challenge for me. He seemed to be present one moment and then "gone" the next. The schizoid relational pattern of being present in a relationship one moment and then needing to withdraw the next is described by Harry Guntrip as the "In and Out Programme" (Guntrip 1969: 36). While Clark was easily overwhelmed by my presence and my comments, my failure to respond at the right moment could plunge him into an experience of futility. My empathic failure in the early stages of treatment could result in Clark feeling "lost" and "not real" for several weeks. I often imagined our relational connection as a fragile net that was tenuously stretched over a great abyss.

In the early periods of analysis, Clark had few words to describe his own experience. He came to his sessions, was mostly silent, and left looking defeated. In these sessions, I imagined a small wild animal trapped in a room with me, shaking in the corner. The quality of silence in the room was never quiet, but rather alive with terror. For Clark, primitive archetypal

terror was both ever-present and unconscious. There is an intrinsic difficulty in trying to articulate preverbal experience. When an infant in this
relational pattern perceives a threat as dangerously overwhelming, annihilation fears rush to the fore. Intrapsychic and interpersonal paralysis may be
the result. Alarmed and frightened, the child's affective and somatic development can become arrested, frozen in fear. Over the course of therapy
Clark worked first to become aware of and then to be able to express his
ongoing suffering.

Not hearing, not remembering, and not paying attention all can be
expressions of schizoid encapsulation. A "dismantling of attention" is a
descriptive phrase that Meltzer uses to explain a schizoid child's capacity to
block out perceived threat. Describing the characteristics of encapsulation
further, he refers to "the mind's ability to drop out of existence" (Meltzer
et al. 1975: 6–29). Michael Eigen uses the parallel term, a "blanking out,"
to refer to the same phenomena (Eigen 1986: 112). Both "dismantling of
attention" and "going blank" in the face of perceived threat accurately
describe Clark's inability to remember or pay attention to our interactions.
These cognitively distancing defenses also serve to keep primitive affects
at bay.

When describing a period of derealization, Clark would say, "Last
Thursday, I couldn't feel my skin and then I fell out of the world" or that
"my life seems unreal and my body seems to belong to someone else."
Depersonalization and derealization are states of being that occur in a
phase of a primitive withdrawal, which precedes decompensation. When a
person feels that they do not inhabit their own body and that life itself is
not real, they are hanging on to their sense of self with white knuckles.

Withdrawal into fantasy is employed when mature defenses are undeveloped and insufficient to keep the ego intact. A schizoid person with a more
developed ego may be able to utilize the mature defenses of projection,
idealization, and devaluation. With their facility for mind and the imagination, schizoid patients are particularly adept at employing the more developed defense of intellectualization. Clark could easily use intellectualization
as a defense. He was bright, complex, and had an interesting mind. Without
easy access to his feelings and bodily sensations, the world of the intellect
was a realm in which he could hide.

As Clark's relationship with me deepened, his schizoid defenses began to
loosen their grip, his ego strength developed, and there was considerable
movement in his psyche. Raw archetypal affects of terror and rage made
their way into the analysis. These powerful affective expressions can be
surprising to both therapist and patient. Working together with these
intense affective eruptions over time enabled Clark to forge a more flexible
ego and subsequently live a more related and energetic life. With this release
of libidinal energy, intimations of an authentic self began to appear. As the
psychic contents within and beyond encapsulation emerged, were

contained, and *metabolized* in the context of the analytic relationship, a resultant transformation generated connection to a wellspring of desire.

Transference and counter-transference

Schizoid patients can appear like a deer caught in the headlights. They often experience the therapist as the one who has, or might, hurt them. This is an archetypal transference rooted in primitive terror. Long periods of silence may need to be tolerated while a patient internalizes an experience of safety. Isolated and estranged, they have little experience and consequently little integration of non-threatening relatedness. Fears of emotional or physical engulfment are paramount as schizoid patients have little development in either area, which could help them to negotiate the intensity that a therapeutic alliance entails.

These realities have far-ranging implications for negotiating the development of transference with schizoid patients. When a therapist is perceived as a constant threat to a patient's well-being, an undifferentiated archetypal transference can take many forms: a huge enveloping witch mother, the ice queen with a perverse smile, a seductive malevolent ghoul. Movement from the initial archetypal transference to a more personal one is very threatening, but one that can slowly lead from living in an inner world of imagination into human tears and a personal connection. At best, the capacity to experience the therapist as a kind, helpful but not intrusive person begins to loosen the repression of physical and emotional neglect or impingement. As the images that inhabit the transference evolve over the course of therapy, subsequent personal integrations may continue to take place; the capacity to feel and the capacity to experience oneself as embodied may develop. Subsequent gains in ego development continue with this process.

A therapist's well-meaning expression of warmth or excitement too early in analysis can be experienced as overwhelming and hence destructive in creating this relationship. These patients need emotional space. If carefully modulated, interaction by interaction, trust may begin to build, and the therapist's affective interest in the patient may be more easily tolerated and lay the ground for the patient to be able to loosen the grip of their encapsulation. On the other hand, early transference resistance may become evident in the patient's detached and ironic responses, which reveal an oppositional attempt to construct a cool barrier between them and others. While this barrier was initially erected with the intent of protecting the person from noxious engulfment, it also interferes with reality perception and inhibits input into their relatively closed psychic system. In treatment, this barrier is an impediment to the development of the transference. As we have said earlier, this aloofness is an addressable defense that must be penetrated before the work can proceed.

A schizoid patient's lack of emotional resources and seeming lack of interest in becoming involved with others may contribute to a therapist coming to the conclusion that the patient is depressed. It is our experience that many schizoid patients are often misdiagnosed as having some variant of a depression disorder. Yet when in an encapsulated defense, the depressive's dark tone of guilt is absent. An inability to express feelings, an emptiness and flattened expressions lead us to consider a schizoid character structure. A schizoid person may become depressed after a loss, but restricted affect is different from depression.

An errant diagnosis of depression for a person with a schizoid character structure leaves a clinician misdirected in their interactions and interventions. Schizoid distress is distinct and easy to miss; the _purpose_ of the character defense is to _hide_ by withdrawing into fantasy. Schizoid distress, while it may be stirred up by rejection or betrayal, leads the patient to a cold empty place. Their underlying experience of emptiness is for the most part objectless. If we consider the intrapsychic structure of a schizoid patient, at the core of their personality lies a landscape of barrenness and unreality. This specific archetypal ground may present itself in the image of an abyss, the infinite cold distances of deep space, or permanent solitary confinement in a padded white room. While painful circumstances may evoke these images for the patient, the bleak experience of an abyss has existed for them from their beginnings; it exists in the foundations of their being.

Counter-transferentially, the therapist may experience a number of different responses with a schizoid patient. At one moment, the therapist may be drawn to a counter-detachment, both from the patient and more subtly from her own affect. In response to the patient's inability to articulate or recognize affect along with their substantial fears of being overwhelmed and their capacity to use aloofness as a defense, there is a danger that a therapist will withdraw and pull back, becoming counter-detached. Finding oneself having difficulty paying careful attention to the patient or daydreaming is a temptation that is easy to fall into. Sometimes these are difficult patients to care about; so much silence to endure, such inability to articulate the distress that they are experiencing, so little capacity to connect provides little gratification for the therapist. In the presence of flight from contact and long silences, it may be difficult for the therapist to maintain confidence and resilience.

Through advice giving, expressions of intense interest or overcompensating to make up for the lack of contact, the therapist may be drawn toward enmeshment. Since fears of being engulfed are at the forefront of treatment with a schizoid patient, attempting to connect by caretaking or being patronizing will often quickly backfire. Sorting through these counter-transference responses and interpreting them for oneself and the patient is the crucial work in this field. As the richness of the schizoid patient's inner world becomes apparent and appreciated, another counter-transference response may surface. This appreciation may pull the therapist into a collusive alliance. The therapist may begin to feel that this patient is special and talented and that others are unable to appreciate their gifts. If this collusion continues, the patient may be so gratified that therapy becomes a substitute for the challenges of pursuing outside relationships. This collusive alliance may reenact the patient's relationship with an over-involved parent.

It may be a temptation for a therapist to feel judgmental as the patient reveals an interest in violence. It may be surprising to clinicians who are less familiar with schizoid terrain to discover their patient's interest in horror movies and true crime books; more sophisticated personalities may carefully follow front-line stories about war or the crime scene in local current events. The "gentleness" of a schizoid person seems in contrast to their interest in and capacity to seek out violence and distress in order to observe it. Yet fully considered the schizoid person's interest is understandable, since the schizoid person is the penultimate observer, observing yet separate from the action. It is their nature to be vigilant, wary, and ready to withdraw. In order to feel safe from perceived life-threatening disasters, one does well to be acquainted intimately with the dangers of the outside world.

We imagine that idealization of the imaginal may be a result of schizoid states remaining unanalyzed and unworked in therapists themselves. Unanalyzed schizoid pockets of encapsulation in the therapist can generate several counter-transference responses; distancing in the presence of intense affect, spoiling moments of contact, and withdrawing into fantasy in sessions to manage uncomfortable content. Unanalyzed idealization of imaginal contents, in either the patient or analyst, can lead to a treatment stalemate, which leaves both parties sitting out in the cold. With unconscious schizoid issues, both the patient and analyst's capacity to reach out to the other can be in a state of paralysis. Like the Little Match Girl, the analytic dyad can be freezing in the midst of plenty, looking at life through a frosted windowpane, without the ability to reach out and ask for warmth.

The archetypal terrain of schizoid disintegration: nameless dread, the black hole, and what lies beyond

In psychoanalytic literature, two evocative terms capture the experience of a person approaching schizoid decompensation: "nameless dread" and the descent into a "black hole." (The term "nameless dread" was introduced by Karen Stephen in 1941 to describe the extreme extent of anxiety in infancy.) Later, Bion uses "nameless dread" more specifically to describe an infant's experience in the face of a maternal failure to contain an infant's anxiety (Bion 1967). Several analytic theorists employ the term to describe the wordless experience of eerie and mysterious terror, which precedes schizoid disintegration (Grotstein 1982; Eigen 1986; Tustin 1990). "Nameless dread" is a state of being that describes the pervasive terror of anticipated entry into the dangerous unknown; a terror without subject, a horrible premonition of doom that precedes extinction. Without an attuned caretaker, an infant's experience of this anxiety can remain archetypal, undefined, uncontained, and untransformed.[3]

The "black hole" describes a person's experience of ego collapse and immersion into an objectless unconscious, a catastrophic implosion. The image of a black hole conveys a catastrophic discontinuity of the self, loss of a sense of being alive; a black, psychotic depression, which engulfs one with a sense of losing the very floor of existence. Individuality, consciousness, and the meaning-making capacity in the psyche are lost in the indefinable expanse of archetypal reality.

When a person withdraws from life to a critical degree or withdraws "too far," the energetic power of the unconscious draws one into an intrapsychic whirlwind. Pulled into the *other side*, sealed off from life, struggle is futile, meaningful existence destroyed and any sense of hope is a long distant memory. Imagistically, in a catastrophic schizoid disintegration, one's being disperses into nothingness and then is swallowed up by the dark energy of a black hole. In astronomy, gravitational collapse occurs when the depleted resources of a star can no longer produce an expansive force, a movement into life. This collapsed matter shrinks into an infinitely small size and spirals into an unknown universe. When the radius of this star decreases below a certain limit, the curvature of space that remains seals off contact with the outside world. Light and other forms of energy and matter are permanently trapped inside. The former star has now become a black hole. The process of the final stages of a star and its collapse into know-not-where is an apt metaphor for an experience of schizoid disintegration; reduced and drawn into an icy nothingness, neither light, matter nor hope exist.

We'd like to emphasize that a terrifying and deep annihilation anxiety is not solely the province of pathology. In the first year of life, consciousness has just barely started the process of differentiating from the unconscious. Every infant lives in a state of dependency on a caretaker who may or may not be available, who may or may not be caring. All infants encounter moments when their perception of threat causes immense anxiety. These experiences of threat are amplified by helplessness and the fact that infants cannot verbally communicate their needs or their distress. It is possible for a child in this state to be held and comforted by another, contained. However, defenses of the Self, which emerge in the first year of life, originate when trauma is experienced as catastrophic *and* accompanied by a failure of the caretaker to contain this terrifying experience of anxiety. In the face of these extreme conditions, primitive defenses are employed in a desperate and inflexible manner to prevent an overwhelming disorganization of

Containment

personality, dissolution of cohesiveness, and loss of contact with reality. A heavy reliance on one primary defensive strategy becomes a cornerstone in the development of one's character structure. It is not uncommon for adults to fear or re-experience catastrophic anxiety, especially during periods of stress, abrupt change, and in the process of transformation. Those conditions lay us all open to experience primal anxiety.

When rigid character structures are employed defensively, they can sever our connections to all that lives, and leave us devastated. But when archetypal experiences of annihilation can be related to, approached with reflection, and exploration, even they can bring meaning into our lives. It is possible that our deepest wounds and anxiety states are not solely the causes of suffering; rather, they can become a source of reconnection. Our periodic painful visits to the wound can become an entrance into the great mystery.

Annihilation anxiety and the potential of epiphany

So far, we have considered both nameless dread and the energetic pull into an intrapsychic black hole from the lens of psychology. From the lens of religion, references to unnamable "awefulness" and dark whirlwinds can connote the presence of the divine and have profound spiritual implications (Otto 1923). An overwhelming experience of the otherness of spirit has the power both to infuse us with a profound sense of meaning and purpose and to obliterate our humanity. People have always intuited that an unfathomable realm exists beyond our consciousness; at times we call it transcendent or transpersonal, at others, supernatural. The awful/awesome terrain of spirit can capture and destroy, or captivate and enlighten. When the depleted resources of a person who primarily uses withdrawal as a defense initiate a massive withdrawal from life into encapsulation, we could say they have entered into the unfathomable realm of the gods. Described in Genesis in the Old Testament, they have entered "the darkness of the deep" that precedes creation itself (*Jerusalem Bible* 2000). Encapsulation in the unconscious is an unnatural state of being. This serious transgression can have disastrous consequences. A withdrawal that was intended as a defense to protect and comfort quickly turns icy, isolating, dark, and potentially lethal. ———

The difficult fate of one who undergoes a perilous plunge into the inner world is an archetypal theme that reoccurs in the worlds of fantasy, fairy tales, and myth. When trauma and encapsulation occur before consciousness has had sufficient opportunity to differentiate itself from the unconscious, the structural integrity of the ego is diminished. Thus, separated from an authentic source of libidinal energy that could flow along the ego–Self axis, one is not only at a loss to reach out for what she desires, but also unaware of what she desires. Schizoid encapsulation can seal one off from the human world and keep the person captive in the world of spirit. As an example, abandoned, left in the world to die, and unable to reach out to ask for help, the Little Match Girl in Hans Christian Andersen's fairy tale finally reaches out to the spirit world for solace (Donahue 1995). In the tale, the archetypal grandmother beckons the Match Girl out of life into the spirit world where a real girl cannot exist.

The withdrawing relational pattern and the disembodied self

Earlier we discussed the poverty of affect and bodily integration in a schizoid person. In fact, in the entire withdrawing pattern, a poverty of affect and bodily integration prevails. D. W. Winnicott describes how, for all infants, the process of psyche awakening develops within the infant's body during the process of a *good-enough mother's* "holding and handling" her child in the first few months of life. Within this experience of touch, this awakening of skin as container and boundary of the self, the infant discovers both her separateness and her capacity for communion and relationship. "As the mother introduces and reintroduces the baby's mind and psyche to each other," impersonal archetypal reality becomes personalized, animated individuality is created, and an indwelling takes up residence in the child (Winnicott 1971: 271). It is through the experience of "holding and handling" that the infant becomes able both to differentiate itself from the mother and to develop a sense of self over time. In doing so, the infant develops a feeling of wholeness about herself, and an ability to perceive a sense of wholeness in others. As the child separates from the mother and experiences herself and others as separate, primary defenses become unnecessary; i.e. splitting, denial, and withdrawal. Once the self is embodied, once the ego is at home and alive in the infant, the foundation for confidence, trust, separateness, and love is established.

As adults, the issues of physical detachment and fear of closeness often come painfully to the fore in the lives of people with a schizoid structure in their sexual lives. Theodore Millon posits that for the schizoid personality disorder the "biological substrates for a number of drive states, such as sex and hunger, are especially weak" (Millon 1981: 273). Nancy McWilliams concurs with the observation that schizoid people may be sexually apathetic; "despite being functional and orgasmic . . . some schizoid people crave unattainable objects while feeling vague indifference towards available ones" (McWilliams 1994: 193). The partners of schizoid people sometimes complain of a mechanical or detached quality in their lovemaking. The schizoid person needs and desires feelings of security, closeness, and sexual expression, yet fears engulfment and subsequent regression to a more passive primitive state that sexual closeness might evoke. The schizoid compromise in terms of sexuality is to be apathetic about sexual desire and detached or mechanical in its expression. In the context of describing a schizoid person's sexual conflicts, Guntrip quotes a patient who states "I feel that I ought not to want my wife's breast or any comfort. Sexual intercourse ought to be purely mechanical. [Just as] I'm afraid to let go and let you help me" (Guntrip 1969: 159).

In the next chapter, we explore how counter-dependent narcissistic people and obsessive-compulsive people fear and defend against regression into these cold empty schizoid states. This is not a territory that anyone would willingly fall into. Both narcissistic and pre-neurotic defenses are staunchly erected to defend against such a painful objectless regression. For people with a schizoid structure or schizoid enclaves, a regression can take them into the perilous territory of psychosis.

Joanne: seeking sustenance in the spirit

A person needs a developed ego in order to negotiate archetypal realms. No spirit is kind if it possesses the human. As in the conclusion of the tale "Little Match Girl," her beloved deceased grandmother appears shining and redemptive as she lures the girl out of life into the promise of spirit. Spiritual transformation, however, is not the fate of the Little Match Girl. Each match she lights leads her further into the arms of archetypal seduction and embrace. Her search for comfort and lack of human connectedness ultimately leads her out of life. While she imagines herself swept up to heaven in her grandmother's arms, she dies frozen in the snow. The unconscious lure of psyche, mind, and imagination can be a destructive force in the schizoid personality; can be a chilling reality. The schizoid person must learn to hold in perspective the phenomenal lure of her mind and imagination if she is to develop human life and relationship with all of its down-to-earth limitations.

One woman patient who came into analysis had an inflexible schizoid character structure. Joanne was drawn out West to a spiritual center to study aura balancing and channeling. She was sure that this involvement would lead her into the light. Instead she experienced that her life was becoming more and more narrow, and she was becoming poorer and poorer. She began to realize that she had cut herself off from her family, and was now isolating herself from her friends. She entered analysis with a clearly stated goal of discovering what childhood patterns were limiting her spiritual development. Over the next years we unraveled how her childhood experience led her away from a full engagement in life, and to quest after the cold embrace of isolated spirit.

Some of us have had clinical experience with people seeking spiritual and religious meaning in life, where this pursuit has had a difficult impact on their day-to-day life. Without some ego development as ballast, a deepened entrance into the imaginal unconscious can serve to draw a person out of life. When the divine is idealized as all-powerful, loving, and benevolent, it is far too easy to imagine that surrender to this being is spiritual progress.

However, any archetypal possession is a signpost for future disaster. In certain spiritual circles, there is a knowing phrase: *You have to have an ego to transcend an ego.*

Joanne's disappointing early experiences with her mother left her vulnerable to idealizing her father. As an adult, she came to realize that her mother was depressed and had several hospitalizations for psychotic depression. As a child, in desperation and aloneness, she turned to her father hoping to recreate some of the connections that she had with her mother. Her father was a kind man, but emotionally remote. This combination of factors led Joanne to develop an idealization of her father, and further, an idealization of a father god. In her immersion in church and her spiritual practice, Joanne created for herself a life of deprivation and aloneness. As our work proceeded, she had a dream series where this divine being taught her to fly, and would take her on greater and greater "high" adventures. Meanwhile, her day-to-day life continued to disintegrate. She experienced some transient psychotic episodes which frightened her severely.

Then she had a dream about this god, which terrified her. He led her on another flying adventure, where she followed him beyond the clouds, out of the atmosphere. She had problems with her breathing. He led her into outer space, which was beautiful, serene, and very very cold. At some point she looked down at her body and noticed that frost had formed on her skin, and that she had begun to turn blue. She woke up in terror, and brought the dream into analysis. As we worked the dream, she tearfully realized how her increasing hours in prayer had led her to neglect her body and her home. These unfrozen tears marked a point of return from a spiritual practice that in its extreme worked to remove her from her human participation in life.

Only the gods can live on the Acropolis; it is a serious transgression for a person to seek a room there. Sacrificing an archetypal union (whether conscious or unconscious) with a god can be an important part of healing and becoming embodied in an individual human life. One's humanity will be diminished if possessed by any aspect of divinity. As the Greeks firmly understood, identification with or possession by a god is an act of hubris for which the mortal is severely punished.

It is easy for a person whose psyche is predominantly steeped in the otherworldly pleasures and pain of the imagination to become excited, lured out of life and then destroyed by their inner world, repeatedly. This world of image and thought can be both haven and prison, separating the person from relationships and with their own capacity to take action in the world. In the realm of myth, the continent of Atlantis was said to be an amazing ancient civilization, separated from all other continents by water. The archetypal myth of Atlantis tells of huge crystal palaces, communication by telepathy, great minds with great mental achievements that create a vast ethereal civilization. Atlantis is present in one moment, and like the intrapsychic disintegration of the schizoid herself, vanishes without a trace in the next. This magnificent spiritualized world is swallowed up by the watery depths.

The goddess Sedna: icy abandonment, submerged creativity

We'd like to end this chapter by exploring a myth about a goddess who inhabits these frozen depths; an archetypal presence who may possess and sink her icy fingers into an individual life. Throughout the Arctic, the sea goddess Sedna is feared and venerated. Her story is told by the Sikumiut who call themselves the "People of the Sea Ice," and the Inuit, the "People of the Icy Sea." It is a tale about survival in a forbidden place, the cycles of life and death, of how woundedness can be transformed into treasures, which arise from the deep (Merkur 1991).

The myth of Sedna, like any myth, can be reflected upon from many angles. It remains always a story about itself; it exists in and of itself, a story of a goddess, a story about the creation of animals. Symbolically, we imagine it as a story about early developmental dynamics or as a story about the pattern of a woman's life. If a person becomes possessed by the archetype of the mythic Sedna, it will determine her entire life story. The myth of Sedna is an archetypal story about a goddess and simultaneously it is a story which provides us with a poignant portrait of a human life fated to develop a schizoid form. The goddess Sedna lies abandoned in icy isolation. This fate may be echoed in the encapsulated defense of the schizoid personality:

> A proud girl living alone with her father in a frozen landscape refuses to marry any human suitors, choosing instead to marry a bird. He takes her away to a rock cliff, which is his home. Here her feelings of isolation become unbearable. Through the howling northern winds Sedna's father hears his daughter's cries and comes by boat to rescue her. But the enraged bird-husband chases them and creates a fierce storm with the flapping of his wings. Fearing for his life, the father throws the girl from the kayak into the ocean and chops off her fingers as she clings to the side of the boat. When she continues to hold on, her father beats at her fingerless hands. Frozen by the Arctic sea, her beaten hands crack off. When Sedna could fight no more, she sinks. Her fingers turn into seals, her nails become whalebone and the stumps of her hands turn into polar bears.

At the bottom of the sea, Sedna transforms into a half-human, half-sea creature that controls the ebb and flow of life. When she is content, her hair flows in the currents of the water, but when angered by the actions of careless humans, the natural order of life is disturbed and her hair becomes tangled and filled with lice. She retaliates by withholding the sea mammals from hunters. In order to ensure survival and set the laws of nature right, a shaman must take a spirit flight to the bottom of the sea to appease the disgruntled sea goddess by combing and cleaning her hair in atonement for the people's transgressions. When her hair flows freely again, order is restored. The shaman convinces her to release the mammals which allow the Inuit to eat from the bounty of the sea. What a story!

This is a story about a goddess. Rejecting suitors, marriage to a bird, betrayal, amputation, and metamorphosis; dramatic archetypal themes that are the very stuff of myth. These mythic currents describe the movements of the gods and when they are identified with, can wreak havoc in lives of humans. With that distinction in mind, and without offending the goddess herself, let's turn to consider how these symbolic undercurrents might flow into an individual life. An individual woman with a powerful wounded goddess ruling her unconscious is an apt portrait of a schizoid psyche. Her encapsulated ego is captured in the depths of her unconscious in the realm of the dark archetypal feminine. A personal connection to her body and her feelings remains undeveloped. In addition, her consciousness and a developed realization to her creativity remain trapped in the archetypal realms.

Psychodynamically, when the girl in the myth refuses all suitors and chooses instead to marry a bird, what is happening in human terms? Just as Sedna is not willing to marry a young man, the tenuous consciousness of an infant who will develop along schizoid lines is unable to tolerate relationship. This infant's constitution and particular experience of the world causes her to withdraw from the outer world and form an encapsulated "crustacean defense" in the unconscious. As a result, the child is never again able to participate in full engagement with the world. With this encapsulation intact, her psyche no longer functions as one of a real girl, but more like Sedna herself, a half-human and half-otherworldly creature. We imagine this sea creature as a symbol of an ego encapsulated in the unconscious, of human potential being possessed by an archetype.

In the myth, the girl chooses the bird as a marriage partner. This symbolic choice for the schizoid person represents an over-identification with the spirit in the form of the bird. This possession by the imaginal unconscious paradoxically captures her ego and prevents her from being able to develop a mature conscious relationship to her unconscious world of mind and imagination.

In the myth, after refusing all suitors, and choosing a bird for a bridegroom, Sedna is carried off to barren unpopulated heights where she moans in isolation. Life for an adult woman with this character style is filled with such a fear of intimacy that, over and over again, she carries herself out of life and into her imagination. Once so cut off, she may be overcome with the pain of her isolated remote existence. While longing for contact, the unconscious itself stirs up storms of resistance, which prevent her from relating. Her white-knuckled grip on the boat of consciousness, her tenuous grip on the reality of life in the world, her fragile conscious adaptation is often short-lived. Her schizoid adaptation *cracks* as she encounters the harshness of life and she may fall into the non-human objectless realms of the deep. Just as Sedna sinks to the bottom of the sea, a woman with a schizoid structure can lose her grip in the world and descend into the abyss of her unconscious.

At this juncture of the myth, the great goddess herself leaves her human likeness behind as she evolves into a half human/half sea creature. This is a treacherous moment in a woman's story. Living from the depths of the unconscious itself and taking on the archetypal forms of the otherworldly creatures that reside there can be seen as a metaphor for a person who falls into the depths of psychosis. Possession by the goddess at this level can be deadly. We imagine that for a woman descent into a non-human form is a symbolic expression of depersonalization and derealization; where a person experiences her body as alien and life as not real. Identified with and possessed by the archetype of Sedna, a person is fated to reenact the rhythms of the goddess who releases and withholds life. This rhythm of releasing and withholding is akin to the "in and out programme" of the schizoid; released from her encapsulation she enters a tentative engagement with life, only to withdraw again and return to her depths. When individual consciousness remains captured in the unconscious, archetypal reality encases the personal psyche.

In the myth, when angered by the transgressions of the Inuit people, Sedna's hair becomes tangled and filled with lice when it cannot flow with the currents of the sea. The natural order of life is disturbed. In human terms, we transgress the natural order when the boundaries between what is human and what is divine become diffuse and intermingled. Encapsulation in the unconscious is such a transgression. When human consciousness withdraws from its own world and lives from the unconscious, as we have seen, dangerous consequences ensue. Developmentally, if all had gone well, a child would have become progressively differentiated from the unconscious and its archetypal contents. However, in a schizoid developmental impasse, the child becomes identified with and possessed by the gods and goddesses and all is not right with the world. The appearance of parasitic lice symbolically represents the condition of an unbalanced psyche for the schizoid person. The natural flow of energy between ego and archetype is impeded and the archetypal world consumes consciousness.

As we have explored above in the case of Joanne, in order to become embodied in an individual human life, sacrificing union with the gods is essential. This sacrifice is an attempt to restore the natural order of things. Creating and maintaining the natural order of things is an expression of the archetypal Self. It is the nature of the gods to be wholly other than humans;

majestic, numinous and awe-inspiring. Without a developed consciousness to encounter these aspects of divinity with a full awareness of their Otherness, armed with the appropriate rituals of respect, one tempts fate. Unprepared, we cannot encounter the gods and live. When we are possessed by the *mysterium tremendem*, our humanness is obliterated. There are many instances in myth where mortal existence is overwhelmed by the gods. A Hellenic instance of this disastrous encounter is when Semele encourages the Greek god Zeus to appear to her in his full splendor. In that moment of revelation, she is burnt up by his flashes of lightning and her human life on earth is ended.

Within a schizoid encapsulation, consciousness is adrift among archetypal forces; at times possessed by, at times undifferentiated from, at times in terror of extinction. Like the rhythms of the fate of the continent of Atlantis, at one moment living amongst fabulous crystalline palaces of the gods, at others overwhelmed and unexpectedly thrown into chaos by the waves of Neptune, one's life disappears, one's body dissolves, one's civilization is erased without memory. Union with archetypal aspects of divinity may offer moments of seduction and glory but, like the flight of Icarus, always end in disaster for a person. Human fear turns to terror in these encounters, as the awe-inspiring becomes awful, splendor becomes dreadful, and the glorious becomes infernal. We imagine that for the person with a schizoid character structure an experience of nameless dread foreshadows their inevitable obliteration. This dangerous state of affairs is often symbolized in the dreams. Threatened by demons, haunted by ghouls, and chased by dark phantoms out to God-knows-where, encapsulated existence in the unconscious becomes increasingly terrifying.

Yet as we develop a "face" with which to face god, the face that god shows us evolves (Lewis 1980). As Jung has observed, the face we show to the unconscious, it shows to us. As a schizoid encapsulation begins to loosen and consciousness begins to emerge, the possibility of a meaningful encounter with the numinosum develops. We become more equipped to encounter numinous realms, which offer experiences of the sacred that are inspiring, enlivening, and inspiriting. When archetypal reality is revealed to a person through the archetypes of the gods and goddesses, we may be required to discover our potentials and our destinies.

Archetypally, images of both dark and light spirit exist. Archetypally, spirit is neither light nor dark. However, an individual psyche can experience one pole or the other. Why does the dark face of god appear in the psyche? When the ego remains identified with or undifferentiated from the archetypal glorious bright positive aspects of divinity in the schizoid character the darkness of the unconscious divine gathers and the dark face of god appears in a fury. In this dark manifestation, human fear turns to terror in these encounters, as the awe-inspiring becomes awful, splendor becomes dreadful, and the glorious becomes infernal.

Sedna and the shaman

To return to the myth of Sedna, her head is filled with lice, her hair is entangled and the flow of the currents of the sea itself is impeded. In angry response, she withholds the "bears and seals and whales" who are the sustenance of life to the humans above. The people quickly realize that they have grievously offended the goddess through their failures to honor her by maintaining the practices of right living. They send a shaman to make amends and restore the rhythms of the seasons and the bounty from the sea. Traditionally, a shaman is a healer skilled in the arduous journey to the spirit world. Not unlike the Greek god Hermes, he flies between earth and the spirit world of the gods. In these archetypal realms he can obtain what is needed for healing and return to earth. Intrapsychically, the shaman represents a developed intrapsychic function which can travel into a deep unconscious place and return to consciousness with a boon. The development of this structure is symbolized by the shaman who serves as a transformative bridging function in the psyche.

In the myth, the shaman must descend into the icy waters and soothe the goddess by combing, untangling and removing the lice from Sedna's hair. Just as a woman needs to cleanse herself from a schizoid undifferentiated state, a developed bridging function in her psyche can work to unleash and untangle the conundrum of an encapsulated ego. With a more developed dialogue between the ego and the unconscious, a woman is able to consciously suffer schizoid regressions, nourish a relationship with archetypal forces in the unconscious, and begin to untangle and integrate her physical and emotional energy.

Just as the shaman soothes the disgruntled Sedna by grooming her hair, a person with a schizoid structure needs to become skilled in self-soothing. For a highly defended schizoid person, recognizing bodily sensations and emotions can be nearly impossible. Shut off from her body and her feelings, the capacity to care for herself is seriously compromised. In order to accomplish this task, a woman must first become aware of her distress, anguish, arousal, and pleasure. Only then can she begin to attend to the undifferentiated sensations and anxiety that surface in the process of her embodiment.

For a woman, as a more integrated human life begins to unfold, her creativity may rise to the surface like mammals from the icy sea. Inspiration may be released in a human embodied manner in creative forms that nurture and enrich life on earth. Returning to consider the Arctic myth of Sedna, from the fingers and the hands of the goddess that are severed, new life forms magically emerge that sustain life on earth. As the goddess loses her girlish form, she acquires the divine power to give or take life. Sedna will always be a goddess of life and death residing at the bottom of the sea. But as the people break the laws which she has decreed, she withholds life and brings on death. As appropriate amends are made to her, she releases the sustenance of life again.

As in the tale of the Arctic goddess Sedna, a person with a schizoid structure lives in chilly isolation in a fantastic mythic underworld. As we inquire into this abyss, we can begin to understand the pain of a woman's existence, as half girl and half goddess. Just as Sedna becomes able to release the mammals of her creativity in the myth, the capacity to reside in these depths with some conscious focus can allow a woman to give rise to her creativity. She must be conscious enough to travel into the deep and return with inspiration that can serve her and her world.

The mythic tale of the goddess Sedna provides us with images from the deep that both inform schizoid character and illuminate the process of how desire can arise and restore the meaning of one's life. At the heart of this tale, as in each of our hearts, lies a tremendous mystery. Evolving numinosum enters the human conscious from the furthest shore of the unconscious. Connecting to this numinous source can allow the waters of life to flow again, so the "bears and seals and whales" emerge. Visionaries and artists travel the depths of the psychic unconscious to find this wellspring, which can refresh, renew, and transform human life.[4]

When a person with a schizoid structure becomes consciously able to suffer her own pain, isolation, and descents into the icy abyss and archetypal realms, a capacity to mediate these waters may develop which enables her to transit these depths and emerge with a pearl of great price. A schizoid character structure can undergo a "sea change." No longer possessed by the unconscious, she can come into dialogue with the Self and bring the fruits of the sea to life on earth. She can learn a new language, discover a new paradigm, become a source of inspiration or evolution that can be a treasure for the culture at large. As the lives and work of mystics, prophets, and artists can attest, the true gifts of the unconscious are hard won. Revelations of the *mysterium tremendem* are more than most can bear. Yet a person who has come into an integration of mind, body, and heart may be blessed with inspiration that infuses her own creative work with an energetic mystery and also brings a necessary vision to the world.

Notes

1 Allan Schore and Daniel Siegel have synthesized years of research from what has become known as the "decade of the brain," from attachment theory, neuroscience, developmental psychology, psychoanalysis, and other sciences into what has become known as the study of developmental neurobiology (Schore 1997, 2003a, 2003b; Siegel 1999, 2003).
2 One pervasive developmental disorder that deserves theoretical consideration while describing schizoid phenomena is infantile autism. Similarities to schizoid personality dynamics can be noted in the infant's apparent withdrawal from the outer world, lack of responsiveness to people, and language deficits. In the *DSM*

II (American Psychiatric Association 2000), it is noted that infantile autism (299.0) can be a precursor to a schizoid development. In psychoanalytic literature, there is a distinction between a natural developmental phase that all infants are said by some to pass through in the first two months of life, and pathological infantile autism.

Developmental theorist Margaret Mahler speculated that for the first two months of life all children appear internally focused and not available for much interaction. She called this early developmental phase "normal autism" to distinguish it from pathological autism. There are valid concerns about Mahler's choosing to use the word autistic with its pathological connotations to describe a normal human phase of development. (Daniel Stern challenges this concept on several grounds; see discussion in *The Interpersonal World of the Infant* 1985: 232–5.) Stern quotes a personal communication (in 1983) with Margaret Mahler, where later in her work she concurred with his objection to the term "normal autistic phase." She suggests in that communication that what she had termed "normal autism" may be more accurately termed "awakening." Integrating this input from Mahler, Stern introduces the term "*emergence*" to describe the infant's psychic entry into life which occurs in the first two months. In many ways, tentative emergence or awakening from an "unborn" or encapsulated state might describe the dynamic of a successful analysis with a patient with a schizoid personality or an underlying schizoid structure.

3 Traditionally, there has been no diagnostic precision describing the difference between the disintegrative experience of annihilation anxiety and fragmentation anxiety. We understand annihilation anxiety as an experience of the schizoid layer of the psyche. In Chapter 4, we describe disintegration in the experience of the borderline layer of the psyche as fragmentation anxiety. Briefly, annihilation anxiety is *objectless,* and appears in imagery of emptiness and isolation. Fragmentation anxiety is experienced as *object-full* and is represented in the psyche as images of being bombarded and dismembered (Dougherty and West 2005).

4 To pursue the idea of the contribution that a mystic child or prophet can bring to culture, we recommend *Living in the Borderland: The Evolution of Consciousness and the Challenge of Healing Trauma* (Bernstein 2005). In this creative and articulate book, Jungian analyst Jerome Bernstein describes an evolving new consciousness that he has observed. He pursues how western confusions between the gifts of mystics and prophets and the problems inherent in a non-rational perception of reality reflect the western tendency to split spirit from nature, mind from body. In the context of his work as an analyst and with a 20-year history studying Navaho healing practices, Bernstein synthesizes the development of western consciousness with contemporary complexity theory on the way towards describing his observations of the reality of the *borderland personality*. He understands this phenomenon as a spectrum of reality that is evolving and available now only to those who are sensitive to its transrational presence. Like all spiritual gifts, the people who bear them struggle for collective validation, camaraderie, and appreciation. Bernstein describes how and why western consciousness needs these perceptions for renewal, as we head towards the edge of a chaos of our own making.

Chapter 2

Counter-dependent narcissistic character structure

Independence in a glass coffin

Peter Pan and the archetype of the puer aeturnus

NARRATIVE INTAKE, PATIENT #6882, PETER PAN – NEVERLAND HEIGHTS MENTAL HEALTH CLINIC

Mr. P. Pan is a youthful man; single, appealing, handsome and charismatic. He enters treatment complaining of a vague sense of emptiness and a yearning for a "home he never had." He feels particularly defeated whenever he becomes aware of the signs of aging or fading energy.

Mr. Pan left home at a very young age and claims that he never knew his parents. He frequently socializes with a group of young males who look up to him for his brave, dashing leadership. He is a hard worker with a grandiose sense of his own power. He relates with pride his numerous adventurous achievements, yet he has not developed a professional life. He works out daily to preserve his physique and vitality.

Although it is difficult for Mr. Pan to admit, he experiences his relationship history as somewhat disappointing. While he is certain of his magical effect on women, he has never been able to sustain an intimate relationship; his connections with women have been brief and exciting. While he often yearns for contact, he admits that he does not have a strong sexual drive.

CLINICAL OBSERVATIONS

Throughout the session, this patient was consistently flirtatious. His attempt to control this session by being seductive seemed practiced and shallow. Rather than being empowered by his youthfulness, Mr. Pan seems encapsulated in his youth, locked in childhood. He is puzzled about his sexuality. He has resisted a more mature adaptation to life, and at this point is struggling with the aging process.

This interviewer has some concerns about the patient's reality testing. While recounting his adventurous exploits, he reported that he "could fly." Further clarification will be required in the next session to determine whether this reference is delusional or metaphoric.

DIAGNOSIS

Counter-dependent narcissist. Rule out possible delusional features.

The individual playfully described in this intake report is a thinly disguised embodiment of the archetypal story of Peter Pan. In this rendering, therapists can identify defensive patterns that are definably narcissistic. The counter-dependent narcissistically organized person is seemingly fearless and frequently concerned with appearance. This character style can seem dashing, impressive, and charismatic. He presents a rigid assertion of independence in defense against his deep longing for contact. As an adult, he may appear as confident, a little cocky, a great lover but feels unloved. His personality may be captivating, and he may be perceived as a winner, possibly even a fine leader. However, his repetitive adventures and conquests cannot satisfy his desire to be touched, to be released from his apparent independence. Not only cut off from contact with others, the counter-dependent narcissist is cut off from any real connection with an authentic sense of self. He avoids what would release him, the descent through grief into the nourishing and regulating potential of his inner world. Caught in a continual self-focus, he attempts to create self-esteem by constantly seeking affirmation from others.

In a classic Jungian work on narcissism, *The Problems of the Puer Aeturnus*, the eternal boy, Marie Louise Von Franz's (2000) describes the puer as a man who is arrested in adolescent psychology: impatient, unrelated, with difficulty settling down, perhaps living a provisional life. Idealistic, without guile, and given to flights of imagination like a child, he lives for the pleasures of the moment, often unaware of the consequences of his choices. The unconscious pressure of a psyche inflated with possibilities coupled with a reckless lack of discipline lures this person into impossible adventures, many of which are doomed to failure. As Von Franz describes it, identifying with the limitless potential of this archetype can ensure a life of dilettantism. The combination of this high-flying identification and an inability to relate on a human level makes analysis most difficult. Von Franz offers the analogy of a pilot flying an aircraft straight up into the air: nothing can be accomplished in analysis until the plane runs out of fuel and begins to fall.

Identification with any aspect of an archetype is more than a human life can support. Such an identification can distort developmental stages of growth and cause rigid defense systems to form. Developmentally, when the natural dependency needs of a child in this relational style are thwarted, a counter-phobic defense forms around an inner emptiness. Given certain constitutional intrapsychic predispositions and detrimental environmental factors, the archetype of the puer aeturnus can become so predominant in a human psyche, promising access to a magical existence beyond the clouds and above the world of adult relationships and responsibilities, all the while distorting the dynamics of human character structure as they begin to consolidate.

While a person captured by the puer archetype struggles with a history of woundedness and archetypal inflation, he is also heir to the playful creative spirit of the child. Jungian author James Hillman observes that we see in the puer a "vision of our own first natures, our primordial golden shadow . . . an angelic essence as messenger of the divine" (1979). The archetype of the puer and the puella aeturnus is alive with the energy of eternal renewal, creativity and play. Released from the defensive grip of rigid narcissistic character structure, inspired imaginative poetic beauty can spring into mundane, profane reality. For a person with a narcissistic character structure, life can be both limited and inspired by the archetype of the puer and the puella.

Initially, Jungian theorists used the puer archetype as a way to speak about narcissism, a metaphor that exemplifies a person whose development seems caught in a youthful identification. In fact, the story of Peter Pan is frequently used in Jungian literature to amplify the dynamics of narcissism. As we will discover, however, Peter Pan is a character who illustrates one particular presentation of narcissistic character structure, the counter-dependent form.

The world that a child explores after achieving some mastery in the primal phase and before the pre-Oedipal conflict constellates is what we recognize as the narcissistic phase of development (note Matrix, p. 6). All of the pre-Oedipal character structures reflect some natural and inevitable degree of failure in early relations that support the development of a flexible ego structure, i.e. we could say that they all have "mother problems." In fact, all three phases in the Matrix are pre-Oedipal and dyadic by definition since they describe psychological dynamics and character issues in operation in infancy, in the separation individuation phases, and in the period before a separation from the mother has been successfully attempted and completed and triadic relations become possible.

However, when we examine the archetypal and developmental under-pinnings of narcissistic dynamics, we discover that three distinguishable forms of narcissism emerge. In addition to Peter Pan in the fairy-tale realm, there are many different kinds of stories that embody the dynamics of youth and age. In Chapters 5 and 8 we will explore how other stories more accurately embody the dynamics of the seeking relational pattern and the antagonistic relational pattern: for example, the *good daughter* is one manifestation of dependent narcissism; and the *proud princess* portrays another in alpha narcissism. All three of these adolescent mythic images of narcissism carry an undercurrent of sexual play; they flirt, spar, and seduce. An adult human sexuality that has lost its innocence and moved into the world of adults, developed a capacity for intimacy, marriage and parent-hood, has not yet made an appearance.

Tale

The youthful spirit of Peter Pan, armed only with his boyish bravado and charm to protect a tribe full of lost children, is a uniquely apt image to explore the specific dynamics of counter-dependent narcissism. *Peter Pan* was first written for the stage by Scottish playwright J. M. Barrie in 1904, and only later rewritten by him as a children's book. Here is our summary of the tale (Barrie 1991):

> The ideal, if conventional, Darling home is first visited by the magical Peter late at night after the three Darling children have gone to sleep. He flies through the open window of the children's bedroom and enters unbidden. Once there, he is quickly scared off by Nana, a large and affectionate sheepdog that barks a warning and chases him out the window, but not before she snatches his shadow in her teeth. Alarmed, Pan flies off into the night sky, leaving his shadow behind. Greatly distressed, Peter returns to find it and he becomes grief stricken to discover that he can't get his shadow to "stick on." He sits on the floor and sobs; his crying awakens Wendy.
>
> Inquiring about his tears and in an attempt to make contact, the polite Wendy asks him what his mother named him. Peter defensively replies, "I was not crying . . . . and I don't have a mother!" He thought them very over-rated persons. Ultimately, Wendy learns that Peter feels his life began when he left his parents and decided to remain in childhood. Feeling compassion for this unusual fellow, Wendy comes to his assistance and sews his shadow back on. All the while Peter Pan struts, brags, and shows off. By the time he flies out of their bedroom window, she decides there never was a cockier boy.
>
> Peter comes nightly to the window and takes the Darling children out on incredible adventures. He teaches them to fly, and eventually

takes them to visit Never Neverland. This magical island is a place where children without mothers never grow up. The Darling children learn that Peter found the island after he ran away from home on the day he was born. He left in haste when he heard his parents talking about the realities of adult life, responsibilities, hard work, and pain.

Once on the Island of Lost Boys, the children hear the tale of the fearsome pirate, Captain Hook. We soon learn that Peter's powerful nemesis, this dread and dangerous pirate, bemoans his lonely life. In one adventurous struggle, Peter chops off Hook's arm. One afternoon while Peter is away, the children and the Lost Boys are kidnapped by Hook's pirates who line them up to walk the plank. By his wit, guile and strength, Peter saves the children and defeats Hook again. The lonely old pirate falls into the sea and is devoured by a crocodile that stalked him. In gratitude for saving the lives of her brothers, Wendy offers to kiss Peter. Peter bashfully declines.

After this great battle, Peter returns the children to their home at their request. Overjoyed to have their children returned and touched by his story of a brave and lonely life, Mrs. Darling offers to adopt Peter. Peter declines this offer of family and a home and flies off into the night sky alone.

The archetypal themes in the story of Peter Pan are alive in the background of the life of a person with a counter-dependent narcissistic character structure. The mythologem of a *motherless* childhood and subsequent denial of the importance of mothering, a *can-do* adaptation to the world that can result in great bravery and an adventurous but lonely life, are characteristic of the counter-dependent's defensive use of withdrawal from the mundane and flight into the otherworldliness of the imagination. However, a person cannot live in the eternal world of fairy. The realities of life's tasks and the pressure of primitive affect straining against an encapsulated character structure threaten fragile narcissistic cohesion.

On Peter's first visit to the staid home of the Darling family, this enchanted being alarms the instincts of the "grandmotherly" family pet Nana. After being startled by her barking, he flies off through the window as Nana captures his shadow in her teeth. Consistent with the puer psychology, flight in the face of the conflicts inherent in embodiment reifies an encapsulated defense. Remaining unaware of the effects that withdrawal has on personal relationships is one way to be out of touch with the shadow. When withdrawn from human connections in flight into the Never Neverland of the unconscious, we are out of touch with the shadow function in the psyche, which could challenge us, penetrate our defenses, and lead us into further development. In a disembodied state, we can lose touch with our soul and that which could bring our "personal spirit" to life (Kalsched 1996).

A counter-dependent narcissistic person is inflated by the experience of unbounded potential; talent and charisma are often so buoyant and infused with archetypal energy that endless possibilities seem beyond the bounds of human restriction. Flight into these lonely soulless heights can be exhilarating, yet also often empty and meaningless.

Maternal compassion, portrayed in the character of Wendy, comes to Peter's aid as she sews his shadow back on. A developed capacity for empathy and compassion, as well as an authentic capacity to mother, are most often qualities underdeveloped for a person with a narcissistic character disorder. Healing can come about through slow and related work within the transference. Only through the experience of a caring, related presence over time can this person become acquainted with their schizoid underpinnings, begin to acknowledge their shadow, and start on the path to wholeness.

This is not an easy task. The counter-dependent person's defensive cockiness and attitude of superiority keep them encapsulated. In fact, "I have no needs" could be the motto of the counter-dependently organized person. Offers of empathy are often diminished or rebuffed, especially at the beginning of the therapeutic relationship. In an attempt to keep painful experiences and undeveloped affective states unconscious, dependency needs are rejected outright and any appearance of weakness is viewed with contempt.

Yet when on stable enough ground the counter-dependent person can embark upon incredible escapades; the heights of imagination and adventure are never far away. However, adventuring can be exhausting and lonely when there is no one to come home to. A foothold in life's spotlight and applause for their exhibitionistic persona can be the slender thread that keeps the counter-dependent person attached to this world.

Peter's underlying schizoid reality can be imagined as the tribe of Lost Boys who live separately on an island in the middle of the sea in Never Neverland. Repressed, unmet dependency needs live on lost in the far reaches of the unconscious. In the tale, the Darling children hear about the fearsome pirate, Captain Hook, who is Peter's powerful nemesis. Symbolically, we could imagine Captain Hook as an alpha male who, in quite a mysterious way, sets the story into motion and readies a man for transformation. This powerful chthonic masculine energy can be experienced by a man as a breakthrough of shadow contents, generated internally by the archetypal Self. The archetype of the rogue, so aptly portrayed by Captain Hook, could dynamically function in a fairy tale as a presence that moves the story along, a powerful dark force that sets individuation in motion. From this angle, if Captain Hook was a stronger rogue figure who could defeat Peter, a person identified with this story might have a better chance at redemption. In a man's life, Peter's defeat could represent the defeat of an inflated narcissistic defense and encapsulated ego, which would then expose his repressed unconscious experience of weakness and vulnerability. Thus, this once archetypally identified man could begin to connect with his humanness.

But in this tale Peter holds his own with Hook and is not defeated. In one adventurous struggle, Peter chops off Hook's arm. However, Captain Hook is not a powerful enough shadow figure in this story to bring about trans-formation in this fairy-tale puer. As a counter-dependent person ages, more and more acts of daring do seem to be required. The threat for an aging puer of a too one-sided narcissistic character breaking down is ever at hand. In the tale, during Peter's struggle with Hook, the Captain is defeated as his severed arm is swallowed up by a crocodile that ruthlessly pursues him. Close behind a narcissistic wounding and defense is the threat of the emergence of primitive affect, the archetypal beast alive in the unconscious, always ready to swallow up consciousness. After Peter Pan's victory over Hook, an even more enraged enemy has been created. When the archetypal rogue is unable to penetrate the defense, he returns to the unconscious only to rise again another day.

After this frightening encounter with these dangerous and primitive forces, Captain Hook and his pirates, the Darling children want to return to the security of their home where they can be the children that they are, dependent and cared for by their parents. At their request, Peter returns the Darling children to their home. Moved by Peter's loneliness and strength and out of gratitude, Mrs. Darling offers to adopt him. He says no. In declining this opportunity, symbolically an erotic connection that might lead to Peter's transformation is avoided. For a counter-dependently organ-ized person, fears of enmeshment can often outweigh desire for human connection. This risk feels more threatening than continuing to live a lonely encapsulated life. Just as Peter was unable to accept Wendy's kiss, he declines this offer of a home, and flies off alone into the night sky.

The archetypes of youth and age

When a person identifies with one facet of an archetype, another falls into the shadow. We might imagine that in the case of a boy identified with Peter Pan, the embittered, defeated rogue energy of Captain Hook, now swallowed by the primitive energy of the beast, lays waiting in the darkness of the unconscious. Senex is a word that means old man in Latin. Meta-phorically, "senex is used to refer to an exacting concern for order and represents the limiting, depressing qualities of age" (Hillman 1983: 117). How might the tension between being identified with "primordial golden youth" and the disowned dark destructive and limiting aspect of age manifest clinically and dynamically? An early identity with the puer creates a premature encapsulation of a developing ego. Captured by the puer archetype, one is often unable to develop and create something real and meaningful. When he does achieve something, rather than being able to take pleasure in the fruits of his talents, he is often haunted with fears of being fraudulent. A puer remains hungry for attention and affirmation while keeping others at a distance. All the while, the senex complex waits in the unconscious, gathering energy, until it is able to overwhelm consciousness and impose a torrent of castrating criticism, imposing leaden limitations on the youth's naive possibilities and bringing his soaring ambitions and creative endeavors to a crashing halt. Narcissistic encapsulation is a brittle adaptation that threatens to plunge one into the dangers that lie beneath. In the process of aging, this archetypal identity can accrue disastrous consequences in the psyche:

> If puer identification is not worked through or outgrown, an enantiodromia will occur, and the puer will become archetypally bound by the Senex; the high-flying fun-loving boy will hold others to great accountability, become power hungry and symbolically eat up the creativity of others around him. The unlived life of the puer arrives in its negative form. It is not the wise old man that the aging puer encounters in his psyche, but old Saturn, with his crushing limitations. In his discontented bitterness he has become obsessed with structure . . . Whoever lives out one pattern to the exclusion of the other risks constellating the opposite. . . . Like old Saturn who devoured his children, everything new becomes food for the Senex and in the process, he has lost his own child.
>
> (Hillman 1983: 117)

Fairy-tale sisters and puella psychology

The fairy-tale world is populated by many boys and girls who live in an eternal childhood. In order to consider the dynamics of puella psychology, let's turn to discuss the beginning of the fairy tale "Little Snow White," a story of one of Peter's sisters in the land of make-believe (Grimm 1972). Snow White's story opens: "Once upon a time, in the middle of winter, when the flakes of snow were falling like feathers in the sky . . ." The scene is poetically set – it is the middle of winter, snow is falling. We brace ourselves for another story as desperate as the Little Match Girl, another story of the lethal power of ice. However, it seems that Snow White has had some parenting, enough parenting that we find that the story is not about being frozen in ice, but encapsulated in glass.

Forced by her father's new wife into premature and defensive independence, she is thrust into the dangerous woods alone. For her own safety, she rises above having needs. She becomes a picture of purity, a picture of empty independence. Subtly superior she moves in and takes care of a house full of dwarves. She is a little mother, all knowing about the needs of others; she succeeds where her own mother failed. This domestic adaptation serves to hide her grief at the loss of her mother, the subsequent Oedipal loss, and defeat at her father's remarriage to the wicked stepmother. This role works to cover the shame and humiliation she feels about not having a mother who loves her, and having a father who would leave her in the hands of a witch.

A person with a schizoid character is symbolically frozen in ice, while the more developed narcissist is entombed behind glass. While no one saw the Match Girl, there are many eyes on Snow White. At least this girl can be seen. There is some life to be redeemed, and at least somebody tends to her and protects her. Nevertheless, the wounding that Snow White experienced with an essentially absent father and an envious, vain, and vicious step-mother left her affects unmirrored and subsequently abandoned to live on in a girlish state.

Upon reflection, the archetypal motifs that we considered in the cold empty turf of schizoid reality appear beneath the surface and more subtly in the tale Snow White. Schizoid character style describes the developmentally earliest step within the withdrawing relational pattern. Counter-dependent narcissistic character structure emerges as a child develops out of the primal phase and into the narcissistic phase.

As the tale proceeds, images of snow evolve into images of glass. This motherless girl is tricked by her dark stepmother witch who poisons the sweet young maiden. Snow White lives on in a death-like sleep for many years, alone and separate from the world, encased in a glass coffin, yet still admired and worshiped by many. The dwarves in their grief exhibit Snow White in a glass coffin. Like many tales of a sleeping beauty, when the puella has been cursed by the dark mother, her death can release the heroic animus from the unconscious. Unfortunately in our day world, there are many girls being admired and worshiped while in a passive death-like state after being poisoned by a dark mother, there are many sleeping beauties still waiting for the prince to arrive.

The fields in which both the puer and puella flower are rooted in an archetype that generates symbols that portray youth and old age, regardless of gender. Cultural gender differences dictate the different expressions of puer/puella psychology and can mask the universal nature of this arche-typal conflation. Much of the Jungian literature focuses on the puer and does not articulate the parallel but different psychological issues for the puella.[1] Youth and old age manifest in different cultural realities as well. In a counter-dependently structured narcissistic girl, her relationship to the feminine remains archetypal since there was not enough opportunity with her personal mother to fill in her experience with personal relatedness. She identifies instead with her father, and identifies herself as a father's daughter. As such she cannot afford to relinquish her identification with her father and forge an attachment with her mother, with girls and women in general, and with her own femininity. Hence much of her personal sense of self, as well as her connection to the archetypal Self, will remain in the unconscious.

When a person grows up in identity with the archetypal puer or puella, we speak of the archetypal reality split off in the unconscious as the senex or wise old man and the wise old woman or the witch. Either way, when there is ego identification with a youthful image, the corresponding image of old age falls into the unconscious. Thus a puella-identified woman may "hold forth" as a wise old woman, yet everyone in her presence feels the prevalence of the immature girl adopting a posture of wisdom. In the same way, we can all imagine an aging puer professor giving a university lecture with the attitude of a cocky young boy, or a defense department official giving a report with arrogance and without humility.

Symbolically, we have seen so far several classic fairy tales portray the defenses of counter-dependent narcissism. Like Snow White in her glass coffin and Peter flying off to the Island of Lost Boys, aloofness, superiority, inaccessibility, and encapsulation are graphically illustrated. The strong, silent, dashing, competent hero, alone, riding high on his horse, to another adventure is a familiar male depiction of counter-dependent narcissistic traits. Like the brave and lonesome cowboy riding off into the sunset, the encapsulation and isolation of the narcissist are often idealized and described as *withdrawal into splendid isolation*.

Whether male or female, when intrapsychic and interpersonal factors conspire to create a narcissistic encapsulation, an impenetrable "youthful" persona is created to interact with the world. This limited persona accurately reflects the reality of an arrested internal development. Premature narcissistic encapsulation interferes with a full emergence of an ego–Self axis that would provide a person with a solid connection to the archetypal Self, the wellspring of meaning for us all. When thus restricted, an inflexible character structure obstructs the flow of psychic energy. It prevents the ongoing development of an internal structure necessary to develop realistic ambitions and ideals that would support the creation of a grounded and related adult life. The resultant inner pressure of primitive exhibitionism and grandiosity exerts a moment-to-moment demand to perform, while inner life is a vast internal emptiness. Thus conflated with the archetypal Self, the counter-dependent person is frequently left vulnerable to attacks of inferiority when he experiences himself as merely human.

However, not every child is destined to become fodder for hungry old Saturn. A narcissistic encapsulation can be "worked through" when one differentiates from the Self and comes to respect the energetic influence towards integration and wholeness. Becoming aware of a dynamic opposition in the psyche, holding the tension between youth and age consciously, a creative synthesis might arise. But with self-cohesion in such a delicate state, the puer and the puella identified person is ever threatened; a brittle transparent adaptation could easily fail to protect them from the danger that lies beneath.

Case vignette: Emily, romantic and unmothered

Let's turn from clinical theory and the archetypal terrain of the puella aeturna to consider an individual and personal story about these dynamics. As we'll observe in considering a case vignette, inflated by the archetype of the puella aeturna, Emily, who was always ready for another adventure, avoids any real relationship and was unable to settle down. She's always a girl, seemingly seductive, performing, and romantic. She is very serious about her appearance, which with much effort is meticulously constructed. She is a fun-loving magnet for men. She "plays it" over and over again, until it is boring. Interpersonally, she is impenetrable. Her capacity to seduce combines easily with her girlish charm. In social situations, she entertains her audience, scattering the fairy dust that makes her the life of the party. Her bright and lively adaptation can often divert a casual observer from the painfully empty inner reality that the counter-dependent person lives.

While she fills her life with others, she carefully guards against entangle-ment. In her inner life, she has prophetic and synchronistic dreams. Her fantasies are wildly romantic, grand, and non-personal. With her easy access to imagery, she uses the fruits of her unconscious defensively in therapy. In her sessions, she exhibits a fair amount of devaluation and contempt towards me. However, Emily is now approaching middle age and her relational poverty becomes evident to her within the context of her aging beauty. She enters therapy with the expressed purpose of becoming a Jungian analyst. With further work, it became apparent that she entered analysis in response to a rejection by a man who was supportive to her and whom she was beginning to allow herself to get close to. With the pain of rejection so close to the surface, access to her charisma and charm was threatened and she sought out treatment. Almost immediately she was able to understand that her daydreaming about cosmetic surgery represented a problem and not a solution.

It seemed to me that her treatment moved very slowly, a reflection of her seemingly impenetrable encapsulation. Her sessions included frequent reports of successes, triumphs, and intricate dreams. While her sessions were filled with interesting words, they seemed also pushy and labored. Quite unexpectedly, Emily got a prestigious job offer out of town. She decided to take it, was flattered, excited, and off to a new adventure. Much like Peter Pan, she "flew off alone into the night sky," to a new life in a high-rise apartment. I thought that she said goodbye to her friends and me too easily, prematurely resilient. Surprisingly to her, the first several months in this city where she knew no one were incredibly difficult. Her doubts about her aging appearance and the pain in her loneliness increased. It became more difficult to be "happy" socializing with strangers. She found herself crying at work several times, and was afraid she was going to "crack up." She deeply feared being shamed by her coworkers in the face of her tears. She phoned me in crisis. Her home in our town had not sold yet and she decided she still had the option of moving back and chose to do so.

Once she reentered analysis, her sessions were often wordless and tearful. She has a dream:

> Emily saw herself as six months old, hungry and crying for her mother. When her mother arrives, instead of being fed, she is held face forward towards a camera, in a stiff white gown.

The image stayed with her and troubled her. In analysis, she begins to remember other incidents where her previously idealized mother was cold, beautiful, and unresponsive. As Emily became aware of what she had missed as an infant, first she grieved and then became thoroughly enraged. She associated this rage with her mother, a rage she felt towards the other women in the lives of *her* men, and general distain with all women, including me. It took much time and fortitude on my part before this archetypal projection of "the evil stepmother" became conscious and untangled. In the long process of disentangling, one archetypal projection gave way to another and her rage transformed into anger.

Very slowly, Emily began to experience me as the Great Mother. She became increasingly able to share her neediness and vulnerability. She would cry quietly when she felt valued, held, and received. There was a period when she wanted only to talk about her favorite foods. She imagined that her hungry child was being seen and related to. Gradually she was released from her glass encapsulation. Idealization is the normal pathway along which the energy of the Self unfolds; it develops the pathway that allows us to become more fully ourselves. Having the security and support by an idealized one to *be* is necessary for the experiences of joy and creativity as well as comfort and security. This numinous experience in childhood also creates a foundation of support which can be sustaining through other developmental challenges and builds and strengthens the relationship between the ego and the Self.

Of course, this process of forming an idealization that empowers and does not ensnare can occur over the course of analysis. As an analyst can evoke and hold the idealized projection consciously, the analysand can begin to integrate its contents. If the analyst unconsciously encourages the process of idealizing, the analysand can be left to wither in a dependent position. Sometimes idealizing projections come to an unfortunate conclusion in a rapid devaluation and an abrupt termination. A best-case scenario resolution would be when over time an analysand begins the process of integrating the idealization into a rightful connection to the Self while at the same time developing a realistic perception of the analyst in human terms through the process of de-idealization.

It is easy to imagine the fairy tale of "Little Snow White" in relation to Emily's story. Lonely and envied, Snow White was exiled into a lonely wood, and Emily's nascent ego was exiled into the vast emptiness of the unconscious. When first wandering in the forest of the unconscious, the regressed ego suffers the isolation that is inherent in a schizoid regression. A strengthened consciousness can emerge from encapsulation only when the defensive narcissistic structure collapses and tears and empathy fill the emptiness with human contact.

Freud and neo-Freudians on narcissism

Freud described "primary narcissism" as an infant's autoerotic phase, the love of oneself that precedes the capacity to love another. Subsequently, he developed the concept of "secondary narcissism" (Freud 1914). He described secondary narcissism as libido regressing back to the self when love is impeded by slight or loss. Also, it was Freud who first introduced the use of the Greek myth of Narcissus to describe narcissistic phenomena (Freud 1914). Narcissus, a beautiful seductive youth, was cursed by the goddess Nemesis, the punisher of heartless lovers, to fall in love with his own reflection in a pool, never recognizing the difference between himself and an image of himself. Narcissus became the center of his own world and could not turn to see another. His own image stirred in him a longing that kept him captive, dissatisfied, and constantly unfulfilled. Although Narcissus was in love with his image, it could never satisfy his longing. Caught in this false and empty existence, he was fated to live and die alone. The themes of beauty, heartlessness, emptiness, and unfulfilled longing present in this tragic myth accurately portray the predominant issues of the counter-dependent narcissistically structured person.[2]

The work of D. W. Winnicott (1958, 1960, 1965, 1971) sets the stage for the work of many later theorists on narcissism. Winnicott was a British pediatrician and psychoanalyst whose work directly focused on the relationships of mothers and their children. He observed and described how developmental dynamics can go awry as a result of an unfortunate child and parental *fit*. An energetic mismatch can interrupt a child's developmental sequence either by not supporting or actively interfering with their explorations in play. Winnicott states that only in a "facilitating environment" can a child acquire the capacity for creating spontaneous gestures. In his early work he concludes that in relation to a "good-enough mother" a child is empathically met and supported, and can develop a capacity to express uniqueness and live in a natural state of "going-on-being." A good-enough mother, by his definition, is able to mirror the broad range of a child's affects, including both love and aggression. In the context of this kind of emotional support, a child builds confidence in himself and in the process of relatedness. The capacity to relate-in-the-moment, authentically and creatively, develops out of these early interactions. Within the context of this living connection, it becomes possible for a mother to evoke and then metabolize the child's innate sense of omnipotence and grandiosity through "dosed" or appropriate experiences of optimal frustration. As a result of this related process a child may develop the ability to accept the parameters of reality, which of necessity include maintaining an authentic sense of self while accepting real limitations.

However, when an experience of good-enough relating is not present for a child, his experience of living authentically is severely threatened. Because of experiences where a child felt his sense of being threatened, Winnicott posits that the vulnerable "true self" regresses into the unconscious while a protective "false self" forms to protect it and remains in place to interact with the world. He suggests that this "true self withdraws into cold storage" under experiences that threaten its sense of identity. A defensive "false self" adaptation is another way to conceive of the premature narcissistic encapsulation that we have been discussing in this chapter. When Winnicott used the term "true self," he was not talking about a fully formed personality inside refusing to reveal himself. He was talking about a potential for the "direct and personal experience of living which remains undeveloped because of a lack of suitable facilitating conditions" (1965).

In the last 30 years, psychoanalytic literature about narcissistic phenomena has increased exponentially. Social theorists have observed that increased awareness of narcissism is a reflection of trends in the general American population. In response to the Victorian models of behavior in Europe, hysteria was prevalent in Freud's era. However, the American cultural myths of limitless frontiers and potentials, vast resources, and personal freedom have contributed to the emergence of an adolescent, puer culture in the USA and fostered the incidence of narcissism (Lasch 1978). Reflecting this cultural reality, Kernberg and Kohut are theorists who have a pivotal influence on contemporary clinical thinking about narcissism. While continuing to preserve Freud's drive theory, Kernberg (1970, 1975, 1984) posits a structural model of narcissistic character pathology which he states forms as a result of repeated rejection of the child by manipulative parents whose capacity for empathy is impaired. The internalization of these distorted object relations results in a structural defense that holds a brittle narcissistic cohesion together. This "pathological self structure" is evidenced in an intense fear of criticism and use of isolation, which attempts to protect against an experience of inferiority, which could dissolve a fragile structural cohesion and allow an overwhelming influx of primitive affects. Simply put, a narcissistic defensive structure is an attempt to keep a sense of self together in the face of a powerful inner pressure to fall apart. Kernberg also suggests that the narcissistic person perhaps has an innately strong aggressive drive, which fuels this internal pressure of affect (1970).

Kohut posits a paradigmatic shift from considering the phenomenon of narcissism from the prism of a Freudian drive model to a deficit model (1971, 1977, 1984). Kohut focuses upon core defects originating in inter-personal failures, which result in an unstable cohesion of one's personal sense of self. With this shift in focus from drive conflicts to the central structures of personality, Kohut moves from a biologically based theory to an interpersonal one which results in a separate "psychology of the self".

While noting that narcissistically wounded patients evidence an excessive concern with themselves, Kohut focuses on their lack of self-esteem, lack of the presence of guiding ideals, and an absence of the capacity for being empathic with others. For Kohut, the child's need to be empathically met by a parent is vital. It is Kohut's conviction that aggression itself is a disintegrative reaction to inadequate parenting. Kohut understands that narcissistic self-structures arise from two specific developmental failures. The first involves the child's inability to convert archaic grandiosity into appropriate exhibitionism and self-esteem. The second is the inability to establish and work through an idealized parental image.

The developmental process of converting archaic grandiosity into self-esteem requires that a child be empathically received and mirrored enough by a good-enough parent. Once in place, integrated self-esteem enables a child to explore and display their unique capacities and interests and be admired for them by that parent. The empathic mirroring process gives the child enough support to express and integrate the "grandiose self" in their own unique way. It is through experiencing this necessary process of being empathically received and mirrored by the mother that an individual develops the capacity to have empathy for others as well as to develop a healthy sense of ambition, and self-esteem. Second, the failure to constellate and integrate an idealization of a parent contributes to a narcissistic deficit. If all goes well, a child could form a self-merger with an idealized parent. A consequent idealization forms, which when resolved could transform a child's natural archaic omnipotence into an inner sense of guidance, direction and ideals. When integrated, these qualities would enable her to feel powerful and confident enough to bring forth unique expressions of creativity into the world.

A gradual process of internalization can work to repair the original structural deficit. It is through this process that "the basic fabric of the ego" is created. In psychotherapy, as in a child's development, the development of the capacity of empathy and transformations of archaic exhibitionism and grandiosity are achieved in minute interactions over time. Because of honest and well-held experiences of the therapist's empathic failures, devel-opment and healing occurs through a process, that Kohut describes as "transmuting internalizations." In the process of realizing that "the one who holds me in esteem did not intend to wound me, she only made a mistake," the child or patient can internalize love and support, as well as begin to develop the capacity for empathy.

Kohut also recognized the importance of the healthy development of narcissism. Narcissistic achievement is what allows a person the appropriate use of exhibitionism to be able to express one's creativity in the world, the capacity to have realistic ambitions and the energy to act on them, and develop the capacity for human empathy. A living connection with a structurally sound sense of self also enables a person to discover what is meaningful to them, as well as what is in accord with his or her own ideals.

Kernberg and Kohut's perspectives diverge and converge to create a complex picture that coalesces around their clinical observations of the phenomenon of narcissism that includes an inordinate focus on the self, an internal experience of emptiness, and a shame-based lack of self-esteem, which strives to limit their interpersonal exposure by rigidly avoiding close personal contact. McWilliams (1994: 175) colorfully proposes that narcissist's "need for others is deep, but their love for them is shallow."

In *Prisoners of Childhood: The Drama of the Gifted Child and the Search for the True Self* (1975), making Winnicott's work more available and developing her own perspective, analyst Alice Miller highlights the dilemma of an intuitive child raised by narcissistic parents. She observes that these children can be more sensitive than most to unstated affects, attitudes, and expectations of others. In that family constellation, she observes that it is not unusual for one particular talent to be assigned to a child. The child may be designated as genius, as a special child, a favorite daughter, or favorite son. This child is then often burdened with a projection of their parents' sense of specialness, talents or his or her unrealized potential. While carrying these projections may be inflating for a child, their own feelings go unmirrored, and their uniqueness goes unnoticed and unevoked. In turn, the child develops a narcissistic character structure or "false self" to conform to their parent's desire that they be special in a particular manner. When the child does not or cannot hold their parents' reflection, parental disappointment can be very wounding to a child who works so hard to maintain their special status. In addition, because of their undeveloped inner life, they can only retreat to their inner emptiness. In this process, however, the narcissistic child may be more aware than most of unstated affects, attitudes, and the expectations of others.

Because of the centrality of parental approval for a child with a false self adaptation, this special child may go to great lengths to care for their parents. Manipulative parents take advantage of these efforts and the child's resources become drained and abused. Clinically, we can understand the haughty presentation of self, as well as an inability to empathize with others, in our adult counter-dependent narcissistic patients as an inherent consequence of their character structure. This defensive structure is a place to which the patient frequently and unconsciously returns to, to defend against feeling unloved, unwanted, and used.

Case study: Joan – perfect image, shadowy daughter

With easy access to mind and the imagination, the counter-dependent narcissistic person primarily identifies with image and then becomes identified with *themselves as an image*. One of the primary dynamic defenses that is employed is positive inflation (Edinger 1972). When positive inflation is paired with narcissistically required perfection, we find the image of self that is identified with must be beautiful and esthetic. Her house must be beautiful, her husband must be handsome, and the kids must be wonderful. This is not just her life, it is *her*. Her one aim is to be above it all. The positive inflation which she associates with herself and all others narcissistically used by her stands in unstated contrast to the devaluing of all those beyond her walls. She pulls this off by using the defense of devaluation, as we discussed in depth earlier in this chapter. Remaining as pure and encapsulated as Snow White is a lifestyle that supports her psychic integration. A flaw in the picture evokes her fears of disintegration into schizoid emptiness. If the image fails her, all is lost. Therefore she will work desperately to maintain her image: "My life is beautiful – without question!" The perfect image functions as a glass wall behind which the encapsulated narcissistic person lives. The rigidity and the impenetrability of this glass wall enable her to maintain her psychic integration, yet cut her off from open and dynamic contact with both the inner and outer worlds. Fearing both the impact of affects and actions and the threat of schizoid regression, she precariously depends upon her defensive structures. Yet, like glass, these structures can quickly shatter. Given that her defenses are inherently susceptible to shattering, the counter-dependent narcissistic person is painfully vulnerable. She knows all too well that for her hurt can be devastating.

We can see the counter-dependent dynamics of required perfection and identification of self with image active in analytic work with a woman named Joan. Joan had been the favorite daughter of a popular politician. Her mother was his beautiful loyal wife, an energetic and competitive public relations woman who seemed to drive her father's career. Joan reported that her life had been picture perfect until her daughter Jessica reached adolescence seemingly in a dark turmoil. Joan had an adoring husband, beautiful and well-behaved children, and an enviable career on the faculty in a law school. She was accomplished and self-confident. While she was admirable and admired, her subtle superiority provoked envy from others. Joan began therapy as a result of concern she had about a radical change in her daughter, Jessica. Jessica became discouraged in middle school, apparently subsequent to a disappointing academic performance. Although Joan and her husband pulled out all the stops in avid encouragement – tutors, after school classes, remedial computer programs – it began to become apparent to them all that Jessica would never be able to compete at the level her parents hoped for. Soon after that, Jessica became increasingly withdrawn from and angry with them both.

Jessica began to dress, as Joan described, with a "dark eccentricity." At first Joan responded to her daughter with what she perceived as gracious offers to buy Jessica new clothes that were more appropriate for a girl her age, have her hair done to make her feel better, and repaint and fix up her bedroom to lighten her mood. Jessica responded to her mother's cajoling by upping the stakes; day by day, odd dangerous looking jewelry began to appear at the dinner table. Friends with attitudes dark and sullen, who seemed to be considerably older than Jessica, began to appear at their door. At this point, Joan denied the extent of these troubling changes in Jessica, and responded by withdrawing from her daughter. Jessica in turn began to wear all black, painted her fingernails black, and finally dyed her beautiful blond tresses black. Joan found herself in a panic. She tried to write off Jessica's goth persona as a phase, yet she felt incredible shame about appearing with her in public, and angry about being exposed to this dark and untidy world. Where had she failed? This was the first blemish in her well-constructed life, the first chink in her armor. It was at this point that she sought out analysis. She loved her child and the degree of shame that she felt about Jessica's appearance was shocking and sobering to her, as was her inability to constructively intervene in what she perceived as an increasingly dangerous situation. All of this wounded her sense of pride on many levels.

After several years of analysis, Joan began to appreciate how the defensive perfection that had provided her with such success in her life up to now made it impossible for her to manage this crisis with her daughter; in fact it had actually fueled Jessica's acting out. The depth of her shame became the ground upon which her capacity to develop empathy was born. She recognized that she used her brilliance in an unrelated manner that evoked envious responses from others. Over time, Joan became able to recognize the ways she devalued others to feed her sense of being. Joan was able to work with the realization that her perfect adaptation to life was a defensive compensation for the shame she felt as a child when her own witchy mother used and rejected her in order to maintain her mother's image of perfection. Joan came to understand that at a young age she rejected her connection to herself as a woman.

Joan adapted to her mother's rejection by deciding that if she was above reproach in her appearance, her intellect, and her home and family life, then there would be no grounds on which others could shame or reject her. In fact, it became her strategy to reject them first and rise above conflict. She was able to comprehend that while·Jessica's phase belonged to Jessica, symbolically it was a representation of her own dark, despised, and rejected shadow. Jessica was at the mercy of her mother's unconscious insistence that she act out her mother's shadow. About this time, Jessica went off to college and the dark intensity of her persona, as well as her anger, began to recede. Supported with these changes and these insights, Joan began to feel more alive in her body, she began to experience her terror of feeling, and she began to feel. She began to desire. Eventually she grieved. Gradually, gradually she was released from her glass encapsulation.

When a counter-dependent narcissistic patient enters analysis, there is typically little transference that can be analyzed. The glass wall of their character structure ensures intrapsychic containment and interpersonal distance.

Jung and Jungians on narcissism

Jung and subsequent Jungian theorists led the way into considering what had formerly been arenas of undifferentiated pre-Oedipal development. Early Jungian theorists, notably Jung, Von Franz, and Hillman, utilized the puer image to talk about a whole range of early psychological phenomena. We might say that puer psychology was an early attempt to differentiate and elucidate Oedipal character issues from a Jungian perspective.

One pivotal difference between the works of Freud and Jung is that Freud was more focused on Oedipal guilt and "father" issues, while Jung focused on pre-Oedipal shame and "mother" issues. Perhaps because of the context of his own life and training in Victorian Vienna, and in response to his internal structure and personality, Freud's focus on the Oedipal arena and the development of neurosis was a logical consequence. Narcissism as such was not explicitly addressed by Jung. We would suggest that as a result of his experiences at the Burgholtzi, as well as the profound impact of his own character and personality, Jung's psychology focused most directly on pre-Oedipal material and had a more maternal focus.

Freud viewed regression as a defense, most often doomed to failure. Jung's break with Freud coincided with the development of his concept of a creative regression and its publication in *Symbols of Transformation of the Libido* (Jung 1956a). In a purposeful regression in analysis, Jung describes how libido travels into and beyond the wounds of early childhood into the collective unconscious.[3] There, transformation can occur where realignment with the Self takes place and the person can proceed renewed. Edinger would later describe this purposeful regression, renewal, and progression as repairing a break on the ego–Self axis (Edinger 1972). Thus for Jung, regression can be a purposeful movement back into the earlier experiences with the mother and ultimately into the collective psyche for renewal.

From the initial work of Von Franz and Hillman, later Jungian theorists developed these concepts more clinically and analytically: most notably, Kalsched (1980), Satinover (1980), and Schwartz-Salant (1982). Jungian authors continue to contribute to psychoanalytic work on narcissism. After this initial work on the puer, Jeffrey Satinover went on to imagine into issues related to the narcissistic dynamics in Jung's personality and psychology, and the hysteric issues and character in the work of Freud. Nathan Schwartz-Salant went on to explore links between narcissism and the individuation process and symbolic aspects of borderline character. Donald Kalsched continues to delve into a Jungian integration of contemporary object relations theory in relation to pre-Oedipal issues.

The narcissistic phase: counter-dependent, dependent and alpha narcissistic character structures

As we have stated, Jungian puer literature relates to and describes what we differentiate into three different forms of narcissism; each character structure being modified by the archetypal ground from which it emerges. In the withdrawing relational pattern, narcissistic dynamics with an underlying schizoid pattern used defensively work to keep this puer aeturnus off the ground, flying from one adventure to another, with little authentic contact with others. The counter-dependent puer and puella take off on their puerile flights into the mind, into the blue yonder of exploration, which can often prevent them from settling down into stable careers and in-depth relationships. Their romances are often long distance and perfect or empty and mundane. The hard work of interpersonal relating involves intimacy and the risk of exposure that the counter-dependent narcissist cannot tolerate. With the cognitive and imaginal talents that are available from the unconscious, their accomplishments can be many – brilliant, inspiring and breath-taking. Functioning at lower levels, they can get into a pattern of seeking their missing self-esteem and lovability through various cognitive musings; academic programs get started and abandoned, formulas get worked out and not written down, great novels are planned but not published, artistic careers get lived out imaginally, but not on the canvas. Grandiose strivings create unrealistic goals and fuel dreams that are a set up for failure. She plans to be a be a rock star but never learns to play an instrument or sing, he has great visions of being a scientist who cures cancer but never takes a chemistry class; he dreams of being rich and having a large family when he is unable to hold down a job or date.

As we explore in Chapter 5, a dependent narcissistically structured person is ever on a quest for a new erotic or romantic conquest, or perversely possessive. The dependent puer and puella sometimes identify with the archetypes of the "anima woman" and the "Don Juan man." In dependent narcissism, the *flight* defense is acted out in the context of others, sometimes into others. These *youths* often seek their esteem, lovability, and identity through ultimately unsatisfying relationships.

In Chapter 8, we consider in depth the dynamics of narcissism in antagonistic relational style. The person with an alpha narcissistic structure acts out a relentless pursuit to dominate others. Like a bully who uses and abuses power unwisely, he defeats his friends and foes alike. These same defeats often become his undoing. Seeking esteem through triumph, a strong constitution and physical energy are used in the service of personal success, by accumulating ultimately meaningless victories. Left languishing in the world of action, the alpha narcissist becomes estranged from the states of being that make an individual life worth living in the first place.

At the opposite end of the spectrum, in all three narcissistic variants, individuals whose structure is formed in the narcissistic phase can be puffed up and rulebound, arrogant and officious. In this manifestation, the narcissistic person has identified with the senex. In fact, they need to relate to the spontaneity of the puer to become whole.

Amanda: hard-working competent puella

A counter-dependent narcissistically structured person may appear, on the surface, in many different guises; often quite different from Peter Pan and his high-flying exploits. For example, Amanda does her "high flying" academically (Leonard 1985). Grounded in the mental realms of the psychic unconscious, she has access to great academic and organizational feats. Hardworking and competitive, she plays tennis and is on the debate team. In contradistinction to Peter's constant play, she seems to be busy at constant "work." She is a whiz intellectually, gifted and articulate in school. She is well put together, albeit in a conservative manner. Charismatic, yet lonely, in command socially, yet suspicious of emotional and sensual relationships. While she may prefer heroes and football players, she chooses dates that do not make demands on her immature sexuality. As the puer aeturnus has his identity caught up in the mother complex, the puella has her personal sense of self, captured by the father and the world of the father.

We could imagine that symbolically Amanda is conflated with one aspect of the goddess Athena, the classical Greek Athene. Like Athena, Amanda is a father's daughter who will most likely function efficiently in the world, in the academic, corporate, or political world. In the psychology of the puella, the girl is caught in the intense psychological field between the father and the daughter, especially if her mother has resembled the goddess Metis; her mother may have been experienced as absent, disappointing, or rejecting. It may take much time and many wounds before Amanda can access her connection to beauty, rage, sexuality, and wisdom. Yet all the while, shadowy more ancient aspects of Athena gather in the unconscious, waiting for recognition. In Amanda's case, the archetypal energies of Metis and Medusa were unconscious and yet to be discovered and integrated into her personal sense of self. As we have considered in Chapter 1, a powerful human conundrum exists when a person has identified with an archetype. Yet this singular focus is a lens through which we can observe archetypal dynamics that can possess or enrich a woman's life.[4]

Olympian virgin Athena: victorious and invulnerable

Striding into a room 42 feet tall, she resides in the Parthenon on Olympus, the "apartment of Athena," triumphant over a city that was named after her. Sprung from the head of her father, fully armed with a great war cry, Zeus was said to be her only parent. Brilliant, intellectual, brave, chaste, dauntless, with a great capacity for the strategies of war, she was the patron of warriors, a protector of heroes, and a father's daughter par excellence. Majestic and full of dignity, she is a goddess with ancient history and tremendous power. Athena is both the inspiration for and in her classical form, a product of classical Greece. In many ways, she symbolizes the pinnacle of western culture and was at the same time its muse. Woe to the woman who is identified with this kind of power, and woe to those who love her.

It is easy to appreciate the positive aspects of the fair gray-eyed Athene. This goddess offers organization, support for the polis, justice, and order. Her virginal encapsulation allows her to remain steady, focused, and dedicated to higher, thoroughly impersonal principles. She is a public figure, always in view, but we register that there is never a mention of a home life. In fact, Athena is a goddess who will not tolerate others seeing her while she is vulnerable. When Tiresias sees Athene naked, vulnerable, she strikes him blind. Yet with a nod to her epithet of being just, she gives him the gift of wisdom and of prophecy (Kerényi 1978). Identification with this classical aspect of Athena would be a superhuman frame on which to construct a narcissistic defensive structure; a seemingly triumphant and competent archetypal façade over a lonely girl who is ashamed that she feels unloved.

To travel to the bottom of these mysteries, we will have to meet all three aspects of this great goddess in the context of an individual woman's psyche, the ancient Metis, Athena herself, and the first beautiful, then terrifying Medusa. In addition, one curious note in this myth is that as an infant, Athena was attended to by Aidos, the goddess of shame.[5]

Pre-classical aspects of Athena: Metis and Medusa

Symbolically, while sifting through the layers of collective history, we can concurrently imagine our way into the personal history of a person with a narcissistic defensive structure. While the illustrious Athena of classical

Greece generates overwhelming martial power there are many tales that tell of her origins, archetypal and geographical, in places reputed to be even more ancient than Greece, the dark foreign soils of the other realms of Africa and the Orient. Unearthing these earlier mythic expressions helps us to uncover and discover Athena's chthonic nature. Most familiar to us is the image of Athena popular in fourth and fifth century Greece. Earlier versions of the myth of Athena live in the shades of history and indeed form the shadow of their classical counterpart (Pratt 1994). From the moment of her miraculous birth from the head of Zeus and throughout her reign, Athene is accompanied by symbols of two other goddesses: a wise owl at her shoulder that is a symbol of her devoured mother Metis, and a shield which bears the image of the beheaded serpent-tressed Medusa. In addition to the fully armored father's daughter who tends to her beloved city and worships her father as exalted god, alive within a more inclusive multilayered perspective in the archetype of Athene are several other divine aspects. Athena's more complete tale informs us of maternal wisdom and includes the passionate and beautiful Queen Medusa.[6]

Themes that are familiar to us about Athena run through all classical Greek mythology. We hear how tribal primitivity is overcome by heroic might. Zeus conquers Metis, and Athena conquers Medusa. We see these storylines again and again, as we consider myths that spring from powerful conquerors over more land-based agrarian peoples and their goddesses and gods: the dragon or the beast must be slain; the gorgons must be killed; the monster who is seen as the embodiment of the evil principle must be overcome. Exploring myths symbolically, we can come to understand that lurking within these monsters is an earth deity, a lady of the underworld, who has her own riches to offer, a lord of the animals. In the psyche of the counter-dependent narcissistically structured woman, these monsters can be symbols for her uninhabited body and connections to torrents of unconscious affects. When these "monsters" are consciously encountered, suffered and related to, they can open a path to individuation.

Metis is an ancient goddess, the defeated earth mother of wise counsel who is devoured by her jealous and power-hungry husband Zeus. Myths and images of Metis are necessarily fragmentary because of the distant place in history from which she emerged and lived. Evidence of her early incarnations in image reveal her close association with the Great Mother archetype and the earth mother. In the beginnings of a North African myth, Medusa was not born a gorgon or a monster, rather a mortal Libyan queen who is conquered and then punished by the Greek gods and heroes (Fontenrose 1959: 285). Athena is said to have transformed Medusa into her monstrous form, as she was envious of the queen's beauty.

A larger and more complete survey of the archetypal terrain of the goddess Athena can help us to imagine a person with a schizoid or underlying schizoid character structure. A woman's single-faceted identification

with the classical goddess Athena can give way to an archetypal heritage
of great diversity and great wealth. Considered psychologically, when a
woman is singly identified with the armored father's daughter Athene, she
must encounter and make meaning of her relationship to the once beautiful,
exiled, and shamed Medusa in order to lay claim to a relationship with the
wisdom that is her archetypal inheritance (McGrew 1988). A woman can
come to know the strategies and resourcefulness of the classical Greek
Athena, experience the beauty and queenly graces of Queen Medusa, as
well as suffer the banishment and shame of the Gorgon that may lead her
to a whole experience of herself. There, she may come to have an experience
of the wisdom of Metis. Medusa, Metis, and Athene are eternally a part of
the same archetype. It is our limited human consciousness that has made it
seem otherwise.

With this vast historical context in mind, let's turn to consider how these
archetypal motifs live and even rule in the psyche of a counter-dependent
person. The doors are wide open for the development of an unconscious
identity or conflation with the Olympian Athene when a girl child is met
with an absent or intrusive mother. Feeling unloved, neglected, or rejected
by one's mother breeds deep feelings of inadequacy and shame. Without an
early physical and emotional relational connection developed between
mother and daughter, a girl can grow to feel uncomfortable in and removed
from her own skin. If circumstances are right and there is a father in the
house, she can attempt to overcome these painful feelings about herself and
her body by idealizing and identifying with her father. Internally, this
situation is akin to the myth of Athena, the motherless daughter of Zeus.
The counter-dependent stance defends against earlier feelings of being
unloved or inadequate, of being too vulnerable to the presence of the
mother. Like Peter Pan, she may deny the importance of having or being a
mother. Like Athena, she may consciously feel that she belongs solely to
her father.

As a girl distances herself from her mother, she also loses a valuable
connection to the archetypal Self. Just as Metis lost her power and visibility, a woman can lose her capacity to connect with her own authenticity.
As we discussed earlier, an Athena identification can be used to create a
false self structure to attend to the world while she encapsulates her
vulnerabilities and shame. Symbolically speaking, an Athena identification
seals over the underlying archetypal reality of Metis and Medusa. In the
process, this woman is left to live her life in an empty armored shell.

Facing the Gorgon: regressive work in analysis

Uncovering the primal realms of shame and rage with a person with a
counter-dependent structure is a piece of work that is easily missed or
avoided by a therapist for several reasons. The counter-dependent

narcissistic person's charm, their relief about progress that is made in other areas, and the primitivity of their repressed aggression can all conspire to keep the therapist from "going there." These affects can be a fearful thing to evoke and encounter. If the therapist may be hesitant about going down this path, the patient who has utilized her image of perfection to make a life may feel paralyzed about proceeding. Facing this Medusa will deconstruct her sense of self. "Medusa may represent powers which were previously hidden and denigrated that we are forced to connect with, in order to live facing up to our murderous, vengeful, envious feelings of woundedness and shame" (Pratt 1994: 118).

Yet it is through this encounter with the deepest shame and fear that a rigid counter-dependent narcissistic character structure may be defeated and come into greater relationship with the Self. When a person is blinded to the depths of their primal experience, they can live a life out of touch with patterns that inform wholeness.[7] Athena, Medusa and Metis are not only three ancient goddesses but also components of one archetypal reality that can guide individuation. Just as the story of Demeter and Persephone can be imagined as one of ongoing separation and reunion within the psyche, the dynamics in the myth of Athena, Medusa and Metis, working in concert with a receptive consciousness, can contribute to both an enspirited and grounded personal life. The result of this "is not in a primitive reunification with the all-embracing maternal, but an active creative transformation of powerful, unconscious energies; carried out by one self-contained and magnificent feminine consciousness" (Elias-Burton, as cited in Pratt 1994: 123).

Notes

1 For a developed and insightful Jungian perspective on the stages of a woman's development, see *Female Authority: Empowering Women Through Psychotherapy* by Jungian analysts Polly Young-Eisendrath and Florence Weideman (1987).
2 The myth of Narcissus, which can be used to amplify counter-dependent narcissistic dynamics accurately, does not represent the mythic themes present in the lives of those people who have dependent and alpha narcissistic structures. We will consider in depth how the archetypes of Dionysus and the Predator respectively are alive and present in those forms of narcissism in Chapters 5 and 8.
3 For a rich archetypal amplification of creative descent, Jungian analyst Stanton Marlan explores the paradoxical image of *The Black Sun* (2005) and the meanings of darkness. This paradoxical image accompanies not only the darkest intrapsychic experiences but can also reveal a luminescence that is the light of nature itself.
4 For a very lively, poetic and meaningful rendering of Athena and her work in the psyches of women, see Annis Pratt's, *Dancing With Goddesses: Archetypes, Poetry and Empowerment* (1994).
5 Sandra Edelman has pieced together a wonderful bounty of mythic reality and personal story in *Turning the Gorgon: A Meditation on Shame* (1998). She leads us down the path of her own dream world and analysis to uncover the treasures she

found beneath the ground of classical Greece. Her scholarship on prehistoric mythic sources seemed notable to us as well.

6 As cited in the exquisite *Sailing the Wine-Dark Sea: Why the Greeks Matter*, classical scholar and champion Irish storyteller Thomas Cahill notes that while acknowledging the symbolic truth of myth, he states: "One can easily exhaust the reader by alluding to one too many scholarly controversies. I cannot refrain, however, from at least mentioning that many reputable scholars – Peter Ecko, Ruth Tringham, Mary Leftkowitz, and Colin Renfrew, to name a few – doubt (or even vigorously dispute) the importance of the earth goddess worship in prehistoric Greece" (Cahill 2004: 276). We would add that mythic veracity aligns with developmental realities in the human psyche. In all of our psyches, the reality of the mother is primal.

7 For an elegant rendering of the contours and dynamics of the inner world, see Murray Stein's *Jung's Map of the Soul: An Introduction* (1998). This work weaves together the spiritual and psychological in a seamless manner.

Chapter 3

Obsessive-compulsive character structure

For the perfectly tidy, the wolf stands hungry at the door

"The Three Little Pigs" is a story that begins when these good pigs are sent out into the world by their depleted mother to seek their fortune. The boys leave home prematurely, with boyishly polite manners, wanting to be good little pigs with a minimal capacity to protect themselves (Steel 1994). Consequently, psychologically the story is more about the building of defensive structures and less about the seeking of fortunes. We see the obsessive compulsive character structure portrayed symbolically in the Third Little Pig, who works hard with great precision so that he is safely encapsulated in his sturdy brick house, which protects the developing ego from the wolf at the door. The less rigid defenses, the straw house and the stick house built by the first two little pigs, were simply not enough to protect the good little pigs, the developing ego, from the wolf – the life of the body, affect and especially aggression. We can learn something about obsessive-compulsive character structure from the nature of the brick house. First, bricks are made with earth baked dry; affect is extracted from

life. Second, the dried out matter which remains is methodically placed, brick by brick, with mathematical precision. The bricks themselves are firmly cemented into place. This is one solid defense.

Withdrawing into encapsulation, devoted to work and discipline, unprepared to overtly use aggression and being dependent upon the methodical mind are all textbook traits of the obsessive-character structure.[1] The obsessive-compulsive individual's profound feelings of anxiety and vulnerability cause him to seek shelter and safety by conforming to family and community roles, behaviors, and values before he has been able to differentiate his own. Defensive conformity internally collides with the need for autonomy, which results in feelings of anger and rage at those upon whom he depends and fears.

Since the prospect of taking on the broader world without adequate internalized support can be very threatening, rigid defenses become solidified. Unable to develop a more flexible means of coping, the obsessive-compulsively structured person stations himself metaphorically behind a brick wall. From within this defensive fortification, the person works hard and tries to be faultless. However, the unconscious may present itself in the form of autonomous obsessive thoughts and the desire to commit compulsive acts. In the face of sexual and aggressive feelings, he feels a particular threat to his characteristic style of encapsulation. In times of perceived overwhelming challenge and extreme anxiety, these fortifications are designed to protect against painful regression into schizoid terror. This pre-neurotic defensive encapsulation creates a solid barrier to the flow of energy along the ego–Self axis.

Defensive encapsulation and overreliance on the mind and reason can both rob one of access to developing an affective and somatic life, as well as limit access to imaginative resources and creativity. When rigidly in place, this character structure limits access to the wellspring of vibrant and living images and thoughts at the root of one's archetypal inheritance.

Case vignette: working for what is right and compulsively doing what is wrong

A man called up who insisted on developing much of the initial frame of treatment on the telephone. Immediately, he wanted to know all the rules. He was a retired FBI agent and now worked as a law enforcement consultant. At this point in his life, he found himself surprisingly and inextricably drawn to spending hours on porno sites on the internet. Tormented by guilt, afraid of losing his valued position, and in terror of a nervous breakdown, he reluctantly sought help. His life had always been securely defined by discipline, hard work, and a conservative attitude; he "lived by the book." At home, the same principles had ruled. He talked matter of factly about his loyal wife, well-adjusted children, and position in the community, adding however that he felt terrified that his internet behavior would *blow this house down*. He feared being out of control, he feared being discovered, he feared ultimately being destroyed.

In treatment, we had to uncover the meaning that this fascination held for him and discovered it to be in part a projection of his disowned aggression. He never could have imagined that he wanted to blow down this *faultless* image. His primitive aggression was such a tremendously ego-alien aspect of his personality that it took several years of challenging work to differentiate himself from his rigid moral code in order to develop enough internal security to tolerate his affective storms without constellating intense anxiety and fears of disintegration. Not only his relentless guilt, but also his terror had to be carefully contained and interpreted. It was a long stretch of time before he could begin to reflect upon his rigid need for control of himself, as well as others. Ultimately, unbaked earth, the moist dirt of human body and affect, can be the agent that leads to embodiment for the patient who is stranded in a defensive commitment to order. In the tale, the Third Little Pig not only builds a brick house but also learns how to trick the wolf into the pot of boiling water. We might interpret this psychologically as the obsessive-compulsive person's need to step out of his ever so good smarts and become effectively aggressive. Once the wolf is "cooked" and the instincts are transformed into a digestible form, a person with an obsessive-compulsive structure can begin to relax their rigid defenses and tap into their renewing sources of spontaneity and imagination.

Developmental dynamics

Entering the pre-neurotic phase: from dyadic to triadic relating

Having weakly managed earlier developmental challenges, a person with an obsessive-compulsive, hysteric or passive-aggressive character structure enters the pre-neurotic phase of development with some structural deficits. Differentiation of ego from the unconscious in the first year of life may only have been partially accomplished. Karen Horner (1991) originally introduced the term "pre-neurotic" to signify a level of ego/object relations that is more developed than borderline organization and less developed than neurotic ego organization. At this level of development, an individual's psychic energy need no longer be directed primarily towards the differentiation and consolidation of the ego. Ego has had sufficient internal and environmental support to begin to separate from the unconscious. Now that the ego is relatively differentiated, negotiating a relationship to the larger world is the next developmental task. Extracting himself from a primary concentration within a dyadic relationship, looking forward and being challenged by the complications of a triadic relationship, he is in an in-between phase. He is no longer in the arms of the mother, and not yet fully engaged in the classic Oedipal struggle. Pre-neurotic character structures reflect the way a child has engaged with the issues of the two to four year old as he is faced with further challenges of separation, autonomy, guilt and desire.

All three character structures in the pre-neurotic phase are created as defenses of a shaky ego in an attempt to manage the pre-Oedipal developmental demands of separation from the mother and the capacity to move towards the father and the world. The obsessive-compulsive person accomplishes this difficult task at the price of conformity and repression of desire. The hysteric accomplishes this by keeping her seductiveness with the world superficial and unconscious. The passive-aggressive person appears to passively submit to environmental demands while burdened with tremendous resentment. In the context of this compromise, all three structures interfere with a free-flowing energetic exchange between the ego and the Self.

Woundedness in the pre-neurotic phase results in the ongoing experience of shame and guilt; shame regarding difficulties with dependency and guilt at the anger and resentment for those on whom they depend. For the hysteric in the seeking relational pattern, undigested archetypal affect is expressed in seductive behaviors in a desperate attempt to be and stay connected. On the other hand, these seductive behaviors are often dissociated or denied. To admit into consciousness the need for both autonomy and connection to another in a libidinally charged situation brings about fears of premature separation from the mother, which may evoke a descent into the affective chaos that is yet unresolved. They feel shamed about their "badness" and guilty about their desires. The passive-aggressive person situated in the antagonistic relational pattern also suffers shame and guilt; shame about their weakness and "apparent submissions," which fuels their guilt-inducing unconscious passive-aggressive acts. Their need for autonomy is expressed passively through self-defeating aggressive maneuvers.

Returning to consider the withdrawing pattern, in Chapter 1 we observed that in the tale of "The Little Match Girl" a person with a schizoid structure does not suffer concerns about shame or guilt. She is frozen in terror that her existence is constantly threatened. She is deeply withdrawn, paralyzed and unable to reach out for help. For the obsessive-compulsive person in the pre-neurotic field, the task is to defend an unsteady ego while faced with the challenges of individuation and the arousal of desire. The need for autonomy is expressed in their quest for perfection, which surfaces as conformity. Their desires are harshly censored and overridden. These unconscious desires are also the source of an ongoing pervasive sense of guilt. The Third Little Pig knows how to survive. However, he must keep his needs for erotic connections and aggression at bay.

In the obsessive-compulsive individual, as in the entire withdrawing pattern, a poverty of affect and bodily integration prevails. A personal quest for faultlessness, a devotion to duty and work, a tendency to claim the moral high ground, and a need for control serve to encapsulate them from others. Defensive encapsulation robs one of the opportunities to learn important relational skills at critical moments in development, which further impedes the capacity to develop the skills needed to participate in mutuality. It is important to become conscious of defensive encapsulation early in treatment, as the process of analysis itself may reinforce this pattern of defensive withdrawal when an analysis is allowed to remain solely in the realm of the mind, dreams and the imagination.

A conundrum of terminologies

Obsessive-compulsive personalities do not always suffer obsessions and compulsions

It has been frequently said with good reason that obsessive-compulsive personality structure has been wrongly named. Obsessions are thoughts and compulsions are acts performed to prevent the negative consequences threatened by the obsessions.[2] In and of themselves, these symptoms do not constitute a character disorder. There has been a long history of confusion around the diagnosis of obsessive-compulsive personality disorder (OCPD) which we introduced above. This uncertainty has been further compounded by the fact that obsessive-compulsive personality disorder has changed names many times over the years. The following are examples:

- Psychoanalytic terminology: anal character
- *DSM-I*: compulsive personality
- *DSM-II*: obsessive-compulsive personality
- *DSM-III*: compulsive personality disorder
- *DSM-III R*: obsessive-compulsive personality disorder
- *DSM-IV-TR*: obsessive-compulsive personality disorder
- *ICD-9*: anankastic personality

Added to this diagnostic confusion is the fact that obsessive thoughts and compulsive acts are *symptoms* that occur in several different character disorders, most notably schizoid and paranoid personalities. Obsessive-compulsive personality disorder per se is characterized by the rigid need for perfection, excessive discipline, preoccupation with orderliness, inflexibility, a lack of generosity, scrupulosity, hyper-focus on details and rules and excessive devotion to work. Only a small number of those with obsessive-compulsive disorder (OCD) have the entrenched defensive personality traits that would meet the criteria for obsessive compulsive-personality disorder (OCPD). Despite its similar name, obsessive-compulsive *personality* disorder does not always involve the symptoms of obsessions and compulsions, but rather as a personality pattern it is characterized over time by a pre-occupation with rules, schedules, and lists, perfectionism, and an excessive preoccupation with work.[3]

The clinical syndrome obsessive-compulsive *disorder* is clearly differentiated in the *DSM IV-TR* (American Psychiatric Association 2000) from obsessive-compulsive personality disorder by situating the disorder on Axis 1 and the personality disorder on Axis 2, thus clearly differentiating the clinical syndrome from the deeply entrenched personality structure that seeks control, especially of angry impulses. Obsessive-compulsive disorder (OCD) is a highly comorbid clinical syndrome that has numerous origins and occurs along with various Axis II personality disorders. In other words, one can have OCD and not have an obsessive-compulsive personality disorder. A therapist can treat a person's OCD and never come close to affecting their personality disorder, although the patient may gain a good deal of symptom relief. Therefore, a therapist's capacity to differentiate the clinical syndrome from the personality disorder is important. Currently obsessive-compulsive personality disorder is not seen as either in the same spectrum of illness or as part of a continuum with OCD (McCullough and Maltsberger 2001: 2341–52). In fact, the majority of individuals with OCD do not meet the criteria for obsessive-compulsive personality disorder.

Many clinical syndromes (anxiety, somatoform, depressive, affective, and dissociative disorders for example) diagnosed as Axis I disorders arise from deeply entrenched personality disorders and have a different significance to different underlying dynamics. McWilliams gives us an example. While the obsessive-compulsive's rigid striving for perfection is designed to satisfy negative parental complexes, the narcissist's drive for perfection is a response to an intense need to believe in their own intrinsic superiority (1994). As we have noted in our Matrix (p. 6), both the counter-dependent narcissist and obsessive-compulsive people are ultimately defending against fears of regressing into schizoid terror states with their exaggerated need for independence and control.

It is interesting here to note that not all obsessions and compulsions are problematic. Some fears and subsequent repetitive actions are a source of comfort and a welcome part of daily life. We use them to soothe ourselves in times of transition or when we feel out of control of something; as seen when we ritually calm children with bedtime stories or wear our lucky socks to baseball games. Normal worries, such as contamination fears, frequently increase during times of stress. Obsessive-compulsive personality traits, like all personality traits, are also adaptive and contribute to the fabric of human life. These conscientious individuals are "capable of being devoted, emotionally steady, and reliable" (Oldham and Morris 1990: 66). This steadiness provides leadership and continuity to society. Their capacity for caution and thorough attention to detail creates personal and cultural structures that protect and inform. Their natural capacity to observe and maintain detail has been utilized to explore, record, and map new terri-tiories, geographic and intrapsychic as well in deep space and particle physics. This kind of mental and imaginative thoroughness over time has resulted in the development of cultural infrastructure and engineering; be it aquaducts and wells, finding safe paths in the forrest, or designing and constructing interstate highway systems.

Case vignette: differentiating OCD from OCPD

In therapy, differentiating OCD from obsessive-compulsive personality disorder is constructive in determining long-term goals. The following is a case example that illustrates this difference. Following her mother's death, a 38-year-old single woman with severe OCD who was in a major depres-sion began treatment. Her depression and OCD symptoms emerged with force soon after her mother's death. She had become so immobilized that she was unable to leave the house and was being attended to by neighbors. Her particular obsession was scrupulosity, which most often involved her fears of being in a state of sin and being damned by God as a result of looking at men and having sexual thoughts. When she had a sexual thought, she experienced it as autonomous and intrusive and she would be compelled to go to confession in order that she "get right with God" so she could continue her life without fear of damnation and the paralysis that followed it in her psyche. Most vital for her however, was that confession stopped the obsessions. She might obtain some relief for an afternoon, but soon she would begin to doubt herself. Did she confess the sin exactly in its entirety? It seemed these confessions were never done exactly right. Did she really feel regret at the moment she confessed? Had her confession contained every detail of the sin? Then the compulsion to confess would return in an attempt to stop the tormenting obsessive thoughts. Often these periods of deep conflict and depression were so overwhelming that she simply gave up and stayed home.

With this patient, it may seem straightforward to begin to contemplate the psychodynamics at work: her mother complex, separation issues, dependency, and fears about her sexuality. At the same time, while suffer-ing the sudden onset of symptoms at a time of great stress, her OCD symptoms tended to wax and wane over time. Sometimes they seemed little more than background noise; at others they produced severe distress. In her severely depressed and confused state, her ability to maintain herself while living alone was in question. I recommended a psychiatric consult and saw her twice a week. The psychiatrist diagnosed her with bipolar disorder, major depression, and obsessive-compulsive disorder and treated her with an anti-seizure medication effective for bipolar disorders and a non-SSRI antidepressant for her depression. Over the course of the next two months, as the medications began to take effect and their dosage was corrected and determined, the depression and the debilitating obsessions and compulsions began to subside. As the therapy deepened, it became apparent to me that she did not have the drive for perfection and controlling rigidity of an obsessive-compulsive personality disorder. In fact, her pervasive style of detachment, absence of friends and solitary internal style of relating to the world, along with an insistent imaginal creativity, allowed me to understand the schizoid nature of her character. Her analysis was able to proceed from there.

Inner conflict that results in a vicious cycle of symptoms

Obsessions are thoughts that occur repeatedly and autonomously. They are unwelcome, disturbing and intrusive. People who have obsessions most often recognize that they are not rational, but that recognition has no impact on their appearance. Obsessions are accompanied by uncomfortable feelings, such as fear, guilt, disgust, doubt, or a sensation that life has to be lived perfectly. Things have to be done in a manner that is just so to protect themselves or others from harm, and from their immoral impulses. Individuals try to make their obsessions go away by performing compulsions, thus a vicious cycle is created.

Compulsions are repeated acts designed to release the person from the grip of the obsession. However, this relief is usually temporary. A compulsion is a neutralizing strategy to decrease anxiety. For example, people with an obsession about contamination may compulsively wash until their hands become raw and inflamed. An obsession about harming oneself or others may be addressed by repetitive checking; repeatedly checking that the stove or iron is off. Excessive religious or moral doubts are linked with counting or praying compulsions. Forbidden thoughts can give rise to compulsive ordering or arranging. An obsessive need to have exactly the right thing can result in compulsive saving or hoarding. Unlike addictions, compulsions do not tend to give the person pleasure. The rituals are performed to obtain relief from the discomfort generated by the obsessions. Anxiety is modulated by incorporating control. Activities are confined to those permitted by the controlling and rejecting other. Intrapsychically, moralizing and perfectionism work to keep the needy parts of the self under control (Benjamin 1996: 246–51).

The central conflict for an obsessive-compulsive person is between obedience and defiance. Their interpersonal style and intrapsychic structures reflect an internal schism that can neither be escaped nor resolved. A poised and reasonable persona may serve to obfuscate how intensely conflicted an obsessive-compulsive person is. This structure is perhaps the most deeply conflicted personality disorder. While the obsessive-compulsive structural compromise solution incorporates the values of powerful others,

it submerges individuality. The more adaptation there is, the more anger and resentment.[4]

Theoretical antecedents

Much has been written about obsessional neurosis and obsessive-compulsive personality disorder. However, it was with Freud's work that psychoanalysis turned from observing the symptoms of obsessions and compulsions to identifying the personality structure that generated these symptoms. In accord with his developmental model of psychosexual stages, Freud first coined the term "anal personality" to characterize the conflicts of the obsessive: withholding, control, and an over-concern with dirt. Freud attributed anality to its coincidence with toilet training. The obsessive individual's conflict with aggression is related to these early power struggles with maternal figures. For the obsessive, a severe inner conflict between submission and autonomy results in a central ambivalence that is reflected in lifelong difficulties with taking initiative and procrastination. Freud's term "anal character" captures the obsessive's extreme conflicts with guilt and desire; the need and the desire to evacuate and the shame, guilt and pleasure associated with defecation, as well as the power struggle with the parents. The compensatory character structure that the obsessive person develops serves to embrace the values of the powerful others, while remaining cut off from his own needs and desires. This concession is achieved at a cost. A core part of the self is angry and knows that he has been sacrificed.

Building on Freud's observations of the obsessive's tendency for parsimony, rigidity and righteousness, in "Character and Anal Eroticism," Ferenczi (1925: 259–97) portrays the obsessive's quest for perfection and tendency to judge others for not living up to their high standards in the term "sphincter morality." In 1933, Reich aptly noted that people with obsessive-compulsive structures who displace their aggression are more forceful and those who repress this internalized anger become more self-righteous. Nancy McWilliams observes that the basic conflict in the obsessive character is between rage and fear; rage at being controlled and fear of being punished (McWilliams 1994: 282). The obsessive person fears making mistakes and facing punishment for being less than perfect. Obsessive-compulsive people appear to have learned that there is a sanctioned but limited sphere of acceptable conduct. Sperry describes the obsessive-compulsive personality's emotional style as grim, angry, frustrated, and irritable (Sperry 1995: 138). The constant balancing act that their internal schism requires makes these individuals highly susceptible to anxiety.

Bearing internal conflict by restricting desire and conforming to collective expectations offers cultural validation and is paid for in cash by our western culture. McWilliams observes that the obsessive-compulsive personality disorder is the most prevalent personality organization in technological societies, emphasizing the values of scientific rationality over feeling, sensing, listening, playing, and daydreaming: "People with personalities organized around *thinking* and *doing* abound in Western technological societies" (McWilliams 1994: 280).

Conforming to perceived cultural norms validates a conflicted identification with the father world and renunciation of dependency needs, which is thematic in the obsessive-compulsive structure. Contemporary studies have turned to focus on interpersonal dynamics, noting difficulty in self-esteem and self-doubt, difficulties in managing anger and dependency (Gabbard and Menninger 1988; McCullough and Maltzberger 2001; Gabbard 2005). A person who has an obsessive-compulsive disorder strives for mastery over all anger, even resorting to appearing to be deferential and obsequious to mask their hostility.

Obsessively structured individuals were punished for failure and were given few, if any, rewards for success. These were children who grew up in an atmosphere with little warmth where the emphasis was on control. The most they could hope for was to avoid criticism or punishment. Benjamin observes that as children and adolescents they may have been subject to intractable intimidation and relentless coercion to obey and follow the rules, without question or regard for their own needs (Benjamin 1996: 246–51).

Jung on obsessive-compulsive personality

Jung comments directly on obsessions or obsessional neurosis almost solely in contrast to hysterical neurosis, a common psychiatric focus in his time. He notes that obsessional tendencies increase under stress and quotes Janet's observation that *abaissement de neuveaux mental* is enough to release the play of contraries from the unconscious in hysteria and obsessional neurosis (Jung 1909: para. 29). Jung proceeds to observe: "While the hysteric complex emphasizes the affective component, the obsessive gets caught at the level of cognition" (Jung 1909: para. 184). Thus, Jung's thinking is concurrent with our placing the obsessive-compulsive personality structure in the realm of cognition and the hysteric personality rooted in the affective.

Jung also refers to obsessions and compulsions frequently when addressing the compensatory functions of the psyche (Jung 1928: para. 702). For example, when unacceptable instinctual thoughts or impulses arise and challenge a self-definition, anxiety increases and the pressure of obsessive thoughts and compulsive behaviors functions to bring these dark urges into consciousness:

It is a notorious fact that the compulsion neuroses, by reason of their meticulousness and ceremonial punctilio, not only have the surface appearance of a moral problem but are indeed brimful of inhuman beastliness and ruthless evil, against the integration of which the very delicately organized person puts up a desperate struggle. This explains why so many things have to be performed in the correct style, as though to counteract the evil hovering in the background.

(Jung 1968b: para. 282)

Personal and archetypal dynamics

Obsessive-compulsive character development: conform or individuate

In order to separate from the grip of the unconscious parental complexes and establish a cohesive sense of identity, people with obsessive-compulsive character structures consciously seek to be above blame, while secretly resenting the conformity they feel required to assume to attain that goal. In order to manage their undeveloped and resentful feelings, they minimize the experience and meaning of affect, both their own and others. As a result, their feelings are muted, suppressed, and rationalized. With an active mind and a paucity of feelings, they can become very concrete – "Just the facts mam." This concretization interrupts the flow of spontaneity, desire, and thus creativity.

Obsessive-compulsive character structures obstruct access to the resources of imaginal unconscious and interfere with the capacity to relate sensitively and intimately with others. The internal quest for faultlessness and scorn for the excesses of "time, dirt and money" may provide some success in our competitive world but generates a constant state of inner conflict. This conflict may be expressed as moral superiority or rigorous self-criticism. These defenses interfere with a fluid dialogue between individual consciousness and the archetypal Self. The wellspring that could endow a life with meaning is *dammed up* by the development of a too rigid character structure. This dammed up libido then fuels the "senseless" obsessions and compulsions that emerge from the unconscious.

The high moral ground frequently occupied by a person with this structure both validates sensual and emotional sacrifices and relieves anxiety. Living from these pristine moral heights, they often "criticize others as too casual, self-indulgent and incompetent" (Beck et al. 2003). Needless to say, "they do not usually recognize that they judge others in accord with rules that they themselves unconsciously detest" (Millon 1981: 226).

For the obsessive-compulsive person, intrapsychic structures supporting the development of a lively personal life remain undeveloped. When the archetypes themselves appear as raw and unmediated expressions of the imaginal, the resultant images and ideas have enormous power. Highly defended ego consciousness interferes with internal access to the unconscious and this person may seem unable to engage in creative fantasy or remember their dreams. The dreams and fantasies that do break through can cause great anxiety, which is frequently managed by judging these contents of the unconscious as bad, useless and meaningless. Their inner world is ego alien to the person. For the obsessive-compulsive patient, when an archetypal component confronts the ego, the child or person withdraws into a defensive encapsulation; separated both from others and from themselves into an empty and dry but well-lit place. We can imagine how their internal dryness and feelings of emptiness attract obsessive-compulsive people to hysterics, who are affectively rich and dramatic. Mythologically, the great god of reason, the Golden Apollo stands alone on Mount Olympus in archetypal reality. Like Apollo, a person with an obsessive structure can have an orderly existence, but live an unrelated and empty life.

Order in chaos, and chaos in order

The primary defenses used by the obsessive-compulsive person include isolation of affect by means of rationalization, intellectualization, moralization, and displacement as well as undoing and reaction formation. These defensive patterns allow an individual to appear conscientious and objective. However, the person must also manage the internal turmoil of unresolved struggle between obedience and defiance which threatens to upset their carefully developed balance. The obsessive-compulsively structured person must guard against both external eruption of anger and the internal disruption of unacceptable emotions and impulses.

Interpersonally, the obsessive-compulsive person's insistence on doing things according to logical and rigid rules angers others. Some become aware of their impact on others, but do not understand it. Others appear indifferent to the negative emotions they evoke in other people. In fact, if confronted with the anger of others, obsessive-compulsive individuals are inclined to believe that these people have no right to be angry.

Withdrawal, encapsulation and annihilation anxiety in obsessive-compulsive personality disorders

Individuals with obsessive-compulsive character structures have unworked schizoid issues or *schizoid enclaves* in their personalities. Defenses are developed against experiencing annihilation fears suffered in the primal phase. Terrors of regression into dissolution and loss of a sense of self are highlighted in the obsessive person's desperation to hold on to concrete reality. These enclaves are highly defended against in analytic work. Cited in Spensley's book discussing the work of Francis Tustin, it is noted that in the treatment of obsessives, black hole paralysis contributes to "therapeutic impasse, negative therapeutic reaction and the problem of endless sterile intellectual dialogue where treatment has focused on paranoid fears and has failed to recognize and appreciate the significance of autistic 'black hole dynamics'" (Spensely 1995: 67).

As we introduced in the schizoid chapter, defensive encapsulation works intrapsychically to create the illusion of a protective covering to recreate an intrauterine experience prior to the painful experience of vulnerability that accompanies separation. Encapsulation within this imagined protective space, serves three interlocking functions. First, encapsulation provides intrapsychic protection from the awareness of the initial experiences of premature traumatic separation. Second, an encapsulated defense against this awareness of traumatic separation is vital because without it a traumatic regression into an objectless intrapsychic black hole may occur which would sever the person from all inner and outer connections, a regression into objectlessness. Finally, encapsulation enables a denial of dependency on connections, which have proved to have fearful consequences. Depending on the degree of an encapsulated defense, the cost to subsequent development can be enormous. Persons with schizoid, counter-dependent and obsessive-compulsive psychological structures are all susceptible to encapsulated regressions when under stress and during regressive work in analysis.

In obsessive-compulsive character structures, there are intrapsychic encapsulated enclaves, and surrounding them hardened defenses. We can reach a symbolic understanding of these three encapsulated character structures in the withdrawing relational pattern if we compare the image of *ice* in the Match Girl's tale, to Snow White's *glass* coffin, to the *brick* house that the Third Little Pig constructs. In all three cases, we can see a structure in the image that is constructed to protect an individual from a descent into intolerable anxiety. We have observed that it is through regression into the primal phase that the obsessive-compulsive person can access whole-making functions of the archetypal Self and resolve the regression with more freedom to connect with their authenticity.

"The Red Shoes"

Conflict between conformity and a desire to engage in the exciting unknown

Themes central to the dynamics of the obsessive-compulsive character appear in the fairy-tale world of Hans Christian Andersen in "The Red Shoes."[5] We observe in the tale a vicious cycle. Emerging desire is abruptly cut off by a stern censor, creating an obsession and compulsion. While Karen, the girl in "The Red Shoes" is not repeatedly checking doors or washing her hands, she is compulsively dancing. Although the character Karen does not have the specific obsessive-compulsive personality disorder traits of being perfectionistic, she does struggle with the obsessive's conflict between conformity and a desire to engage in the exciting unknown. Let us now turn to the tale:

> Once there was a pretty little girl who was so poor, she did not have any shoes. One of the old women in the village with kindness sews a pair of shoes for Karen from scraps of red material. On the day of her mother's burial, wearing her red shoes, Karen is noticed by another old woman who takes a fancy to her, and brings her into her home. The old woman casts aside Karen's well-loved shoes, and brings her up to be a proper young woman.
>
> In preparation for Karen's confirmation, the old lady whose eyesight is failing, takes Karen out to buy new shoes. Karen finds a new pair that she loves; they fit, and the old lady who cannot see their color buys them. Wearing her pretty new shoes to church, throughout the ceremony of her confirmation, Karen can only think of her shoes. When the old bishop speaks of her covenant with God, Karen's mind is not on his words.
>
> Against the instructions of the old lady, Karen wears the red shoes to mass the next Sunday. On the way into church, an old invalid soldier tapped her shoes on the soles and adds, "Remember to stay on her feet for the dance." Throughout mass, Karen can think of nothing but her red shoes. She even sees them reflected in the wine. On the way out of church, the old soldier remarks again about her pretty dancing shoes, and once these words set her dancing, her feet will not stop. The shoes have taken full command of her feet, her will is not her own. Only when they are removed, can Karen stop dancing. Even after this dangerous encounter, Karen cannot resist stealing glances at them tucked away in her closet. One night as the old lady lies ill and dying, Karen slips on the red shoes and goes out to the great ball. She began to dance, and when she does the shoes take over and dance her out of the ballroom, out of the city gates, and into the dark forest. Unable to stop, she tries to pull off her shoes, but they have become attached to her feet. With no recourse, she dances day and night without rest. She dances through meadow and field until she comes to the churchyard.
>
> Dancing toward the open church door, an awesome Angel dressed in white bars her way. Sternly he declares that she must dance until she becomes pale and as thin as a skeleton. He commands that she dance without pause so that every proud and vain child in the village can see and fear her fate. She dances, she dances, she dances. With torn and

bleeding feet, she arrives at the solitary cottage of the Executioner whom she begs to cut off her feet so that she can stop dancing and repent. The executioner chops off her feet. Still dressed in the red shoes, her severed feet dance into the dark forest. Supplied with a pair of wooden feet carved by the executioner, she limps into the village with the intention of repentance and a return to the church.

However, when she approaches the church, the red shoes appear dancing in front of her! [The compulsions go right on without her!!!] She flees in horror. Taking refuge as a servant in the minister's house, she turns to her psalm book and directly asks God to help her. The heavens open, the sunshine fills her heart until it breaks, and her soul flies on a sunbeam up to God, where no one asks her about her red shoes.

Karen comes from abandoned beginnings. She has been subject to rigid demands for conformity and caretakers who are more concerned with appearances than the wishes of a child. Always hovering in the background of this story as well is a vengeful and primitive morality that induces guilt and fear. Ironically, being swept away by the body's expression of freedom and pleasure could be an obsessive-compulsive person's worst nightmare. Psychologically, it could indicate a dissolution of ego defenses that leaves one *out of control*. Symbolically in "The Red Shoes," there is a direct correlation between repression and compulsive dancing.[6]

"The Red Shoes" is not a tale of redemption for the person with an obsessive-compulsive character structure. Karen is not the portrait of a person who individuates through her character structure; quite the contrary, she is defeated by it. Psychologically, we could say that she never develops enough of a cohesive sense of self to manage the internal conflict between the need to conform and the need to individuate.

Karen is described as delicate and very poor. In human terms, we might imagine a character structure that lies on a weak foundation. Like the Little Match Girl before her, with no father who attends to her and a mother who dies as the story opens, she is cast into the care of the ancestors, left to the mercy of the archetypes.

Her feet are clothed in red. The foot can symbolize the phallus, while the shoe is an image of the vulva. The foot can also be imagined as an image of the soul. Symbolically, we could posit that the young girl in this story is faced with and ultimately overwhelmed by her budding sexuality. One can say that this is a story of the fate of a young girl who grows up without parental concern and guidance into a repressive Christian culture. One could also say that this is the story of a young girl who grows up without parental concern and guidance and is therefore without sufficient ego development and subject to persecutory archetypal energy, which in the tale arrives in the form of the Executioner and the avenging Angel.[7]

Karen is pressured by unmediated archetypal excitement, unmediated in that she has had no caretaker to help her integrate and manage it gracefully. This excitement, which could be the beginning of the unfolding of a young girl's sexuality, instead becomes an archetypal force that possesses her. Karen's premature arousal leads her into trickery and deceit. It appears that she gets away with tricking the old lady into buying her a pair of red shoes. She gets away with it, but in truth, dynamically, it gets away with her. She could think of nothing other than her red shoes. They become her only focus, to the detriment of her growth and development. Again, we feel the absence of the mediating influence of a human mother. This kind of internalized mediation could afford the obsessive-compulsive person the opportunity to digest or transform these archetypal energies into a human dimension and to acquire some balance. This would, in turn, support the development of a sufficiently strong ego. An integrated sense of balance could face the compelling excitement of the red shoes without becoming over-aroused and carried away.

The red shoes were Karen's obsession at this point in the tale and the dancing soon became her compulsion. Her obsession was so extreme that while she was being confirmed into the body of Christ as an adult Christian, blessed by the bishop, she could think of nothing but her shoes. While Karen may have the desire to be close to God, she still seems to have the desire to dance to her own tune. She dared to wear her red shoes on the very next Sunday, and did so by means of both boldness and trickery. In doing so, she summoned up an archetypal force, the old soldier, an animus figure, who activated the power in the shoes and set her to compulsive dancing. A young girl in life with this inner story is caught in the battle between her nascent desires and the restrictions of them. Earlier in this tale, the shoes which became her obsession could be set aside. However, at this point in the tale "they take full command of her feet." When the shoes become "attached" and can no longer be "taken off," we can imagine a rigid character structure fully in place. The angel dressed in white at the church door is a vengeful primitive messenger of God. Karen is ordered to repent, and makes a guilty retreat. This archetypal image bars her access to living spirit and the whole-making function of the psyche. Her sexuality is possessed by the Devil and her spirituality is possessed by this punitive angel. Both the figure of the Devil and the angel block the possibility of integrating sexuality or spirituality, and they order her back into her guilty conflict.

At this point in the tale, Karen returns to confess, sacrifice and repent. This is another familiar theme in the dynamics of the obsessive-compulsive character. If sacrifice and grief can be held consciously, an individual might be able to face and work with guilt. With support and guidance, this repentance might have contributed to the strength of Karen's ego. What might appear out of the tension of the opposites of desire and conformity is the transcendent function of the psyche. This "third" energy might lead to the emergence of transformative symbols, which serve to strengthen the ego and enliven the ego–Self axis. However, in the story, with the connection to her sexuality and spirituality blocked, she turns on herself as she moves towards castration, mutilation and death. She turns to the Executioner, who then amputates her feet. With her connection to the ground severed, her possession by the unconscious is complete. Rather than learning to manage her anxiety, she mutilates herself. Symbolically, this is a killing off rather than a taming or maturing of her sexual and creative instincts. Her compulsion to dance ends at the price of being severed first from her sexuality, and ultimately from life itself.

Finally, in a disembodied penitent reverie, she is ultimately cut off from life, dies and is taken up to heaven. Karen's vision of ascent into heaven is very similar to the image of the death of the Little Match Girl. In human terms, when a person is cut off from their own desires, their soul, they are subject to a deadening. When Karen is executed by the archetype, she gets pulled into the unconscious and out of connection with life. What might have been her access to a wellspring of archetypally inspired beauty becomes a tormenting possession that sweeps her into eternal nothingness.

Case study: sleepless, skinny, tormented and guilty

With the amplification of "The Red Shoes" in hand, let us turn now to a case that reflects the dynamics of a person whose unmediated archetypal feelings persecute her into a state of exhaustion. An attractive and con- scientious 37-year-old woman named Trudy came in for analysis with immediate concerns about a significant weight loss and insomnia. (Trudy had lost 19 pounds, which put her down to a gaunt 91.) Paramount to her were her fears that if these symptoms kept up they would render her incapable of continuing to care for her two young children, aged one and four, without the constant help of her parents. Her symptoms arose over the past six months, the same time frame in which it became increasingly apparent that her one-year-old son had numerous developmental impair- ments. Despite the presence of a supportive spouse, her efforts to cope with her feelings of helplessness and guilt about her son's disabilities and the needs of this child were compounded by her problems in coping with her feelings and the needs of her highly gifted, extraverted four-year-old daughter. Her relationships with both of her children seemed to be com- pounded by the hovering presence of her mother, who was frantic about her grandson's impairments and overly involved with the fast-track education of her gifted granddaughter. Trudy was very grateful for her mother's help with her children, yet struggled with the increased level of anxiety that came along with her mother's frequent presence in her household.

Her insomnia turned out to be driven by her increased compulsions to check: check that all the doors were securely locked and her family was safe from intruders; that all the machines in the house that could generate a spark or fire were safely turned off. She was embarrassed to "confess" her compulsions to me and hoped for reassurance that she was not crazy. She was amazed that she should be caught up in such irrational actions because she considered herself such a rational person. While compulsive behaviors and protective rituals were not new to her, the grip that the compulsions had over her life and their current intensity frightened her.

Trudy had been an owner of a childcare center before she had her own children. She studied child development extensively and now watched with fear and self-blame each time her son was slow to coo and respond to her face, to turn over, to sit up. In addition, her son was a very heavy baby. It was becoming apparent to others that the child "was not normal." She was defensive and guilty about taking him out in public. Her son's condition was in sharp contrast to her daughter's natural tendency to be socially engaging and elicit smiles and attention.

In accord with the severity of the symptoms of depression, sudden weight loss and insomnia that Trudy was experiencing, I referred her to a psychiatrist for an evaluation who prescribed an SSRI antidepressant. The medication decreased the intensity of her anxiety, and her appetite improved over time. Her compulsions to check in the middle of the night were somewhat relieved, but they remained intense throughout the day.

Trudy was an only child, born in 1961 in post-war Germany into a rather stern Lutheran family. The child-rearing techniques of that culture and era were strict and required a child's submission. Her father was a laborer with a commanding presence. Her mother was a childlike woman with great fears and anxiety. Trudy felt responsible for caring for her mother's anxieties, which were many. Her mother wanted to live through Trudy socially, but her daughter's introverted and serious intellectual nature thwarted that desire. Her granddaughter's social precociousness and giftedness seemed to provide the grandmother with an outlet into life that she had long awaited.

The family immigrated to the USA when Trudy was six. She took on school and learning a new language with purposiveness. She remembers working hard at school as somewhat satisfying. Her parents frequently used Trudy to communicate their needs to merchants, at her school, and in their neighborhood, as they felt shame about their broken English. It took lots of time in therapy for Trudy to recognize and admit the shame that she felt about herself and her family. As an introverted girl in a new country trying to learn a new language, her social isolation grew and was very painful to her. Her isolation continues to trouble her.

In analysis, Trudy wanted to be a good patient and used her time in treatment most efficiently. She'd ask me for homework and frequent progress reports. She was concerned about using her family's resources for her own good. From the beginning, her desire for my approval and acceptance was overt. I found her easy to like, although I often felt impatient with her excruciatingly detailed descriptions of events and relentless self-criticism. She expressed the intense level of demands that she made on herself in a very serious and controlled manner. At times, the atmosphere in the room was so tense that it left me feeling exhausted. Yet she seemed hungry to be related to and surprised at my capacity to empathize with her. Her harsh and punitive superego demands seemed a stark counterpoint to my willingness to elicit her thoughts and feelings about her children, her husband, and her mother.

While she could empathize and articulate the feelings of her parents with some detail, she had little experience in expressing her own. She did not seem to be withholding her feelings from therapy, but rather she had no experience in expressing them. Over time, she discovered that she could remember her dreams. Bringing her dreams to therapy formed a bridge into developing a richer emotional life. Her dreams were rich and layered. She was surprised at their depth and expressiveness. They began to help her understand and acknowledge her rage at her mother's intrusiveness and demands.

As our work continued, Trudy and her mother took her son to many doctors, looking for a diagnosis to explain his failure to develop. As we processed these painful experiences, it became apparent to Trudy and to me that her mother's presence was not a support to either Trudy or her son. In fact, managing her mother and her mother's intrusiveness and anxiety often became the focus of these appointments. As I introduced the idea of setting some boundaries with her mother, unconscious material presented itself in her dreams and the therapy took on a new vigor.

Managing the shame and guilt that accompanied the emergence of dreams and memories of childhood sexual play immediately intensified our relationship. At times, she was unsure she could share what a horrible person she was and be able to continue to see me. At the same time, her nighttime compulsive checking behaviors (the stove, doors, toaster, iron, etc.) had increased and caused her sleep to be seriously interrupted again. What emerged were memories of sex play initiated by a girl three years older than Trudy who had lived in her neighborhood. From the years between the time that Trudy was eight and twelve, these two girls engaged in frequent sex play that had a sadistic ritualistic focus. Trudy was clear that the older girl taught her what to do, and that Trudy, even though conflicted, cooperated at first and then seemed to be compelled. The older girl had stolen one of her mother's padded "pointy bras," which Trudy would put on and then act as dominatrix to the older girl, who acted in a passive and submissive role.

Along with the emergence of these distressing memories, Trudy began to access her anger and desire to set limits in different situations. The anger scared and worried her. The irrational nature of her feelings distressed this woman who prided herself on her highly rational worldview. She became angry with me about the undefined nature of therapy, and wondered if I were trying to make her dependent on me by not giving her concrete answers to her questions about the length of treatment. This in turn raised issues concerning dependency and her fear of it. We explored her mother's dependency on Trudy, and Trudy's fears and anger about having to raise a dependent disabled child.

Her dreams often contained the symbol of a key. In time, we connected this image with her compulsions to check to see if the house was locked. One afternoon, Trudy returned home from the store to find her parents in her house watching television and snacking. Her parents dropped over frequently without calling. If she wasn't home they would let themselves in with a house key she had given them and wait until she returned. This particular day, she was tired from not sleeping and burdened by the demands of her small children. She was enraged to find them there relaxing and she exploded. He father immediately chastised her for her outburst and stormed out to his car. Her mother burst into tears and quickly followed her husband.

In our next session, while shaken from the outburst, Trudy was able to make some constructive connections. The key in her dreams, her inability to set limits with her parents, her inability to set limits on putting demands on herself as well as fears about her own anger began to come together. The coupling of the two themes in her compulsions – to check the doors were locked to keep safe from intruders and the need to check to see nothing would explode or catch fire – paralleled issues about a need to develop as a separate person, as well as her fears of her own intense affects. Over time, Trudy came to understand the sexual play she had engaged in as a child as a ritual that echoed her struggles with her mother, an expression of her unconscious anger towards her mother, an expression of a desire for some power and control, her being caught in a scenario where dominance and dependence were enacted.

Treatment reflections

Trudy's work continued and her symptoms subsided. She came to understand how her obsessions and compulsions were related to her level of stress and most particularly were stirred as a result of split-off anger. She began to question the extreme demands for perfection that she imposed upon herself. In terms of long-term gains, she was eventually able to develop an increased tolerance for her feelings in general and came to more realistic expectations for herself as a parent.

Often an obsessive-compulsive patient brings a problem-focused agenda to sessions in the early phases of treatment. It is tempting for the therapist to want to get on with affective and relationship issues. However, premature pressure to access affect can be counter-productive and alienating (Beck et al. 2003). The obsessive person's facility to "make use" of symbolic material is restricted by their character structure. The work of analysis may begin very slowly. This may be very frustrating for a patient or a therapist who believes they need to set efficient goals and measure achievements. Part of the reason that unstructured activities or situations are so anxiety provoking for individuals who are obsessively structured is the lack of safety involved in not knowing the exact rules of conduct or what behavior will ensure safety. The nature of analysis can evoke tremendous fear and anxiety in this person. It is not uncommon that some obsessive-compulsive patients are unable to tolerate feeling out of control and "not knowing what to say" in analysis, they ultimately drop out of treatment. McWilliams (1994) counsels therapists in the early phases of treatment to become aware of and attempt to absorb their obsessive-compulsive disordered patients' unconscious negativity. Further, she highlights the healing potential of ordinary kindness and non-retaliatory responses to their irritating qualities.

Trudy continued to be troubled by her lack of friends. Individuals who are obsessive-compulsive can be exasperating to others without fully comprehending why. It was only over time in my work with Trudy that we developed enough trust for an alliance to be formed where I could process the discomfort and impatience that arose in response to the tension she created. We were able to explore how her serious demeanor and self-criticism contributed to her difficulties to maintaining casual friendships.

Trudy's ability to remember and work with her dreams allowed her to access unconscious material. As she recalled her sex play as a child, many avenues seemed to open up for her. She became aware of her shame about her anger with her mother. With our alliance intact, I was able to invite her anger and criticism of me. Careful processing of this material was integrative and seemed to support a growing sense of autonomy. At the time Trudy ended her work with me, she was able to reflect on the limits of her responsibility for her son's condition. She sent him to day care a few afternoons a week and took up yoga. She began to be able to enlist her capacity for hard work and serious dedication on behalf of herself and her own individuation process.

From Peter Pan and narcissism to Saturn and obsessive-compulsive disorder

The archetypes of the puer and the senex

While exploring the inner world of the counter-dependent narcissist, we considered at length how often the person is animated by and identified with the archetypal eternal puer, the eternal boy. The relationship between the puer and the senex is hand in hand, two polar opposites of archetype of age. If the counter-dependent narcissist is most frequently animated by the archetype of the puer, the obsessive-compulsive is often influenced by the archetype of the senex. Considering the dark devouring dynamics of obsessive-compulsive personality disorder, we come face to face with the powerful creator and death-bringing archetype of Chronus or Saturn. His focus on time, death, and control portray the dark side of an archetype that is central to the obsessive-compulsively structured person. As Saturn pushed his children, one by one, back into their mother's womb, we can see the parallel with the obsessive-compulsive person; while they make lists, chart time schedules and make rules, their potential for expressing freedom and creativity gets pushed into the unconscious. In later generations, in a less primitive phase of human consciousness, another god with very different characteristics rises to the fore. Apollo, classical Greek god of order and perspective is no longer a primordial vengeful father who eats his children. It is possible that Apollo, a sun God, can be activated in the psyche of the obsessive-compulsive person. He illumines the value of order and rationality in a way that only a god can. This archetype can inspire a creative integration of these values in a human life.

Apollo: in the human realm, justice needs mercy if the will to power does not predominate

Apollo was a very powerful god in the Greek pantheon, the principal god of prophecy and divination, of the arts, and of music. He was both the bringer of plagues and the patron of medicine. He was vengeful, punitive, and competitive. Like the goddess Athena, Apollo both portrayed and influenced the essence of high classical Greece, 400 BCE. This apex of Greek culture evolved from the earlier eras of the culture of warriors and heroes, gave way to an era of detailed artistry in architecture, the arts, and medicine, and finally flowered into a culture of citizenry and law. The light of this sun god illumines human matters and brings a measure of the Golden Mean to consciousness (Cahill 2004). The cult practices of Apollo served to contain the faithful who felt trapped in the darkness of their own beings. His rituals offered a penetrating illumination that could be enlightening and transformative (Kerényi 1983).

The spirit of Apollo's epithets, "Everything in equal measure," and "Know yourself," evoked and supported the development of reflective consciousness, dialogue and democracy in ancient Greece. It was Apollo himself who guided the murderous arrow into the heel of Greek's greatest warrior, Achilles. In doing so, the golden god ended an era of rage and military glory. Reason and duty towards civilization's law necessitates destroying that famed warrior's rage, anger, bloodlust, and petulance. However, without the cover of night, constant daylight can ruin things that flourish in twilight or moonlight. Constant sun bakes the earth dry of moisture and creates desert conditions.

Apollo is first of all his father's son. The son of the great god Zeus was devoted to righteous duty. He did not possess his father's passions or the kind of creativity that appears from sudden flashes of lightning. Rather, from his place in the sky he brings perspective, order, discovery, and observation. Like many a person who is captivated by the gifts of this god, Apollo reigned but he never ruled (Bolen 1990). Creativity, robbed of a dark moist place to gestate, cannot foster love, progeny, or generativity. So while the god Apollo occasionally lusted, his advances were often spurned. He was never loved or married.

In the archetypal dragon quest, Apollo conquers and vanquishes the horrible monster, the python who prophesizes in the service of the ancient Gaia, the Earth itself. Considering this as a symbolic victory of reason over matter, thought over instinct, daylight over nighttime, we can proceed to understand how this powerful god would appeal to developing human consciousness, struggling to become independent amidst powerful primal forces. For a child whose developmental needs were devalued and consigned to the unconscious, might aligning with the Apollonian ideal appear to offer sanctuary from the writhing underworld?

We imagine that the archetype of Apollo would be enormously attractive to an anxious child with a shaky ego, whose pattern of withdrawal and encapsulation leaves him vulnerable to dreaded experiences of dissolution. Apollo's grace and poise promise power for a person who is caught in an intolerable bind between conforming and autonomy. Yet the obsessive-compulsive person can also become robotically paralyzed behind the walls of the Apollonian ideals of perfection, equal measure, and the Golden Mean. The righteous laws and vengefulness of Apollo can sever a person from the juices of life and the flow of their own creativity.

Loosen what is too tight

How might animation and revitalization occur for a person with an obsessive-compulsive character disorder? With enough ego strength and reflective capacity, it may become possible to suffer the conflicts between conformity and autonomy, between desire and moralism, possible to become aware of the need to control and impose perfectionism on self and others. With rigid defenses loosened, psychic harmony may begin to reestablish itself. The Golden Apollo ruled at his sacred shrine in Delphi most of the year, yet during appointed seasons he took leave and traveled to the far ends of the spirit world to visit the mysterious Hyperboreans. In those seasons an enantiodromia took place. Dionysus was allowed to emerge and reign at Delphi. As we will explore in great depth in the next chapter, Dionysus is the god of passion and wildness. Inspired by but not identified with either god, holding space for one's human values and space for inspiration, a person with an obsessive-compulsive structure can access the wealth of the flow of their own creativity, maintain more flexibly the gifts of Apollo, look forward to expressions of Dionysian passion, and partake in the wealth of human empathy and intimacy (Downing 1993: 69).

Summary of the withdrawing relational pattern

The curse and the boon of encapsulation

Each of the character styles that lies within the withdrawing relational pattern has a similar feel to it. When we review the symbols that surface in the myths and stories in these last three chapters, we see that the images are noticeably encapsulated. The Match Girl is frozen in ice, Snow White lies sequestered in her glass coffin, the Three Pigs hole up in the brick house. These images portray character structures that wall off life, interpersonally and intrapsychically; the person is unable to break through the barrier of rigid defenses to make authentic contact. This defensive encapsulation is different from the other relational patterns considered in the following chapters, in which contact is emphasized by the seeking pattern and aggression is emphasized in the antagonistic pattern.

The withdrawing character structures tend to rely both creatively and defensively upon the use of the mind and the imagination. Thus, in "The Match Girl," the child withdraws from her pain into the realm of comforting, if deadly, fantasies. Peter Pan magically flies over the city rooftops to the Island of Lost Boys. The Third Little Pig, in his efforts to protect himself from the instinctual wolf, depends on his mind and rigid mental structures to build his brick house.

However, when the ego is developed and the defenses are employed flexibly, the potential of the psychic unconscious can inspire tremendous creativity in the realms of mind, imagination and poetry. Looking through ice, the schizoid person may be able to see into the crystalline structures of eternity. Gazing through glass, the counter-dependent narcissistic person can develop an eagle-keen vision bringing perspective, boundaries, and balance to reality and contribute spiritual wisdom to human affairs. Contributing to the building blocks of culture, the obsessive-compulsive person can offer architecturally perfected grace, technologically informed order, and the strength and fortifications that allow vulnerability to exist in the world.

Notes

1 If we were proceeding solely from a neurobiological cause and effect perspective, we could consider the neurobiological origins of OCD from at least four biological perspectives: neuroanatomy, neurogenic, neurochemistry, neuroethology

(evolutionary neurology). However, from a complex adaptive systems perspective, the interactions of a developing child with their caretakers, their social system, their individual psychology and the Earth itself, we get a more accurate image of the real complexities of human development. If we add to that the effect of the child's physical environment on his body, his rate of metabolization, the impact of physical and emotional trauma, individual genetic loading, the nature of the geography he lives in and experiences of his ancestors and their particular evolutionary adaptations, we understand that nature vs. nurture is a reductionistic outmoded model from which to debate.

2 The most common obsessions are contamination, pathologic doubt, somatic, symmetry, aggressiveness, sexuality, scrupulosity, hoarding, and unacceptable urges. The most common compulsions are checking, cleaning, counting, confessing or seeking reassurance, symmetry, ordering, repeating and other mental rituals (Komor 2000).

3 Obsessive-compulsive personality disorder is the most common personality disorder in the general population – 7.88 percent (Grant et al. 2004). It is one of the most prevalent of three disabling psychological disorders, twice as prevalent as schizophrenia and bipolar disorder. Seventy-five percent of patients who are diagnosed as having obsessive-compulsive disorder are also significantly depressed (Gabbard 2005: 573–9).

4 The *messy compulsive* personality is so ambivalent and conflicted about every possession, every choice and gradation of quantification, that he can become a hoarder who lives an oppressively cluttered and chaotic life.

5 This version of the tale is adapted from Andersen (1976: 289–94).

6 Like myths, fairy tales tell rich and complex stories about patterns of individuation from which many lessons can be learned. In the abundant *Women Who Run With the Wolves*, Clarissa Pinkola Estés interprets the tale of "The Red Shoes" with an emphasis on appreciating the gifts inherent in our *homemade* creativity and not selling it out to *store-bought* values. We understand handmade creativity to be a gift from the wellsprings of the Self (Pinkola Estés 1992).

7 Jungian analyst Donald Kalsched carefully explicates this dynamic in his original and significant work *The Inner World of Trauma: Archetypal Defenses of the Personal Spirit*. He names the dynamic in the psyche that would protect a terrified aspect of the self that withdraws in the hope of protecting the personal spirit, the Self Care System. Once established, the System that was intended to protect is guarded by an archetypal Internal Persecutor, who may then act as an impediment to individuation (Kalsched 1996).

Part II

The seeking pattern

Chapter 4

Borderline character structure: agony and ecstasy

Introduction

In the Museo Templo Major, in Mexico City, lies an awesome stone relief, oval in shape, 11 feet in length. As we study the complex forms carved into the stone's roughly flat, upper surface, we slowly make out the dismembered parts of a female body. Eventually we realize we are looking at the body of a goddess, broken into fragments. The severed limbs, seen in profile, are carefully laid out, in pinwheel fashion, around the frontal presentation of the naked torso, all carefully contained in the oval outline. The contortion of her body parts, the bones which protrude from her cruelly dismembered limbs, the fanged masks mounted on her knees and heels, the snakes tied around each limb, and the skull attached to her belt spell out an image of gruesome death and dismemberment, darkness and chaos. This is an image of the Aztec goddess Coyolxauhqui. The Aztec myth tell us that Coyolxauhqui was outraged when she discovered that her mother, the Great Goddess Coatlicue, had been mysteriously impregnated.

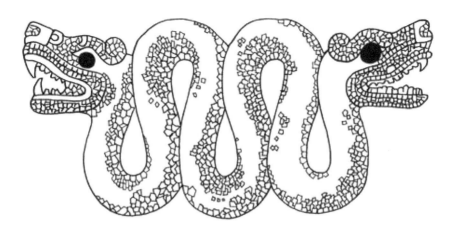

Driven by her sense of dishonor and her rage, she summoned her 400 brothers and together, intending to slay their mother, they advanced upon her. Just as they arrived, the Great Goddess gave birth to her divine son, Huitzilopochtli. This young savior god, painted blue, covered with feathers, and equipped with spear and shield, immediately beheaded and dismembered his half-sister, Coyolxauhqui, whose body fell, breaking into pieces, down the side of the great Serpent Mountain. This awesome stone relief presents a detailed portrait of Coyolxauhqui's broken, dismembered body and thus details the agony of this harrowing tale (Moctezuma 1992: 14–18).

We begin with this mythological image because it presents us with an evocative experience of the *mysterium tremendum* that lies at the core of borderline dynamics. Chaotic, intense affects and crowded, fast-paced, overpopulated and enmeshed interactions tend to govern borderline reality. Developmentally, the borderline character structure is the earliest expression of the seeking relational pattern. This character structure becomes organized around rich and intense, but unembodied and unimagined, affects. These intense, archetypal affects tend to dramatically overwhelm the nascent ego. Thus in the borderline expression of the primal phase we find that the person's inner reality is dominated by tyrannical forces which distort or obliterate reflection and drive the person into wild affective states. These wild states are frequently symbolized in myths and stories as a character, human or divine, being dismembered, that is broken, torn, or cut apart. These states may also find their expression in stories when the hero finds himself covered in ashes or soot, drowning in blood, or burning in flames, or they may appear in the visage of a frenzied, wild animal. Each of these images speaks of the unimaginably intense, inner experience of borderline chaos that is so evocatively portrayed in the Mexican representation of Coyolxauhqui's dismembered limbs.

As clinicians, we have each had experiences with patients who present us with these realms. Taking in a borderline patient is often like taking in a wild and terrified creature, usually right from the first phone call. For example: she enters your office, throws herself on your couch, and intermittently hides or erupts into her story. Like a trapped animal fighting for survival, one moment she may cast her eyes down, the other she may go for your throat. Wild, affectively charged contradictory messages can make every moment of analysis compelling and dangerous. It feels like life is on the line and it may well be. Darkness prevails.

Clinical theorists tend to ascribe a single underlying cause for structural impairments: e.g. the patient is thwarted in her desire for contact (Kohut 1977: 171), or the patient is driven by aggressive impulses (Kernberg 1975: 25). Yet the person with a borderline character structure lives in a world where the intense desire for contact, with others and within herself, generates both connection and attack, both love and hate. At one moment she may be expressing a deeply felt love, at another an equally deeply felt hatred. She uncannily keeps the other enmeshed in her chaos. Although she desperately wants connection, her actions tend to cancel each other out. At this point she typically turns to ruthless attacks upon herself and she may cut her skin, spoil her contacts, lose her job, and ruin her relationships in her wild attempts to seek contact.

This puzzling contradiction may baffle and antagonize therapists. Being on the receiving end of these unpredictable encounters requires the therapist to manage many levels of reality at once. The patient quickly weaves the therapist into her archetypal drama. In the intersubjective field, this drama is most frequently experienced as waves of affect with intangible form. At one point the patient may experience the therapist as the good mother, at another as the vampire, and yet another as the dark angel. Good and bad whip through the room with such affective velocity that at times you both may be cast into near psychotic madness. In this chaotic state, boundaries between conscious and unconscious, as well as boundaries between you and the patient, can become elusive. The therapist must consciously hold in awareness the curative value of living in these experiences with the patient while she carefully sheds light upon them, encouraging the emergence of the patient's reflective consciousness. The therapist must ask herself to weather the storms, receive the desire, and survive the attacks without retribution. The patient needs to experience the therapist as someone who maintains positive regard for her, as someone who cannot be killed off, run off, or in any way diminished. However, the therapist may well feel her own rounds of fear or rage, as well as defensive contempt, scorn or superiority. If she can remain in conscious relationship to her own feelings and defenses, she can remain with the patient constantly, competently, and indestructibly. She then can mediate the patient's affects within the transference, and these wild forces eventually may be developed into an affectively enriched symbolic capacity and interpersonal competence.

As the person with a borderline character structure learns to relate to the affective unconscious, rather than be controlled or possessed by it, she gains access to its rich and creative potential. If her archetypal wildness is honored, respected, and related to, if it is well integrated, she may receive deep nourishment from this life-giving, inspiring underground spring. This nourishment may render her keenly alive, with not only a capacity for involvement in deeply felt, vivid, loving, and loyal relationships, but also in an affectively enlivened spirituality. The cost of inadequate dialogue with this archetypal force is frequently immeasurably intense pain for herself and those around her, while the reward of adequate dialogue can be magnificent depth and vibrancy.

Borderline is a term that tends to be used pejoratively in clinical settings for those patients whose violent lives intimidate those who would help. Countertransferentially, it is extremely difficult for us to access, accept, and contain these places within ourselves; indeed, these experiences may be what we consider to be *other* than ourselves. When this is the case, borderline experience is cast into what we call the shadow, into disowned, dark, and unreachable corners of the psyche. All too often therapists are quick to consider the borderline person not only as "other" but "evil." Indeed, evil is not an unfamiliar word to appear, although generally not in print, in the midst of discussions about borderline patients. The therapist, when she herself is terrified of these dark territories, is likely to become either over or under involved in the heated crises of the patient's life. She may be tempted to try to "fix" the chaos as it is enacted in the patient's life. However, this chaos belongs not only to the patient but also to the therapist and to the eternal realms. Only with real knowledge of these realms in our own psyches and in our own personal lives are we in a position to begin to relate to the reality of these patients.

In this work we use the term borderline in a very specific way to refer to a character structure organized by the predominance of archetypal affect. As we will review in more detail below, the term borderline originated in order to describe any state that lies diagnostically between psychotic and neurotic McWilliams (1994: 42–4). It then became commonly used to designate a broad spectrum of states arising from early developmental wounds (see e.g. Kernberg 1975; Searles 1986). Thus many authors use the term borderline to refer to a rather large group of patients that we differentiate into separate diagnoses. We reserve this term for developmentally very early dynamics and defenses, thus differentiating it from narcissism and pre-neurotic character structures. In the primal phase, we see the borderline person as someone who is informed, if not possessed, by archetypal affects. A person whose character structure is inspired by aggression and who is impaired at a very early moment in life develops a psychopathic character structure. A similarly wounded person inspired by mind and imagination develops a schizoid structure. These differentiations, much like the three differentiations in the narcissistic field, help to clarify and sort out many of the discussions in the literature about borderline phenomena.

Case vignette: thrills to spills

For a number of years I worked with a man, Derrick, who was a physician. Having worked in the emergency room in a big city hospital for some time, he had decided to take a position in a less demanding department in a small local hospital so that he could also be involved in the theater. He had been married several times and was now single, vowing to only date and have fun. Fun, however, was not what his stories revealed. His heart was frequently broken. His dreams were flooded by pursuit and murder. His body was ravaged by intermittent rounds of binge drinking and cocaine use. At 45 years of age, his dashing youth and professional accomplishments were no longer disguising his inner turmoil. The thrill of being on stage was no longer satisfying. He felt terrified that he would destroy everything that he had achieved. He felt terrified that he would destroy himself. Fighting, which had previously been limited to his sexual partners, had now spread to his friends and colleagues. He needed help. He wanted help.

Brilliant and fast-paced, Derrick arrived in my office every session with countless stories of intense dramas at work, on stage, and in bed. Up to this point, intense dramas of one sort or another had served to creatively and effectively vent the archetypal affects inherent in his underlying borderline structure. However, the chaotic and destructive quality of these affects, previously well disguised as flamboyant and passionate theatrical displays, now began to overwhelm his ego, interrupt his personal relationships, and erode his professional life. For months our sessions were dominated by his turmoil. Over time his rage began to appear in our sessions; in addition to fighting with others, and much to his dismay, he began to fight with me. In response to the slightest misunderstanding or lack of attunement on my part, he became enraged. At times, when he yelled at me or left the session slamming the door, he would return later afraid that I would be retaliatory, rejecting, or literally gone.

Derrick's volatility exemplifies how the borderline patient lives in a state in which his intense desire for contact, with others and within himself, generates both connection and attack. The person with a borderline character structure tends to split archetypally imbued good and bad aspects of the self and others and then rapidly, unpredictably, and thus chaotically swing between these opposites. These wild and rapid swings powered by immense and extreme affects are the hallmark of borderline reality. Slowly, very slowly, as Derrick and I stayed with his wild and rapid swings, he began to experience me as constant, competent, caring and indestructible. Eventually, supported by a newly emerging reflective ego, he began to experience himself as coherent and multisided, as humbly and gracefully human.

The treatment of a patient with a borderline character disorder, or even a patient with an underlying borderline character structure, is a complicated, and even daunting, experience. The clinical rule of thumb is to set limits. Yes, we see this as a necessary support for the patient's endangered ego. However, much of the power in the room is well beyond the control of the patient's ego. Therefore, while a conscious reflective ego is being developed and supported, one must forge a dialogue with the archetypal affects that tyrannically drive the person into wild affective states.

Allerleirauh: a tale of the soot-covered sun

The Grimm's tale of Allerleirauh[1] takes us into the heart of borderline territory, providing us with an archetypal story about the wounded and wild child whose voice so often lies behind the desperate behaviors of people with this character structure.

The tale begins

> As the incomparably beautiful queen was dying, she instructed the king to marry another as radiant as she. One day, the king noticed that his now grown daughter, Allerleirauh, was as beautiful as his own dear wife and he fell violently in love with her. Shocked, the princess tried to turn her father from his designs by requesting three dresses and a mantle of fur which were so extraordinary that he could not possibly obtain them. But when the king managed to fulfill her requests, she realized that her only recourse was to flee from his desire. She packed three of her small golden treasures, along with her three magnificent dresses. Blackening herself with soot, she cloaked herself in the mantle of furs and fled to a far forest where she hid in a hollow tree.

We may interpret this story in terms of family dynamics and thus imagine that it tells of real and identifiable interactions in a young girl's life. More symbolically, we might explore how the interactions between the queen, the king, and the daughter portray intrapsychic patterns within a girl's psyche wherein one part (the parental complexes) turns incestuously and abuses another part (the ego). Many theorists suggest that borderline dynamics arise from identifiable physical and sexual abuse. However, at times this character structure emerges even when the family dynamics are not traumatic. In our reflections about this tale, we will move back and forth between the historic and symbolic perspectives.

This story begins with the death of the *perfectly* beautiful mother. Symbolically, the death of the all-too-good-mother heralds the arrival in the psyche of the opposite to what has prevailed, the arrival of darkness and misery. Her dying, and extremely complicated wish to the king imparts instructions that ultimately lead him to an incestuous desire for their daughter. This mother, who appears to be "all-good," in effect casts a spell upon her husband and throws her daughter into a terrifying predicament.

A young girl without sufficient mothering is especially vulnerable to an invasive father. Similarly, intrapsychically, a young girl's father complex, especially when it is in collusion with the mother complex, may be archetypally driven to possess and subjugate the virginal ego. In the story, Allerleirauh first attempts to ward off her father with impossible tasks, but he meets her challenges. In the face of this overwhelming and abusive force, Allerleirauh covers herself with soot and furs and flees into the depths of the forest. Dynamically, the ego hides its beauty, immerses itself in "the-all-bad," and flees into the depths of archetypal reality. Both her disguise and her flight create a critically needed separation. The alternative would be undifferentiated possession by a dominating and abusive father, whether a literal father or a father complex. Such a possession could lead at best to the development of a thoroughly false self, at worst to a psychosis.

Allerleirauh's flight from the father and her enantiodromatic immersion in the darkness of the archetypal realms may appear to be destructive, but for a borderline person it is a necessary step in the emergence of individual consciousness.

This image of Allerleirauh alone in the threatening forests evocatively portrays the borderline character structure. In the face of abandonment, passion, violence, flight, and terror, she fights for survival. Developmentally, when the infant in the seeking relational pattern faces the natural and necessary differentiation between good and bad, she defensively splits her inner reality. She flees into darkness, covered in furs, while the bright side of self goes into hiding. The adult woman with this character structure finds herself flooded by raw archetypal affect. She lives in a state of feeling constant laceration, from both inside and out. She frequently admits that she harbors a conviction that she is truly bad for those around her, that she is a curse, or even an evil being. The intense affective storms that possess her propel her into enmeshment from every angle within herself, as well as with others. Hidden in the forest, cloaked in animal skins, the person remains captive in the darkness.

The tale continues

Led by the keen noses of the huntsman's dogs, the young king of these far lands discovered Allerleirauh hiding in the tree. Covered with furs, she appeared to be a most wondrous beast and the king took her into his royal palace. There she was confined to the depths into which no daylight entered. Living in this wretchedness, she was ordered to do kitchen work and sweep ashes. One feast day, Allerleirauh secretly removed her cloak of fur, washed off the soot, stepped into her dress that shone like the sun and went up to the festival. The king recognized her beauty and asked her to dance, after which she disappeared so quickly that no one could follow her. Slipping into her den, she once again became the furry, soot-covered scullery maid. When asked by the cook to make the king's soup, she made a delicious broth into which she slipped her golden ring. The king loved the soup, was surprised by the ring, and demanded to talk with whomever had made it. Allerleirauh was summoned and appeared. When questioned, she revealed only that she was a poor girl with no father or mother. Declaring that she was good for nothing except to have boots thrown at her head, she denied any knowledge of the golden ring. At the second festival, the same events transpired. Allerleirauh appeared at the ball, fled, sent a golden gift, and once again denied her value and her knowledge. At the third festival, Allerleirauh arrived in her dress that shone like the stars. However, this time the king cleverly slipped a golden ring on her finger and insisted upon dancing with her for so long that when she fled to her den she left her ball gown under her cloak of furs and left one finger not covered with soot. After she quickly slipped a golden gift into the king's soup, she was once again summoned. Seeing her white finger and the ring that he had put on it during the dance, the king grasped her and held her fast. Struggling to get free and run away, her mantle of fur fell open and the star dress shone forth. When the king tore off her mantle of furs, her golden hair shone forth and she appeared in full splendor, no longer able to hide herself. When Allerleirauh washed away the soot from her face, her full beauty was revealed. The king chose her to be his bride. They were wed and lived happily until their deaths.

In the tale, we hear that the huntsman's dogs eventually discover the girl who has fled into the forests. Perceived by others as an untamed beast, her wildness repels yet fascinates. It appears that a very basic instinct, symbolized by the dogs, awakes the ego and brings it into proximity of the king who may be understood to be the animus. Delivered from entrapment in the unconscious, the ego is once again in a place from which it can seek contact, possibly this time without meeting abusive attack. Allerleirauh did emerge from hiding. By appearing at the festival in a beautiful gown, she brought the bright side of herself forward, even if fleetingly. This new presentation of the bright side of the self was neither repossessed by the all-good mother complex nor subjugated by a dominating father complex, but was met by a newly related animus figure. Allerleirauh was then able to engage in a process of repetitive exposure: the various clues hidden in the soups, the various appearances at the balls. Intrapsychically, it appears that the forces that propelled Allerleirauh into the dark had given way to the dynamic exploration of a balance between the opposites.

Just as Allerleirauh repetitively emerges and retreats, we find a person with a borderline character structure making contact and then attacking, improving her life and then destroying it, in what might seem like never-ending cycles. Yet, when these cycles are a series of well-held interactions, it gradually becomes clear that a momentum is growing, a developmental process is occurring. In the story, at the third and final festival, Allerleirauh did not cover herself completely. She no longer hid completely and was therefore accessible to the firm grasp of the king. This encounter led to Allerleirauh's standing in full splendor, able to arrive at the wedding, the celebrated *coniunctio* (Latin for "union"), the marriage of differentiated opposites.

Like the king's direct engagement with Allerleirauh, at some point it may well be necessary for the therapist to become more forceful and direct in his interpretations with the patient. When the patient feels sufficiently valued and safe, these active interactions serve to bring the patient fully out of hiding. Having been met in the moments of her suffering and chaos and accompanied by the therapist, she can now begin to reclaim the bright split off part of self that was carefully hidden and protected in reaction to her early abandonment and abuse.

The therapist's experience of a relationship with a patient with such a profile may be likened to the king's experience in this fairy tale. These patients do bring the richness of the depths of the affectively imbued archetypal realms into our lives in an immediate and animating manner. Yet this richness may or may not be welcomed. If we, as therapists, are not wrestling with our own dragons, if we do not recognize our own despair and our own murderous rages, we will be especially susceptible to being repelled by or fascinated with and ensnared by the patient with a borderline character structure. The therapist may find himself resenting the time and energy he devotes to this particular patient. It is not infrequently noted that borderline patients dominate supervision hours, case conferences, and even therapists' dreams.

The taste of the soup and the promise of the small golden treasures may prompt the therapist, as they did the king, to be insistently curious about where the treasures are coming from, to call the person out of the dungeon and ask over and over "Who are you?" and "Where are you?" The taste of the soup and the promise of the small golden treasures helps us sit in our chairs when the patient asserts, hour after hour, that she is worth, "only a boot in the head," and turns to another round of self-abuse. Eventually, the magical moments at the dance, the wonderful soup and the golden treasures led the king to identify the source of this wealth, and, we must note this, he marries her. While the therapist may lead the patient towards her inner marriage, he could lead himself towards the same. Out of his engagement with this patient, he could deepen his own relationship to the realms of darkness, chaos, and despair – and the full splendor of the golden sun. It is no simple task to open oneself to these chaotic realms yet it is abundantly clear that they can enrich our personal lives and deepen our experience of soul.

The literature

The literature about "borderline personality" is frequently acknowledged to be inconsistent and contradictory. It is intriguing to consider the possibility that these characteristic patterns within the literature might themselves be a manifestation of the phenomena of "borderline" dynamics that are themselves inherently inconsistent, contradictory, and chaotic. People have observed that the borderline patient tends to create chaos, dissension, and splitting among the people in his environment. It is not surprising then to find that the literature about these dynamics suffers a similar fate, remaining fragmented and unintegrated.

We have found ourselves, also, in a quandary created by these contradictions and inconsistencies. We consider "borderline" to be an identifiable personality disorder in accord with the *DSM-III* and *DSM-IV* category (American Psychiatric Association 1980, 1994). In both our personal and clinical discussions, we consistently contrast borderline structures to other character structures: narcissistic, schizoid, obsessive-compulsive structures, etc., considering them each as a distinctive character style. However, we also realize that a number of theorists use the term borderline as a description for a level of development between psychotic and neurotic functioning. From this perspective, any particular character structure, e.g. the hysteric structure, may manifest at a borderline or neurotic level of development. We will review the literature regarding both these positions in just a moment, but first we want to describe how these contradictory perspectives are both woven into our Matrix (p. 6).

As we have described in the Introduction, we use the word borderline to describe a particular personality structure. We have integrated the need to differentiate levels of development by defining several different phases that lie in the "borderland" between psychosis and neurosis. In our Matrix, the earliest level of development is the primal phase, the progressively more developed phases are the narcissistic phase and the pre-neurotic phase. Differentiating these three levels of development enables us to detail the similarities and differences between each phase. Our additional differentiation of the relational patterns allows us to discriminate between interactional styles. Our use of the term "borderline" is thus relatively precisely defined as developmentally very early and based upon an affectively informed seeking relational pattern.

There are a number of general reviews about borderline character structures to which the reader may refer for more details. Particularly clear reviews and discussions may be found in McWilliams (1994), Goldstein (1996), Gunderson (1984), Millon and Davis (1996), and Josephs (1995), while an especially succinct yet inconclusive overview is in Gabbard and Wilkinson (1994).

McWilliams details the history of this diagnosis in such a way as to emphasize the use of borderline as a description of a level of development. She notes that as early as 1890, Rosse observed that some patients seem "to inhabit a 'borderland' between sanity and insanity" (McWilliams 1994: 49). Nevertheless, the less differentiated, classic psychoanalytic model of psychosis-versus-neurosis was predominant until the middle of the twentieth century. At that point, a number of people, notably Gunderson, Kernberg, and Masterson, began to write about borderline states to denote "a type of personality structure graver in its implications than neurosis yet not vulnerable to lasting psychotic decompensations" (McWilliams 1994: 50–1).

"Borderline" as a discrete diagnosis came into prominence with Kernberg's work in the 1960s and 1970s that presented a synthesis of British objects relations theory and American ego psychology. British objects relations theory, notably Melanie Klein, Ronald Fairbairn, and

Donald Winnicott, proposed that character structures evolve through the development of internalized representations of self in relation to others. They assume that the infant brings into the world certain preprogrammed modes of organizing interpersonal experience, certain "universal relational scenarios to which real life interpersonal experience becomes assimilated" (Josephs 1995: 73). These assimilations involve the work of the imagination which "works over actual life experience," rendering an internal reality which is a compromise between the way things actually were and are, and one's wishes and fears.

Using these concepts to develop his ideas about borderline dynamics, Kernberg offers a number of symptoms and "peculiarities" which describe borderline structures. Included are observations that help to clarify the specific borderline dynamics that are of interest to us. He suggests that the borderline patient will present symptoms such as: chronic free-floating diffuse anxiety; dissociative reactions; limited impulse control; conversion symptoms; hypochondriasis; polymorphous perverse sexual trends; addictions; and limited channels of sublimation. He observes that one of the prominent characteristics of the borderline is an identity diffusion "represented by a poorly integrated concept of the self and significant others." He explains that the borderline personality organization has "enough differentiation of self representations from object representations to permit the maintenance of ego boundaries," although the capacity to integrate "good" and "bad" aspects of the self and of others into comprehensive concepts is relatively undeveloped. Therefore, the person's self and object representations remain multiple and contradictory. This structuring may manifest itself in a history of unusually contradictory behaviors and intense alterations between emotional states. This lack of integration limits the capacity for a stability and depth of experience of self or others, to the extent that increasingly distorted perceptions emerge. It is to be noted, however, that these distortions do not eliminate reality testing, as they do in the psychotic patient. Kernberg theorizes that, "This failure to integrate 'good' and 'bad' aspects of the reality of self and others is presumably due to the predominance of severe early aggression activated in these patients. Dissociation of 'good' and 'bad' self and object representations in effect protects love and goodness from contamination by over-ridding hate and badness" (Kernberg 1984: 10–18).

Kernberg also notes that the borderline patient uses a predominance of primitive defensive operations. The neurotic patient employs relatively high-level defensive operations, such as repression, isolation, undoing, and intellectualization, in order to protect the ego from intrapsychic conflict generated by an unconscious impulse. But the borderline employs more radical defenses, primarily splitting and related mechanisms, to maintain a separation between contradictory experiences of both the self and others. These defenses lead to contradictory ego states that are alternately activated. Thus, the borderline tends to experience himself as not a "whole" human being. Kernberg concludes: "These defenses protect the borderline patient from intrapsychic conflict but at the cost of weakening his ego functioning, thereby reducing his adaptive effectiveness and flexibility" (Kernberg 1984: 15–18).

Masterson presents a more detailed differentiation between borderline and narcissistic dynamics. However, he maintains the same general paradigm: borderline is a level of development between psychotic and neurotic. Once again, this is a theory that views borderline as a considerably larger category than we regard it to be. Masterson suggests that borderline dynamics reflect a fixation at the rapprochement subphase of the separation–individuation process at which point a child has developed a certain amount of autonomy but still needs support. Masterson theorizes that during this phase the mother of the child who will become borderline either discourages separation or rejects the child when the child returns for support. In essence, the child experiences rewards for clinging and punishment for self-assertion and separation. The borderline person then tends alternately to cling to another as a potentially rewarding object or to withdraw in the face of re-experiencing the devastating disappointment of rejection. The person's "bifurcated worldview," created by splitting, begins to consist of "a good self image linked to a good mother-image and a bad, inadequate, or deflated self-image linked to the bad mother image." The child will "never fully realize that mother is one, complete person . . . He will continue to think of her as two separate entities, one benevolent, the other wicked." Meanwhile, the good self "engages in immature, clinging, passive, unassertive behavior," and the good mother rewards this regressive behavior. When the bad self, wanting to be active and independent, asserts itself, it is met by a critical and angry bad mother. The mother's tendency to reward the child for clinging and to withdraw from the child's efforts to forge independence become internalized and "locked into the adult's entire personality structure" (Masterson 1976: 78–80). Summarizing Masterson's theory, McWilliams describes "how borderline clients are caught in a dilemma: When they feel close to another person, they panic because of fears of engulfment and total control; when they feel separate, they feel traumatically abandoned . . . neither closeness or distance is comfortable" (1994: 64).

While these theorists have used the term borderline in relation to a level of development, we use it to refer to an identifiable character style, specifically the developmentally earliest expression of the seeking relational pattern. There are a number of theorists who have laid the groundwork for our choice. Gunderson's classic work on defining borderline patients substantially supports the use of the term "borderline" as a diagnostic category. He delineates several criteria that identify borderline patients, including: intense and unstable interpersonal relationships; manipulative suicide attempts; unstable sense of self; negative affects; impulsivity; and low achievement. He proceeds to carefully differentiate this profile from Kernberg's far more inclusive category, "borderline personality organization," as well as from other specific pathologies and character disorders. Gunderson also carefully reviews and gives critical thought to the various psychodynamic formulations of the borderline syndrome. Placing the emphasis upon the borderline person's major interpersonal relationships, he concludes that the characteristics of these patients may be understood as predictable patterns of interpersonal responses, phenomenologically based. He argues that their characteristic behaviors represent changing levels of ego functioning and shifting types of defense rather than the primitive defenses of splitting and projection emphasized by Kernberg (Gunderson 1984). Gunderson's emphasis upon the interpersonal etiology of borderline dynamics is in accord with much of the more recent psychodynamic literature. With the emergence of self psychology and intersubjective theory, a number of writers have argued that borderline patients can be best understood in terms of a breakdown in empathic relatedness. These theorists therefore argue that treatment must involve an actively interpreted transference relationship.

Asserting that borderline is a category with an identity of its own, Jungian analyst Schwartz-Salant observes that a borderline person enters "states of mind that move within and around a border between personal and archetypal, so that aspects of each are interwoven in an often bewildering way" (1989: 9). Speculating that the borderline person has experienced a severe deficiency in empathic responses from significant others, Schwartz-Salant surmises that "the person lacks an internal representation of a positive self" as well as other positive inner figures, and becomes tormented by the negative form of numinous, archetypal experience and has no access to the positive. In a desperate attempt to overcome this dark and disorienting condition, "the borderline person is caught in a drama in which he or she must make ceaseless yet futile attempts to contact other people" (1989: 50–1). Overwhelmed by intense persecutory affects that devastate soul, this person's psyche fragments into a multiplicity of centers in order to survive the despair and dull the pain (1989: 23–8). Suffering from a distortion of the archetypal process of the *coniunctio* both within himself and with others, the borderline person is unable to develop a union within or with others. Facing this reality, the borderline person is bound up with the problem of our time, our cultural inability to actualize the *coniunctio*. Thus: "The borderline person's suffering has a telos, and this purpose, which is achieved by some but tragically eludes others, is also the telos of humankind" (Schwartz-Salant 1989: 225).

The *DSM-IV* has also adopted the position that borderline is an identifiable character disorder, described as "a pervasive pattern of instability of interpersonal relationships, self-image, and affects, and marked impulsivity." Specific indicators include: affective instability; inappropriate, intense anger; frantic efforts to avoid real or imagined abandonment; unstable and intense interpersonal relationships; identity disturbance/unstable self-image; self-damaging impulsivity in such areas as sexuality, eating, substance use; self-mutilating and/or recurrent suicidal behaviors.

Many of these theorists make the observation that the borderline patient has learned undesirable methods of handling a vulnerability to intense and unstable emotions. We see this vulnerability to intense and unstable emotions as being a reflection of learning and development disrupted by the prominent role of the affective unconscious not sufficiently well mediated. The inner and outer landscape of borderline dynamics tends to be full of figures, others with whom the person is in quite constant interaction, if not turmoil. These others inhabit his world abundantly, at times possessively, hauntingly, inescapably. He may feel constantly under bombardment.

Case study: Rachel – the sharp edge of a sword

Some years ago, I was in the midst of working with a woman who was wrestling courageously with a demonic demand that she cut herself. One evening, I came across a poem by Marge Piercy[2] that evocatively captured both her anguish and its possible expiation. The images in this poem helped me contain the session-by-session unpredictability and wildness of our work, and so we begin with these evocative and redemptive words:

The seduction of anticipated pain

You rush to embrace a certain
form of pain like a bright tempered sword
focusing light into a point of blindness
on which you impale yourself.

You thrust into that pain
as into an iron maiden, yank it closed
so that its spikes tear through flesh,
organs until they meet like a grin

of a shark. This is reality,
you say as you bleed there in the dark
of the grinding teeth, this is how
I always secretly knew it would come out.

This is what I am shaped for, the act
for which I have been grown as the apple
is planted to be eaten; I was bred
And hand-raised to this like the pheasant

the state scatters corn to in its pens,
then drops at the roadside in October

to be slaughtered by hunters with shotguns
to whom he runs, hungry, asking for corn.

Outside in the woods of the world, my love,
an owl carries a vole as a pledge to its mate,
the petals of the wild apple tree speckle
the sand and the kingfisher strikes like passion

in feathers to rise with a moon glint of fish.
The only world is neither unjust nor just
but round as an apple and we are made of it
to wonder, to savor and struggle and hurt,

to think, to try to build justice as the beaver
builds her dam, to weather the seasons,
the random bolts of nuisance and disaster, to love
what we can and endure in light and darkness.
        (Marge Piercy, *Mars and Her Children* 1992)

The patient was a young woman, we will call her Rachel, who began analysis with me when she was 26 years old. Repetitively finding herself in a "rush to embrace a certain form of pain," she entered analysis because she had begun cutting herself. Rachel, one of five children, remembered only a few rare moments of warm contact or play with her fearful and protective mother who was excessively concerned with appearance and performance. Rachel described her father as "this world's most predictable jerk." While he was generally sentimental, quite unpredictably and with little provocation he would suddenly blow up and threaten to leave, once and for all. These scenes were followed by a sloppy-drunk remorse, leading into inappropriate affection towards Rachel.

By the time she was six, Rachel had looked forward to getting away from the house and going to school, but when the first day arrived she found herself clinging to her mother desperately, declaring her determination with ear-piercing screams, while two teachers and the principal pried her loose. However, as time passed, she seemed to adjust quite well. She was a very pretty and fun-loving girl, and kids were drawn to her enthusiasm and daredevil recklessness. But in third grade Rachel began to have severe stomach and head aches. She was referred to a therapist who told her and her parents that Rachel had severe separation anxieties and needed help handling her fear and managing her anger. Rachel felt betrayed by his revealing remarks and she refused to see him again. During the next years in elementary school, Rachel picked up, fought with, and dropped friend after friend. Her charismatic energy always seemed to attract another girl, but she suffered each chapter intensely. She began to bite her nails badly and to relentlessly pick at scabs on her body. She felt miserable.

Meanwhile, Rachel's eldest brother, now a defiant teenager, began to have wild parties at their house. Neither parent could effectively control their son; the father withdrew, the mother fretted. Rachel, now 13, enthusiastically threw herself into the middle of the party scene; her first crush was the roughest, toughest of her brother's friends. He teased her mercilessly, which served only to inflame her ardent interest.

When Rachel got to high school, much to her surprise, she found herself fully engaged and excelling in studio arts. Her parents were suspicious of art but appreciated that Rachel was engaged in something that kept her out of their hair. Her friend-after-friend pattern extended to boyfriends who appeared and disappeared at a rapid rate. She became involved more heavily in both drinking and drugs. Nevertheless, she finished off high school with passing academic grades supplemented by an award-winning profile in art and she won a scholarship to a prestigious college of art.

Rachel remembered beginning college in a drugged out, drunken fog, but she rather quickly pulled herself together in response to the truly exciting and challenging studio courses. Following her junior year, Rachel rather abruptly married her boyfriend. After repetitive rounds of increasingly bitter disputes, Rachel decided she could no longer bear her husband's wandering eye. She concluded she was fed up with all men and she packed up and left. After graduating from college, Rachel moved to a city that had a very active art market. She found a group of interesting companions and a first rate gallery through which she began to sell her work with remarkable success. Yet within months she began to experience an intense demand that she cut herself, and she began to use her studio tools to aggressively carve into her body. When she could wrench herself free of this possession to cut, she would flee from her studio, abandoning her work. Soon, her impulse to cut generalized beyond her studio, and she became subject to its grip virtually any time she was alone. At this point she called me.

The first period of analysis

In her first session, Rachel told me a dream she had had that morning:

> I'm backstage in an auditorium – I know I am suppose to perform – a piano piece? – but I have never studied piano. My mother was supposed to come but she's not there – I don't know who I can turn to – I scream for help – from whom? Nobody even hears me. Then this really handsome man comes towards me – he's like a knight in shining armor, sword and all! – but I feel that he is clearly mean, even evil. I panic and try to run but I can't move. – I wake up.

As the dream suggests it would be, our work began with explorations of her mother's terrifying absence. Rachel would arrive with an account of a recent interaction with, or a memory of, her mother. After being with her intense emotions about this scene, at times we could move on to consider how she unconsciously assumed I would repeat this experience. She was deeply convinced that I would inevitably diminish her internal reality, and ignore, discount, and invalidate her feelings. She could not imagine that I would, or even could, stay with her. Slowly, as we worked, difficult but well-defined images appeared of voracious wolves tearing into their prey and scavenger birds picking carcasses apart. These images placed us face to face with her primitive hunger and its drive towards a raw attack upon her body. As these devouring, destructive mother figures shapeshifted into myriad different forms, we carefully and vigilantly witnessed, listened to, and confronted them. I made numerous transference interpretations that encouraged her to express any and all of these experiences directly towards me. At times Rachel experienced me as just like her mother: distracted, ineffective, callous, and superficial. At other times, she could allow herself to experience in me the obliterating power, the impersonal and absolute cruelty, of the death goddesses.

During these critical months, Rachel swung quite wildly between despair and fury. Her despair was punctuated by a conviction that she was at the mercy of her behavior and that the ultimate extension of her cutting would be suicide. Her fury was punctuated by an equally deep conviction that she was so thoroughly bad that she must cut herself so deeply that she die. Propelled by both despair and fury, her drive to cut herself periodically reached an intense peak. Yet she seldom acted it out, and when she did actually cut herself she did not cut deeply. It became clear that her desire was to experience and express her emotions forcefully enough that they felt real and that we both witnessed them unflinchingly. Her primary agenda was about feelings, not action; her intent was to manifest an affective reality. Accordingly, I consistently directed our attention towards her despair and her fury.

Finally, Rachel's impulses to attack and destroy herself began to turn into affects directed towards me. Her incessant demand to cut herself became progressively replaced by an equally intense desire to tear at me, to scratch, bite, and shred my skin, ultimately to murder and devour me. These images and impulses emerged slowly as we consistently examined her persistent attempts to undermine my value and use to her, including repetitive subtle snubs like frame challenges, as well as the more virulent yet covert swipes and thinly veiled attacks upon both me and our relationship. The imagined power of her aggression terrified her at first, but she courageously began to allow herself to see her impulses and images and to say them; she slowly allowed me to receive and hold them.

There is much agreement in our field that cutting provides an immediate relief from desperation, dissociation, or primitive anxieties. It was Rachel's experience that when she cut she felt an immediate release from a numbness that she entered in reaction to being ceaselessly and terrifyingly bombarded by chaotic thoughts and feelings. Cutting created an enlivening reconnection to her feelings but she soon entered another round of being overwhelmed and going numb again. Literal cutting then became the repetitive "solution" that was, in truth, no solution. As she learned to differentiate and find words for her feelings, Rachel realized that her cutting was an expression of fierce archetypal rage. Raw archetypal affect does wield tremendous power, power with a source well beyond the person caught in it. Therefore, it feels other-worldly. Since our culture tends to relegate affects and body to the shadow, cutting appears as a violent eruption from the underworld. Unable to transform archetypal rage into embodied human anger, Rachel had not only turned it against herself but acted it out in numerous ways against others. Even though other people frequently told her that they found her emotional intensity quite intimidating, she experienced herself as fragile and vulnerable, as well as ineffective and powerless.

Over the next couple of years, Rachel continued to confront the agonizing turmoil in her mother complex. In the midst of her grieving her mother's profound absence, Rachel had rarely been able to have any real contact with her mother. At this point, she tried once again, several times. After each of these interactions, Rachel was thrown into tidal waves of emotion, at times into rage, at other times into self-lacerating despair. As we worked through these feelings, she begin to imagine a woman who would come to her piano performance, someone who would help her discover and train her capacity to play. Sometimes this woman was a known person, sometimes an imaginary one, sometimes me. Eventually she sweetly and trustingly found herself imagining being held in my arms. Slowly more and more images (in dreams, movies, and stories) of a positive and loving Good Mother and supportive, truly helpful sisters arrived. At this point, Rachel could recognize that she had continued to reach out to her mother with unrealistic hope, relentlessly seeking to find a sense of self worth from her. Freeing herself of these expectations, she learned to establish boundaries with her mother; with this definition to herself she could make simple, limited contact with her.

The second period of analysis

During the intense work with Rachel's mother complex, I reminded myself that the arrival of the masculine was a prominent part of her initial dream and would probably become an essential part of our process. Fairly soon after the series of sessions in which she felt so tenderly connected to me, her attention did began to turn and it turned quite dramatically. First, she initiated a boundary breaking flirtation with one of her male friends. Retreating from this drama, she began to explore the feelings it had stirred up. She then had a series of dreams about a secretive, cruel rapist. As she courageously faced these horrifying images, she found that she was associating them with her first boyfriend, her brother's rough and tough friend. Was it possible that he had raped her? Her dreams became more compelling. She spent hours, days, and weeks trying to absorb the wrenching emotions that surfaced.

Once her emotions were somewhat contained, Rachel's attention began to turn towards exploring whether or not her early boyfriend had sexually abused her; she wanted to know the *truth*. She called her brother; he was distressed to hear her questions, acknowledging that the guy was an obnoxious bully. Rachel tried a number of times to contact her old boyfriend directly hoping to honestly review their history. He did not respond. With no further clues to follow, Rachel investigated related memories, dreams, and associations. She was reluctant to let go of her search for truth and culpability, but she eventually realized and accepted that being raped was a psychic reality for her, whether or not it had been a literal one.

Having developed sufficient capacity for living with ambiguity about her literal history, Rachel began to increase her receptivity to her psychic reality. Her psyche responded with a torrent of fantasies about men: rapists, lovers, friends, teachers. In the midst of all these images, Rachel had a dream that reminded her of the knight in shining armor from her initial dream. While she had originally been terrified of this knight, she now felt curious and interested in him. Using active imagination during sessions and in her journals, she was able to engage in a series of conversations with him.

Through these conversations, she developed a number of affectively informed insights. She came to see that her father's aggression had impacted her profoundly. His eruptions, which had been unusually violent and overwhelming to the entire family, had impressed her unconsciously as not only inevitable but also as powerful and attractive. The image of the rapist and the archetype of Hades thus gained power over her. Consequentially, not only was she attracted to these dynamics in men, but also her internal masculine took on this character and treated her accordingly. She realized that her initial fear that the knight was cruel and evil reflected her certainty that any powerful male was irresponsibly aggressive, an abusive bully. She also came to recognize that it was the voice of this archetypal bully who urged her to pick up her knife and cut herself.

Rachel would periodically sabotage this demanding work by throwing herself into a flamboyant, chaotic, and destructive relationship. However, she became increasingly able to see these chaotic periods as a defense against both our deepening trust and the insights that were emerging about her father. As she continued her imaginary dialogues with the knight, she began to ask him questions about himself. When she inquired about his sword, she found herself in the midst of a humorous, ribald discourse about phallic power. With his playful coaching, she began to imagine herself wielding this shining sword. Amidst their laughter, nourished by spirit, she began to develop psychic muscle. With his support, she learned to stand up to her internal bully. Now, in response to an urge to cut herself, she could bring forth an image of herself holding the shining sword, wielding beauty and justice not cruelty and chaos. As the urge to cut herself dissipated, Rachel was surprised to find herself experiencing feelings of humor and delight. Thus, she learned to recognize how aggression handled maturely could serve her well as a source of internal coherence as well as of agency in the world. The courage to tame her fear of the knight so that she could develop these dialogues ultimately led her to the place where she felt appreciation, warmth, and love for him. They led her to the place where she felt appreciation, warmth, and love for herself.

This particular period of transformation was not the "she lived happily ever after" end of our process. The psyche simply does not unfold in that way. Yet this work to differentiate and develop a positive animus figure and empower the reflective ego did endow Rachel with increased strengths and resilience which served her extremely well as she wrestled with further challenges from both the personal and archetypal realms. Naturally, she experienced periodic setbacks. Nevertheless, overall we both could see the consistent emergence of an increased capacity to relate to the unconscious, bringing its vitality into her life without being possessed by it. This capacity grew to the point where it was clear to us both that it was time for her to stop coming in to see me. She periodically gets in touch. Her life is rich and complex, not without some amount of chaos, and not without deep, sustaining personal and spiritual reward. As we finished our work, I recalled the poem by Marge Piercy that came to my mind when we began, particularly the last two stanzas:

> Outside in the woods of the world, my love,
> an owl carries a vole as a pledge to its mate,
> the petals of the wild apple tree speckle
> the sand and the kingfisher strikes like passion
>
> in feathers to rise with a moon glint of fish.
> The only world is neither unjust nor just
> but round as an apple and we are made of it
> to wonder, to savor and struggle and hurt,
>
> to think, to try to build justice as the beaver
> builds her dam, to weather the seasons,
> the random bolts of nuisance and disaster, to love
> what we can and endure in light and darkness.

Transference and counter-transference

As we noted above, the borderline patient can deftly weave you into her archetypal drama. Indeed, I became Rachel's bad mother, good mother, invading father, and even shining knight. This rampant use of the other is a potential strength of the borderline person, if they will engage in the analysis of it, bringing it into consciousness. In fact, these interactions become the most effective container for transformation of primal wounds. With many patients, it is difficult to engage the negative transference, but with the borderline, it is generally amply available, creatively so if the therapist is able to hold it.

Countertransferentially with Rachel, during the period when she began to have rageful images, and even more when these images featured her turning on me, I had to center myself quietly and steadily, while keeping my heart open, hour after hour. I learned that Rachel could listen more attentively when her emotions were cool. As we saw in the fairy tale, Allerleirauh struggles not only to conceal but also to reveal herself, sending clues about her worth to the king. This is not unlike the process with Rachel, wherein I carefully followed her into the realms of darkness, into the realms of the affective unconscious. Interaction by interaction, a path was built on which she could emerge. At times this process felt tedious, at times futile, at times frustrating if not enraging, yet I kept my eye on her beauty.

The mythological landscape of borderline chaos

The themes of both torment and beauty that we have discussed theoretically and seen vividly in Rachel's life are creatively woven into the paintings of the acclaimed Mexican artist, Frida Kahlo. Encountering any one of her now famous self-portraits one is required to confront an experience of woundedness spoken out loud. We face her characteristic steady gaze, a gaze into the raw depths of archetypal chaos. In one particular portrait, for example, she strategically places a crown of thorns around her throat. The thorns pierce her flesh, and she bleeds; ceremonial drops of blood mark her chest. This image is deeply rooted in ancient Meso-American mythology, Christian iconography, and the Greek mythologem of Dionysus. The power of this image is not only that it carries the depth and power of these archetypal images, but it also forces us to look at the grim reality of human suffering. Kahlo also hands us a painting of a prostitute, lain out on her bed, her dead body riddled with knife slashes. Chaos prevails: rage, mutilation, blood, agony. This artist spent her life creating paintings that can be seen as an effort to carefully detail the dynamics that underlie borderline reality. Turning towards, facing, the gruesome, overwhelming agony of these realms, Kahlo found a source of creativity that has had an impact upon millions of people who have seen and appreciated her work.

It is the force of archetypal reality woven into human life that gives Kahlo's work its charismatic power. Courageously making the invisible visible, she encourages us each to face and live with these brutal realities which are awesome and powerful expressions of the dark aspect of the divine. These realms are terrifying to behold but they can bring forth the richness of transformation. Some of us are particularly able to face this experience. Some of us are particularly interested in this experience. Some of us live this experience. If we work with people who embody this experience in their character structure, however well developed, we owe them our willingness to know these spaces within ourselves and to enter these spaces with them.

While the archetypal landscape of borderline dynamics is intensely portrayed in Kahlo's paintings, these spaces may be further explored by turning to a more familiar western European image of a dismembered god, that of the Greek god Dionysus. Greek mythology provides us with an abundance of stories about Dionysus, stories that are copious, complex, and contradictory, as befits his nature. These stories portray the mysteriously redemptive potential that resides in the archetypal depths underlying borderline dynamics.

Through his association with wine and intoxicating revelry, Dionysus is perhaps most frequently extolled as the great liberator. In mythic story and in ancient cult practice, when Dionysus first arrives, the well-ordered, routine world is shattered. When Dionysus arrives: "Everything that has been locked up is released. . . . [His presence] bursts chains asunder, causes walls to fall in ruins, and lifts the age-old barriers which keep the future and the remote concealed from the human mind" (Otto 1981: 97). But this expansive, nourishing abandonment is only one part of the story. The archetypal ecstasy, tragically and inevitably, is followed by its archetypal shadow, an agony of dreadful wildness. Dionysus, the god of liberation, the great "loosener," becomes the god of destruction and dismemberment. In a number of stories about Dionysus, we are told that the intense revelry progresses into wild and primitive abandonment as this god and his followers tear apart the bodies and devour the flesh of both animals and other humans. "Liberation" turns into a frenzied attack upon the center, upon unity, upon life itself; archetypal, absolute, and unmitigated chaos prevails. In these stories, we see that Dionysus inspires the emergence of a rapid and repetitive swing between opposites: Dionysus and his followers proceed from revelry to chaos, from ecstasy to agony, over and over again. Dionysus is a god of intense emotion, affective abandonment, suffering, and madness.

These themes appear in poetic and gripping detail in the full-length play, *The Bacchae*, by Euripedes. Here we find the recalcitrant king, Pentheus, lured into observing the ecstatic rituals of the maenads. Meanwhile, among these revelers is his own mother, Agave, who is wildly enraptured by the riotous moment. Without recognizing Pentheus as her son, she leads an attack upon him. Returning triumphantly to the town with Pentheus' dismembered head held high, she slowly realizes the horror of her act and, in incommensurable grief, she is cast into a haunted exile.

It is the challenge of this dance that the person with a borderline pattern is constantly trying to negotiate. The call of Dionysus rings in her ears; she is summoned towards connection, passion, and ecstatic release – and towards the possibility of dismemberment. You may see these dynamics, vividly or more subtly, in yourself and/or any number of your patients. The repetitive, emotional outbursts, her thirst for extremes, her pattern of turning against the one she has loved, possibly even "tearing into" them, each suggests an archetypal invasion of Dionysus. Here we see an archetypal irruption that might lie behind a person's cutting herself. The person's consciousness becomes overwhelmed by the wildness of Dionysus and she may turn on her own body. Or this dismembering process may be concentrated intrapsychically; she may repetitively "tear into" herself, shredding her very own soul.

The core anxiety in the seeking relational pattern revolves around dismemberment. When we were talking about schizoid dynamics we spoke about the terrible annihilation anxiety experienced by the person with this withdrawing character structure. A person with a borderline character structure is plagued by a similarly extreme but very different ultimate anxiety. This person lives with an insistent/persistent anxiety about being dismembered and devoured. Much of the literature about primal, developmentally early, or severely dysfunctional states assumes that the ultimate anxiety is about annihilation. This reflects a bias in the literature towards schizoid phenomena as the basic, underlying state of psyche[3]. Annihilation, deriving etymologically from *nihil*, connotes a state of void, nothingness, emptiness, all of which are characteristic of specifically schizoid phenomena. Meanwhile, what we identify as borderline phenomena are experienced as noticeably different from "nothingness." They are object-full rather than object-less. Borderline experience tends to revolve around chaos, too-muchness, crowdedness, unstoppable bombardment – bombardment that leads to dismemberment. We saw these themes in Kahlo's portraits, themes that are also repeatedly present in stories about Dionysus.

Because dismemberment is such a compelling dynamic in borderline experience, it serves us to note that dismemberment appears not only in the Dionysian rites and rituals but also as a central feature of the stories about this god's childhood. One version tells us that Dionysus was conceived as the son of Zeus, in disguise, and a mortal woman, Semele. Tricked by Zeus's jealous wife, Hera, the pregnant Semele beguiled Zeus into revealing himself in his full splendor. When the great God of Lightning arrived as a bolt of divine brightness he unavoidably and immediately killed his lover. Zeus quickly ripped the unborn infant Dionysus from his dying mother's womb and then stitched the nascent babe into his own thigh, from whence Dionysus was later born, immortal. In another version of his childhood, as an infant, Dionysus was torn apart and devoured by two jealous Titans; but Athena saved his heart and he was born again through Zeus. In both versions we see that Dionysus is twice-born: conceived in mortal and immortal realms, delivered from a mortal and an immortal body; enduring death in birth, and life in death, he is a god of duality and paradox. He is also a god that appears and disappears quickly and unpredictably.

Psychologically, the multifaceted archetype of this wild god wields an intense and chaotic impact upon human consciousness. The intense affect of the archetype, paired with its inherent dualism, appears dynamically in the predilection of the person with a borderline character structure towards emotionally charged splitting. As we have said, in the primal phase the infant experiences the world in primarily archetypal terms. If this experience is not well mediated, the infant's natural capacity to experience differentiated opposites turns into a defensive employment of splitting and projective identification. Both intense emotional splitting and projective identification, manifested as the capacity to stir up distress in others, are the prevalent defences of the borderline person. The inherent duality and the lightning-quick mutability of this archetype can propel a person without a sufficiently strong and flexible ego into emotional extremes and behavioral wildness. One minute the borderline person may declare "I *absolutely* hate you!" yet within minutes he might be saying, "I love you so much!" Having slammed the door, he may turn around moments later and knock forcefully, or just barge back in. Thus we see the face of this quickened god in the borderline person's tendency to live in and create chaos and distress.

Dionysus was also known as the god of confrontation. Wearing a uniquely demanding mask, his eyes, which stare straight ahead, cannot be avoided. He requires encounter from which there is no withdrawal (Otto 1923: 90). Clinically, therapists working with a borderline patient frequently express discomfort with the patient's uncanny capacity for nailing the therapist's vulnerability and, most often, brutally confronting the therapist about it. It is an awesome experience, in any context, to be faced with unflinching eyes that see remarkably accurately, eyes that carry the impersonal archetypal force of Dionysus. This intense, penetrating gaze pervades Frida Kahlo's compelling self-portraits. It is one thing to have someone perceive your vulnerabilities and another to communicate them to you in a human, mediated manner. This is what the developed borderline person can learn to do once she can transform her ruthless insight into related information. However, when the person is more or less driven by Dionysus, her perceptions are expressed in absolute terms that leave one feeling undressed, if not dismembered. Indeed, as we described in the Introduction, when archetypal power is in charge of a mere mortal, we say that the person is possessed. It is through the process of developing a relationship with the archetype that the person claims their humanity. This relationship can evolve, step by step, as the infant with good-enough parenting develops or as life and/or analysis proceeds, in a constructive interrelational container.

Informed by an active dialogue between the ego and the archetypal realms, the person can listen to the archetypal affect and choose to integrate it into human life.

We see this process beginning in the story we mentioned about Agave, from *The Bacchae*. Agave loses herself in revelry; wildly enraptured by the riotous moment, she dismembers her own son. Psychologically, she has gone unconscious, lost her ego-eyes. She is apparently subjected to more compelling archetypal power than the ego can hold. When she returns to her community and sees again, that is becomes conscious, and is confronted with her deed, she is thrown into incommensurable grief. In this story, we see disintegration being confronted and recognized in human terms. It is thrust into consciousness, where it is faced and held in grief. The god and those possessed by him will venture into another round of revelry and chaos while the characters within the story who gain consciousness must submit to the ever-so-human task of living with themselves. Agave is exiled and haunted, thrown into a feeling state painfully familiar to the person with a borderline character structure. Nevertheless, she is now in a position to bear the suffering of being human, and begin to hold the tension between a conscious, individual standpoint and that of the god.

As this story teaches us, it is disastrous for a person to remain possessed by archetypal energy. This lack of differentiation from the unconscious precludes the development of individuality. However, resisting the force of Dionysus is no small feat. This possession may not look inviting from the outside, from where we objectively see the whole story, but participation in the equivalent of a Dionysian rite is a compelling, entrancing and addictive experience for many. Seeing the world from behind the mask of this great god, the person looks out at the world as if from beyond, as if from the eternal realms. Although the archetypal Dionysian presence brings intensity, passion, and emotional engagement and a numinous connection to enlivened spirit, the person must meet this enormous force and hammer it into human terms. When the dynamism of the archetype is met by a sufficiently strong individual consciousness, a creative dialogue may ensue. As this dialogue develops, a person may find herself standing with her feet planted deeply. Holding her human dignity, she may be informed and enriched by the numinous spirit of archetypal affects but not driven by them.

Most of us recognize the moment that Dionysus arrives in our lives. These are times when you dance, sing in a choir, play a hard game of soccer, or climb the highest peak and you experience a remarkable emotional, spiritual, or sexual release, a loosening of your usual state of mind and being. Or you may recognize this force when you get absolutely furious at your friend and are trembling with rage. These moments are humanly essential. Indeed, when a person does not allow the adventurous, intensely affective, wildness in her nature to find expression, she will be inviting a confrontation from the god. As we have seen, Dionysus becomes enraged and aims to drive a person into madness when she does not honor him and relate to his realms.

Final thoughts

We opened this chapter with a brief, intense portrait of the Mexican goddess, Coyolxauhqui, whose dismembered body is portrayed in a great stone relief in Mexico City. As we proceeded, we saw how the themes of this compelling myth are manifest in the lives of people informed by borderline dynamics. The intense affective enmeshment with her mother that led Coyolxauhqui to her murderous attack, the crowded landscape of her arriving with her 400 brothers, the feeling of being broken or torn apart, are images and themes that we have seen in numerous forms above. Yet this story also clearly holds another and extremely important image: the arrival of the divine son. This arrival informs us that all this suffering, all this chaos and apparent disintegration, mysteriously yields something of inestimable value, the birth of the divine child, the true self.

While borderline dynamics can indeed be overwhelming and destructive, they may also be the source of rigorous emotional honesty, vibrant and engaged interactions, and a soulful individuation process. These dynamics not only express the richness and fecundity of archetypal affect, they also carry the redemptive potentiality of an affectively enlivened spirituality.

Notes

1 This story as we tell it is adapted from the tale "Allerleirauh," number 65, *The Complete Grimm's Fairytales* (1972: 326–31).
2 "The seduction of anticipated pain," from *Mars and Her Children* by Marge Piercy, copyright © 1992 by Middlemarsh, Inc. Used by permission of Alfred A. Knopf, a division of Random House, Inc.
3 See for example, Contemporary Kleinian psychoanalyst Thomas Ogden's work in *The Primitive Edge of Experience*, 1994. In this work, Ogden proposes the developmental stage and intrapsychic territory that underlies and precedes all paranoid schizoid experience is an "autistic-contiguous experience." Ogden's concept describes a phase that makes use of defensive withdrawal and "hard objects" to feel contained. Using our matrix, the "autistic-contiguous" experience describes schizoid structure. However, it does not accurately describe the chaotic experience affective experience of the borderline.

Chapter 5

Dependent narcissistic character structure

Dependence in the service of connection

Introduction

In this chapter, we turn our attention to a character structure that is culturally both acclaimed and discredited. The suave romantic, the dedicated board member, and the inspiring teacher: these are figures in our cultural and personal landscapes with whom most of us are familiar. At times, we experience them as loving, generous, entrancing, and persuasive. At other moments, we may experience them as shallow and insincere, self-involved, controlling and invasive, or engulfing.

Common to each of these figures is an identifiable character structure, dependent narcissism, with its relational pattern of seeking others. At times the individual with this character structure may be using this pattern creatively: he may be both deeply connected to the other as well as rooted in his own core sense of being. However, it is also possible that he may employ this pattern rigidly and the development of narcissistic dynamics used defensively then leads the person into persistently enmeshed interactions. In this case, we see him desperately requiring the attention of another person in order to feel intact and to prevent a regression into the borderline chaos of the first year of life. Extending the examples above, we

find that the romantic is depending on his lover's words, the look in her eyes, in order to feel whole; the board member is spending countless hours in service to obtain those responses from others which make her feel worthwhile; the inspiring teacher pours his heart into his teaching because without his students' admiration he would fall into unfathomable despair.

Fueled by the intense affect characteristic of this relational pattern, the person with a dependent narcissistic character structure tends to seize upon one person and then another in his desperate search. This intensely emotional, relentless search for the missing "other" is typically directed outward, towards a literal other, while what is missing actually lies mysteriously hidden within. Intense affect, high drama and entanglement with others are used as a defense against the development, differentiation, and expression of authentic feelings. Unable to gain access to the underground springs that the defenses are effectively hiding, the person roams the world searching, always searching, seeking, always seeking, employing one person after another in his quest. This narcissistic use of others is palpably unsatisfying to both the person himself as well as to those he acquires.

Many great literary figures are caught in the throes of this pattern. For example, Ophelia, the maiden in Shakespeare's *Hamlet*, aptly portrays this character structure. In this story, Ophelia, a lovely young woman, falls passionately in love with Hamlet who has returned to court following his father's death. Swayed by her adored father and trusted brother who are concerned about Hamlet's dangerous determination to uncover the truth about his father's murder, Ophelia, effectively separated from her own feelings, agrees not to see Hamlet. Focused on his mission, Hamlet at one point accidentally kills Ophelia's father. The death of her father who has been the center of her life, coupled with her grief about Hamlet, break Ophelia's gentle mind and, wandering about in madness, she is drowned in a nearby brook.

Here is the story of a young woman who is so desperately in need of her father's approval and so passionately in need of the prince's love that when she loses both she goes mad and dies. Mary Pipher, the author of *Reviving Ophelia*, turns to this story to examine the psychology of young girls. Pipher notes that Ophelia has no inner direction, that her value is experienced solely through the approval of her father and Hamlet. Tragically, she is torn apart by her efforts to please. Pipher makes the case that our culture encourages young girls "to put aside their authentic selves and to display only a small portion of their gifts" (Pipher 1994: 20–2). A popular, even iconic painting of Ophelia by Sir John Everett Millais captures the romantic and tragic intensity of this maiden. In this densely colored, sensual Pre-Raphaelite image we see Ophelia afloat in a brook with flowers around her, drowned but mysteriously beautiful.

There is reason for us all to be seriously concerned about the tendency for this character pattern, with its deep archetypal pull, to be culturally reinforced among adolescent girls. However, we also find people of all ages, including a significant number of men, struggling with this ultimately unsatisfying search for the value in life in the other's loving glance, approval, or attention. While Ophelia, bereft of both her father and Hamlet, does kill herself, we rarely see the person with a dependent narcissistic character structure actually commit suicide. She may resort to a number of emotionally loaded suicide threats, but these generally serve to further engagement, one way or another.

Ophelia's story represents the unfolding of an archetypally informed character structure that appears in many coats and colors. When this structure is defensively rigidified, it weds relentless affective intensity with impenetrable narcissism to the extent of creating chaos intrapsychically and interpersonally. However, when the rigidity of the defenses is minimized and the ego–Self axis is relatively unencumbered, this structure allows for a deeply felt, even ecstatic, relatedness supported by an admirable capacity for empathy, kindness, and generosity.

Theoretical considerations

Dependent narcissism as distinct from dependent personality disorder

For those readers accustomed to using the *DSM-IV* diagnostic manual, the character structure we are describing as dependent narcissism might seem indistinguishable from dependent personality disorder. It does bear some resemblance to this diagnosis, but it is essentially different. According to the *DSM-IV*: "The essential feature of the Dependent Personality Disorder is a pervasive and excessive need to be taken care of that leads to submissive and clinging behavior and fears of separation" (American Psychiatric Association 1994: 665). These dependent and submissive behaviors arise from a self-perception of being unable to function adequately and their goal is to elicit caregiving.

While the people we meet with dependent narcissism may exhibit a number of these indicators, we see the goal that underlies these behaviors as rooted more in *a desperate search to gain the attention of the other, optimally the other's approval and/or declaration of love* than in a concern to be "taken care of." The person with a dependent narcissistic character structure generally knows that she can "function adequately." Indeed she is frequently a high performer because high performance wins respect. Her concern is more deeply rooted in an inner sense that the source of love and meaning lies in the other. Only the other's attention, preferably her declaration of love or approval, provides the narcissistic gratification that keeps the personality intact and sufficiently cohesive. Consequently, she is invariably searching to feel loved, admired, respected, etc. She is constantly seeking the other. This aim may well lead the dependent narcissist into behaviors such as difficulty expressing disagreement or going to excessive lengths to win approval. However, her goal is to be admired in order to secure an experience of being seen, rather than gain "nurturance and support" to bolster a "lack of self-confidence."

The narcissistic nature of this character structure is evident not only in the person's excessive concern with himself, in this case concern with his being loved and admired, but also in his use of other classical narcissistic dynamics and defenses to secure this goal. In this character structure, the tendency to idealize and/or devalue others, as well as the presence of self-aggrandizement and/or self-diminishment, appear cloaked in intense emotionality that fuels enmeshments with others, while the ego tends to be inflated with powerful, raw archetypal affects. The person's determined efforts to secure the loving glance from others is fundamentally exploitative, though this aspect of the relationship is generally well camouflaged and tenaciously denied. He therefore carries, consciously or not, a deep sense of shame.

The excessive concern with himself is often rather difficult to perceive because his life story is typically scripted around the other. This script may feature his love, devotion, or service to the other and the person himself tends to see his generosity and warmth as special gifts that others deeply appreciate. Yet, when these dynamics are being employed defensively, this perception is inherently grandiose and inflated. On the other hand, the person may concentrate upon his apparent helplessness or vulnerability in the face of the power of the other. This person tends to experience himself as self-sacrificing, even a martyr, or as disempowered or of little consequence. Again, this experience is inherently grandiose, but in this instance it is deflated. Caught in a narcissistic defiance of limitation, he is unable to accept the reality that someone/something is missing, so he searches for it endlessly. Whether apparently "giving" or "getting," he is forever hungry. The person's desire for contact drives him to seek the other's attention again and again, yet his narcissistic defenses block him from authentic contact, rendering him not only insatiably hungry but also psychically impenetrable. Defensively, the person experiences his disappointment and hunger in terms of what the other is not giving, not in terms of his own impenetrability.

Theoretical discussion about narcissism in general

In the Introduction, we noted that we use the term "narcissism" to describe a number of developmentally normal, indeed essential, dynamics. A child entering the narcissistic phase is challenged to manage grandiosity, exhibitionism and omnipotence, and the progressive development of a relationship between the ego and the Self. If the environment and fit between parent and child are good enough, the child will develop healthy narcissism that would manifest as competence, coherence, resilience and the emergence of a creative dialogue between the ego and the Self. However, if the environment and fit at this stage are relatively inadequate, the child will begin to employ narcissistic dynamics defensively in order to maintain psychic integration.

These dynamics are carefully delineated in two seminal Jungian works on narcissism published in the early 1980s by Schwartz-Salant and Kalsched. You may recall that in Chapter 3 we briefly told the story of Narcissus, the beautiful, seductive and arrogant youth who rejected all suitors and then fell in love with his own reflection in a clear pool of water. In *Narcissism and Character Transformation*, Schwartz-Salant (1982) details how the myth of Narcissus can be seen as a complex portrait of narcissism that highlights the relationship between the ego and the Self.

As Schwartz-Salant points out, when Narcissus rejects the many calls into relationship, he is ultimately faced with his own reflection. Schwartz-Salant argues that the reflection Narcissus sees in the pool shows not only his ego but the Self (1982: 90). As Narcissus falls in love with this reflection, we see his need to possess the Self and its archetypal beauty and potency. In this inability to reckon with the otherness of the Self lies the expression of an ego–Self merger that is neither personal nor archetypal but a combination of both. Narcissus remains tragically stuck in a middle ground, neither human nor divine (1982: 102).

Schwartz-Salant weaves together ideas about how the disruptions that lead to narcissistic defenses arise from archetypal as well as personal sources. He details how the processes of mirroring and idealizing described by Kohut lead not only to the development of self structures, but also to the emergence of the relationship between the ego and the Self. He suggests that the mother's mirroring of the child's Self encourages an internal exchange of reflections between the ego and the Self. This exchange provides the child's ego with a full inner ground for development without which the psyche resorts to defensive narcissism instead of healthy narcissism. Employing grandiosity in a negative, defensive way, the child splits off negative emotion which then "is usually turned back onto the Self, manifesting as intense self-hatred" (1982: 88). The dynamics of idealization also contribute to the development of the relationship between the ego and the Self, since the child first experiences the spiritual aspect of the Self by projecting it on to the idealized parents. If the child is deprived of the opportunity to experience and reassimilate this projection, he is consequently robbed of access to the Self (1982: 43–4).

Kalsched emphasizes the essential role of *interpersonal* reality in "the gradual transmuting establishment of the inner personal-true self, the indestructible, immortal soul of man that Jung called the Self" (1980: 67). Kalsched makes the case that the narcissistically injured patient is hungry for an interiority that arrives with the establishment of an inner true-self.

He suggests that interiority evolves through the gradual development, within relationship, of underlying structural capacities for internalization. This mystery of psychic internalization endows one with a sustaining feeling of personal solidity and separateness.

Kalsched explains this process begins with the essential participation of baby and parent, patient and analyst, in a transitional area, a bipersonal field in which the child's self is not yet an internal reality but is found partially within, partially outside in the "other." At this point the Self, as an image of wholeness, is alive only in the in-between: "The ego–Self axis is not yet an internal reality but is constellated between 'me' and 'You'" (1980: 51). In this bipersonal field, when the child receives sufficiently accurate mirroring of her true self and receptive engagement with her idealizations, these energies are transmuted into psyche and "become incarnate in the individual as a coherent interior self and corresponding self image" (1980: 52). These inter-personal experiences migrate internally and, forming an inner mirror, they constellate an internal axis of energy. The development of an ego–Self axis is not a given, but is a potentiality that develops within a relationship with another. Individuation is first a bipersonal event and then an internal pro-cess; the process wherein the child experiences both self and other in para-doxical union is essential in order for the process of interiority to emerge. When the "miracle of interiority" eventually happens: "At this moment, the mirror breaks, the universal 'We' becomes I and Thou; self is born along with other . . . at this moment Narcissus sees through his illusion" (1980: 73). Leaving behind the image-realm with which he's been unconsciously identi-fied, the person is then able "to involve himself in life and relatedness on the basis of what he feels *internally* . . . [this leads to] an interior life reflectively in dialogue with the reality of otherness and especially in dialogue with the reality of others as separate persons" (1980: 48).

When a child does not experience a good-enough mirroring and engage-ment in the bipersonal field, they remain fixated at the level where image and reality are experienced as identical. In this case, the ego–Self axis is not vitally polarized and the capacity for internalization is damaged. A pseudo self is developed and the true self, the enfeebled subjective internal self, goes into hiding. "The narcissist gets reflected and reflected and reflected, but the mirror never 'swings inside' as it were, because (appar-ently) only true self – made real in relationship – will 'return' to its home. For the narcissist, everything stays outside in the veil of ten thousand things" (Kalsched 1980: 65).

The dynamics of dependent narcissistic character structures

As described above, defensive narcissism is a manifestation of the extent to which the ego is conflated with the Self. For the dependent narcissistic, archetypal affects inject narcissistic defenses with enormous fuel. Developed to protect the person from further interpersonal rejection and intrapsychic pain and chaos, these affect-loaded defenses frequently throw the individual into high drama. The dramas may be about romantic escapades, a thrill and a spill, an ecstasy and an agony, a high and a low. Or they may center upon big events, possibly lasting for years, for example, an extended family drama of Shakespearean proportions. Caught in this archetypal inflation, without interiority, the ego remains unable to facilitate the development, differentiation, and expression of individual feelings.

A person with this character structure may become desperately attached to the unobtainable other, one specific human being, never veering from her desperate determination that he is the one and only answer, as we saw in the story of Ophelia. On the other hand, the dependent narcissist may well shift this projection from one person to another when the ever so human fallibility of the "loved one" fails to satisfy. Some years ago I saw a woman named Vivian who revealed her dependent narcissism in such a shifting pattern; she once proudly described it as "serial monogamy." Each relationship was larger than life in its emotional intensity, and each began with her finding the perfect love, her true soul mate. As time passed and she became disappointed in her hero-of-the-year, her idealization of him gave way to devaluations and the relationship eventually failed. As we proceeded in analysis, she discovered that she skillfully played the role of the anima woman, the woman that a man desires.[1] Although adept at seduction, she experienced power as lying in others, not in herself. The fact that others found her compelling only added to her defensive use of seduction. It became clear that she knew far more about others than she knew about herself. Her busy social schedule only intermittently distracted her from how much she hated her life and how she hated herself. Employing grandiosity in a negative way, she directed her intense affect against herself, suffering endless rounds of bitter self-recrimination and self-loathing. Within the temenos of our work, instead of looking for a new man to satisfy her insatiable hunger, she began to face the chaos of her inner world. As we reached far into the narration of her childhood, she began to become conscious of just how unseen, unloved, and in danger of attack she actually felt. Claiming her grief, rage, and desire she was ultimately able to transfer the use of her considerable power from seducing and entangling others into capacity to assert her own authenticity.

Dependent narcissism as distinct from other character structures

A dependent narcissistic character structure emerges out of the developmental landscape of borderline dynamics. At this point, however, narcissistic defenses begin to eclipse the earlier defenses of the Self. The experiences and images of the person with this character structure are thus far less fragmented and dismembered, less gory and full of blood. This person may well drive herself into exhaustion and even illness in her attempt to court others, though she is less likely than the borderline to actually cut herself. Her life may well revolve around intense, complex-ridden and frequently unsatisfying relationships, but these relationships do not tend to be as conflicted, explosive, and emotionally violent as the relationships of a person with a borderline character structure. Even so, this person has only recently emerged, developmentally, from borderline reality and any significant absence of the affective connection to the mirroring and idealized other threatens regression into primitive borderline chaos, where the newly developed cohesion of self structures would be endangered. Thus the narcissistic ego–Self conflation is tenaciously defended. Nevertheless, a regression into the raw and chaotic borderline landscape may well be required for the person to develop a creative ego–Self dialogue.

Intense, affect-loaded entanglements differentiate a person with a dependent narcissistic character structure from a person with a counter-dependent narcissistic character structure or a person with an alpha narcissistic character structure. For instance, a dependent narcissist may find adventure in the turmoil of a great love affair. Meanwhile, a counter-dependent narcissist might turn to yet another intellectual project, while a person with an alpha narcissistic character structure might find that they thrive on high endurance, competitive sports. Of course, a dependent narcissist might love the climb if it featured a remarkably friendly guide, or she might engage in a demanding sport if she found just the right coach or just the right team. As we recognize these differences, we are reminded that the shadow elements that bear the fruit of wholeness lie in the relational patterns that are other than one's own. Thus the person with a dependent narcissistic character structure might do well at some point to develop her capacities to undertake adventures alone, with triumph as her goal.

Each of these forms of narcissism finds its expression in terms of puer or puella dynamics. As we noted in Chapter 3, the classic puer aeternus, Peter Pan, is seen to fly high; with little authentic contact with others or himself, he resists stability and commitment, favoring a round of applause over emotional contact. The counter-dependent puella is set to be forever young, quite distinctly on her own. This counter-dependent pattern is in marked contrast to a typical dependent puer/puella who would dive into one relationship after another, hungry for another "intimate" encounter; courting with deep and charismatic feelings and counting on his or her forever youthful vitality to win the admiration of the other. Meanwhile an alpha puer/puella might be found roaming through life, eager for the next conquest, shifting from one arena to another, one deal to another, one victory to another, appearing forever strong, bold and powerful. The split-off senex or figure of wisdom that is submerged in the unconscious for each of these character structures wreaks havoc with the person's life until "old age" arrives to be reckoned with in the forms of limitation, rage, grief, depression, or defeat.

Case vignette: Mary, a controlling, rageful mother

The dynamics of age versus youth were actively at play in the life of a woman named Mary who worked with me a number of years ago. When Mary first called me she was 40 years old. Her husband had left the family ten years earlier and she had "successfully" raised their two older children, but her youngest daughter Lisa, now 13, was quickly becoming unmanageable. Mary had relied heavily upon Lisa's youthful exuberance to lighten the endless household tasks and to enliven their lives. Mary was proud of having created a close family and her daughter's behavior mystified and threatened her.

Mary talked wistfully about the many years when Lisa had been obedient and helpful,"willing to work her fingers to the bone." She wept and wailed about her "baby's" present errant ways. Lisa had begun to act surly, disobedient, and disrespectful and she presented one reason after the other to be out of the house. Mary was certain that these reasons were excuses if not lies and she had begun to collect evidence that Lisa was hanging out with "the wrong crowd." Mary searched Lisa's room high and low, read her journal, eavesdropped on her telephone conversations, all in search of the keys to the many "undoubtedly dark secrets" she knew her daughter was keeping from her. Mary began to present Lisa with unusually restrictive curfews, requirements for confessions, and instructions to withdraw from specific friendships. Lisa became progressively more insolent and evasive. Mary felt like her heart was going to break and she began to feel terribly depressed.

Reluctantly but steadily Mary turned her focus from her enmeshment with Lisa to explorations of her own childhood. Her father had died when she was young, leaving her, rather like Lisa, a babe in her mother's arms. Mary and her three older siblings had served their mother well, working by her side in the house and in the family business. Mary remained her mother's "pet" until she met her husband and they moved into a nearby town. As she explored her numerous memories, Mary gradually realized that she had never really left her mother's arms. She had always counted on her mother's adoring gaze, then her husband's, and then, much to her surprise, Lisa's. She could see how her desperate need for Lisa's love had spurred her into bossy, controlling, and invasive maneuvers. As she began to recognize just how much she counted on Lisa for her own validation, she understood why she was so fiercely resisting Lisa's attempts to lead her own life.

In the midst of these realizations, Mary had a number of dreams that truly horrified her. They featured violent, sexual, and intensely emotional scenes that she could barely stand to recall, much less recount. Among these dreams was one of a huge, black, rapacious bird that was pecking out the eyes of all the cats in the neighborhood. She also had a dream in which she was drowning in swift and turbulent, muddy, thick flood waters, and one in which she was watching as a handsome, charismatic man was seducing, raping and killing several of the girls in Lisa's school. In several dreams she found herself utterly enraged, yelling and screaming at her husband. She patiently learned to live with these images: asking them questions, listening to their answers, challenging them, exploring them, allowing them to course through her veins. These dreams guided her into the discovery of and the capacity to tend to many layers of her soul that had remained underground. As she dared to unveil her own "dark secrets," she could feel her grip upon Lisa losing its hold and she could sense her depression lifting. Mary could now appreciate that she had been projecting not only her own desires for separation and independence, but also her own chthonic underworld, on to Lisa. Lisa had been acting out what Mary herself had needed to develop so many years ago. One morning she came into my office and announced that she must be cured because the night before she had chosen to read her own journal, not Lisa's!

A fairy tale: learning to serve the self

The theme of obedient servitude, to the extent of working one's fingers to the bone, is central to the Grimm's story of "Mother Holle."[2] Here we also find clues to its transformation.

> A lovely young maiden lived with her widowed stepmother and an ugly and idle but favored stepsister. The stepdaughter, forced to be the Cinderella of the house, had to sit every day by the well and spin till her fingers bled. One day, when she dipped the shuttle into the well to wash off her blood, the shuttle slipped out of her hand and dropped to the bottom of the well. The stepmother sharply scolded the girl and insisted she must fetch it out again. Compliantly, though sorrowfully, the girl jumped into the well and promptly lost her senses. She awakened at the bottom in a flowering meadow into which she walked. Along the way she was asked to remove baked bread from the heat of an oven, and shake ripe apples from the tree. She was compassionately responsive to these requests. She then came to the hut of an old woman who had frightening, large teeth. About to flee in fear, the girl heard the old woman invite her to stay. The woman introduced herself as Mother Holle and after she instructed the girl to shake her bedding, "till the feathers fly – for then there is snow on the earth," she promised her that "you shall be the better for it." The girl took courage and entered

her service. All went very well for sometime, before the girl felt sad and homesick. Surprisingly, Mother Holle was pleased that the girl longed for her home again and she offered to show her the way because she had served so truly. She led the maiden into a large doorway where she was showered with gold. When her stepmother and stepsister saw her glory, the stepsister pricked her own finger to obtain blood and, throwing her shuttle into the well, she attempted the same descent. In the meadow, she could not be bothered to respond to the bread or the apples. When she came to Mother Holle's house, she was not afraid. She entered her service expectantly, but soon became lazy. Mother Holle quickly tired of this disrespectful girl and led her to the great door where she was showered not with gold but with a big kettleful of pitch that clung to her for as long as she lived.

This story paints an apt portrait of a person with a dependent narcissistic character structure. The unloved stepdaughter, her beauty hidden by hard labor, desperately needs approval and love from her caretakers. Working her fingers to the bone, her blood is shed in an attempt to obtain approval from the other. Yet she receives only envy and rejection. Unable to protect herself from the ruthless demands of the mother complex, her willingness to go to extremes in service to others may well drive her into exhaustion and even illness. Even with her ceaseless efforts, further demands are heaped upon her. Then, "accidentally," she drops the shuttle down the well and she must retrieve it.

Psychologically, the maiden's accident and the stepmother's scolding are agents that move the story towards transformation. Descent in sorrow to the bottom of the well is the girl's descent through despair and loss into the wellspring of meaning. In this underground place, the archetypal realms, servitude itself can awaken sources of transformation. When she responds to the requests of the bread and the apples, true to her nature, she serves them well. She feels appropriate fear and awe in the presence of the numinous, awful Great Mother, represented here by Mother Holle with her frightening teeth.

What does it mean that her service to the Great Mother generates snow? It's our sense that a little cooling off is what the dependent narcissistic person needs. Their heated and industrious pursuit of the love and approval of the other leaves insufficient room for retreat and engagement with her own source of being. Snow covers, protects, and insulates. The snow in "Mother Holle" falls like feathers, with spirit; it is not a rigid defense that kills, as in "The Little Match Girl." With her service to the Mother, the maiden in Mother Holle learns to make a contribution and become an individual part of the great rounds of nature. She discovers how to transfer her servitude from seeking the validation of others to finding meaning in serving a Self figure in the otherworld; and her envious stepsister, her own envious shadow, is finally tamed. Mother Holle says about the service the girl is to perform for her that "you shall be better for it." This is a moment most of us can recognize when we are finally released from a personal complex and become aligned with a meaning which extends beyond ourselves. This is the moment when we can truly understand how service can hold spiritual value.

The maiden's service to the Great Mother continues until she begins to feel homesick. We may be surprised that Mother Holle is pleased with the girl's longing to return home, to be human. However, in cycles of transformation there is a right time to descend and a right time to ascend; the gods themselves recognize and appreciate our necessity to live human lives. Though she is now showered in gold, she is still merely mortal.

Case study: Paul, a charming but desperate "courtier"

The intense and dramatic dynamics of dependent narcissism appeared throughout my work with a man named Paul with whom I worked several years ago. Paul was charming, fun, and sophisticated; and, when he first called, he was in emotional pain that he found bewildering. He was a well-recognized sculptor in my community and frequently applauded for his dynamic workshops. However, in the years leading up to his call, his age had began to show and the attention he had won so easily all his life was no longer quite so available. Younger women no longer regularly fell in love with him. His wife of many years was no longer entranced; his grown kids returned home rarely. The chronic distrust of his colleagues now began to bother him. Both his art and his teaching were losing their vitality. The vague distress and desperation he had kept at arm's length throughout his younger years could no longer be ignored. Both personally and professionally, Paul had been stubbornly critical of self-reflection and psychological analysis, explicitly holding the psychotherapeutic process in scorn. He had firmly believed that only love in close relationships could heal. Nevertheless, at this point, he felt compelled to seek help because, to his great shame, he was now struggling with impotence, depression, and an occasional, "uncharacteristic" fit of rage.

Notes about the analysis

Early in the analysis, I learned that Paul was a "well loved" only child of a devoted mother whom he described as beautiful, but frail and emotionally distant. His father, as devoted to his wife as his wife was to their son, was a proud and successful farmer. His mother identified herself as an artist, though her work often remained unfinished and was never displayed. Paul and his mother shared a romantic vision of the sensitive artist, and they collusively held the father's elemental connection with the land in some contempt. When Paul was nine, his mother became ill with cancer and died.

Bolstered by a healthy dose of charisma, Paul had developed a powerful, though ultimately unsatisfying, dependent narcissistic character structure, robustly inspired by the puer.[3] Throughout his life, his constant and remarkably successful acquisition of testimonies of love from others had protected him from experiencing the intense distress that was driving his insatiable search for attention. The power of his defenses was abundantly clear to me when we began our work because Paul repeatedly employed his wit and sophistication to charm me; he attempted to court me just as he courted the many women in his life. In doing so, he was defending against the very issues that he consciously wanted to address. As we gradually analyzed his numerous seductive ploys with me as well as with others, he began to explore what was lying underneath his desperate maneuvers.

Early in this process of unearthing his long buried feelings, Paul went through an extended period when he seriously considered leaving the analysis. His defenses were being directly challenged and they naturally went into motion. They mounted numerous convincing arguments that I was clearly not the one to help him, that this was a futile project and that the obvious move was to quit our "ridiculous" work. In one session, I encouraged him to explore the possibility that his defenses were mobilized to protect him from the deep affect that would confront him when he gave up his search for the other. That night, Paul had a simple and clear dream of the two of us standing side by side, facing an immense night sky. We said little about the dream but Paul's pressure to leave the analysis abated and he turned back towards his feelings with an apparent increased sense of inner strength well rooted in the relationship with me and in the Self. Paul himself referred back to this image off and on as we worked together.

As Paul ventured willingly and unwillingly into the rich but terrifying affective underworld, there were of course many sessions of apparent inactivity and some periods of recourse to his seeking from me, lovingly or with fury. However, progressively there was less and less sense of affect used defensively to create entanglement, within himself, with others, or with me. Not surprisingly, as Paul developed the capacity to relate to his own emotions, he experienced profound grief and intense rage about how abandoned he had been as a child. Paul eventually realized that as a young boy he was drawn to his mother's allure, but was afraid that in his boyish exuberance, he would hurt her. "Concluding," as a preverbal child, that his instinctual aggression and natural omnipotence were potentially destructive, he learned to effectively hide his authentic self and serve his frail mother. Sparing her from any affect that might be distressing, he cut himself off from the opportunity to explore and develop himself, particularly his aggression. His fear of her vulnerability and his certainty about his omnipotent destructiveness were "confirmed" with his mother's early illness and death.

Paul's explorations of the underground springs of affect that he had protected himself and his frail mother from all these years, was not an easy journey. Each step involved our handling his fantasies about how I was faring: Could I tolerate his grief? Could I survive his rage? Would I allow him his own identity? It took some time to work through Paul's unconscious conviction that he, his very being, would harm the woman he was with. Eventually, he realized that he also feared she/I might retaliate, if not by dying then by turning on him aggressively. We explored numerous interactions between us in the light of these feelings and questions. He explored how enraged he was at his mother for entrapping and using him and for devaluing his father. As he continued he developed a well-honed capacity for sorting out his narcissistic fury from his authentic rage. As he developed more relationship to this raw and wild affect, he discovered that it was the source of potentially creative anger. Not only did it help him define what he himself truly wanted, but it also helped him build effective boundaries that could mitigate entanglements with others.

As Paul gained access to his fierce, chaotic and well-hidden affects, particularly his rage, he felt progressively less pressure to compulsively seek out romantic sources of gratification, including from me, and he consequently felt wonderfully "freed up." As he gained more access to the archetypal realms which had previously been hidden by his narcissistic defenses, he had a series of dreams of powerful, impressive male figures. He initially saw these dreams as bringing him images of a masculinity that compensated for his father's "weaknesses." Yet as he stayed with the images, he also began to review his memories of his father. He remembered how, as a toddler and youngster, he would play in the fields while his father worked the land. He began to see his father as robust and strong, patient and attuned to nature, and steadily present for, though not abundantly related to, his son. As Paul worked with this new awareness of his father, he confronted the fact that both he and his mother had thoroughly devalued his father's world. He began to see the extent to which both he and his father were slavishly tied to her approval. The enlivening energy from his dreams and from his restructured memories helped to further support Paul's separation from his mother complex and he began to develop a new connection to his father, to masculinity, and to the world of nature.

Throughout our process, Paul stayed with his wife, during periods when their interactions were filled with seemingly endless rounds of turmoil and distress, as well as periods when it seemed there was no life whatsoever between them. However, eventually their symbiotic and enmeshed marriage shifted towards a respectful, mature and fulfilling relationship, and, much to Paul's delight, their grown children sought them out more frequently. Over these years, Paul discovered that as he developed access to and valued his own internal source of meaning not only did his relationships improve, but also his depression slowly lifted and his experiences of impotency gradually decreased. When we terminated our work, we both felt he was in a position to richly live his life, individually as well as lovingly in relationship.

Notes about the transference and countertransference

Both the transference and counter-transference played invaluable roles in my work with Paul. Early in our process he let me know many times, virtually in every session, that he thought I was wise, kind, and powerful and that I was helping him immensely. I could feel the desperation in his need for my love and approval. His determined idealizations coupled with his desperation taught me how tenaciously Paul was defending himself against his deep unconscious pain. The transference dynamics with a person who has a dependent narcissistic character structure are an especially rich source of grist for the mill, but they are also surprisingly difficult to work through. This apparent contradiction stems from the fact that the defenses of this character structure are readily enacted in the relationship. Thus, the relationship is amply available, yet the person's unconscious, defensive use of the relationship is stubbornly impenetrable. The person is reluctant to let go of these defenses because, as in all character structures, defenses protect against retraumatization as well as regression, in this case into borderline chaos.

Over time Paul's idealizations of me turned into devaluations. As he plunged into his new found fury at the disappointments in his life, I was no exception. He did not fail to point out and rail against the moments he experienced me as insufficient, inadequate, and even cruel. Frequently these feelings were authentic. However, we'd occasionally find ourselves back in his old patterns and his attacks would have the smell of attempts to get me to react, to engage with his defensively motivated entanglements. Clearly, at this point, interventions aimed at discharge would only have contributed to a further entrenchment of the pattern. At times explicitly, more often implicitly, I attempted to receive and mirror the authentic feelings hidden behind his entangling maneuvers.

During these years with Paul, I had to wrestle with my own growing impatience and retaliatory impulses. It was not hard to notice that Paul received interpretations and personal connections I offered not only with enthusiasm and flattery or angry manipulative attacks, but also with an impervious wall off which these interpretations and interactions would bounce. He did not control our sessions in the way a counter-dependent narcissist tends to by requiring me to shut up and listen. Rather, he constantly aimed to get something from me, something he then paradoxically could not allow in. It frequently felt like we'd do the same futile exercise over and over. At these moments, it seemed as if our work had become simply another round of his endless sucking. I felt "used" and discarded. It felt to me at these times that he was utterly impenetrable and that we were getting nowhere. Nevertheless, eventually, this seemingly endless process gave way to interactions that had an entirely different sense to them. Not only were these differences reflected in Paul's life and his dreams, I could feel in my body and in my associated reveries that authentic feeling was emerging. These feelings were no longer aimed at me, but at his own individuation.

Demeter and Persephone

The themes we have identified as frequent motifs in the lives of people with a dependent narcissistic character structure are perhaps nowhere as captivatingly and powerfully portrayed as they are in the great and sacred Greek story of Demeter and Persephone, Ceres and Prosperine in Roman times. As we will see, both Demeter and Persephone can be seen as symbolic representatives of these themes. In this myth we find merger and violation, the cruel severance of and wild swings between opposites, the relentless searching for the other, and/or a descent into the darkest depths, all accompanied by intense rage, grief, and despair.

This story[4] begins simply by naming Demeter, the awesome goddess, and her daughter Persephone. Then, Persephone reaches out to pick a lovely spring flower:

> Hades, God of the Underworld, rose up in his golden chariot and abducted the maiden, whose screams eventually, but too late, reached her mother's ears. Persephone was carried away to become Queen of the Underworld, while Demeter, who was once young and gay but was now besieged by grief, roamed the earth, desperately searching for her lost daughter.

As we will see, Demeter's quest for Persephone ultimately leads to Persephone's seasonal return. Symbolically, we might say that Demeter represents the conscious ego, the part of the personality that remains above ground, while Persephone represents the true self hidden in the underworld. From this perspective, it is through Demeter's seeking and affective turmoil that Persephone is eventually allowed to emerge, transformed. Persephone's descent into and reemergence from the Underworld, as an image of the emergent dialogue between the ego and the Self, then represents an accomplishment that heralds the birth of a new promise and potential for the psyche.

We will develop this interpretation, considering in particular the moments when Demeter's story may be seen to portray particular archetypal patterns that can inflate a human ego, creating dependent narcissistic defenses. Yet we will also add the perspective that Persephone too may be seen to represent an archetypal configuration that can inflate consciousness.

In this manner, we will consider both Demeter and Persephone as figures symbolizing archetypal energies that can inspire but also destructively inflate a human psyche. When the ego is conflated by the archetypal realms, dialogue between ego and Self is precluded and the person lives out a collective, archetypal pattern instead of her individuality. Let's begin by examining what each of these goddesses may represent.

Persephone symbolizes the archetype of fresh springtime budding. Her presence promises new life. We sense that she is innocent, a virgin, unpenetrated. We can also sense that she might remain this young forever, thus portraying the defining attribute of the puella who is eternally young, abundant, ever blooming. A person living out his particular aspect of Persephone might appear like the case of Vivian, mentioned briefly above. Living out the archetypal pattern of the puella, Vivian sought one romance after another, while she had little access to her own inner life. It is clearly no accident that the flower Persephone reached out to pick was the narcissus. We are, in effect, invited into the landscape of narcissism.

When Persephone reaches out to pick the narcissus, Hades arrives and abducts her, taking her into the Underworld. It is important to our enquiry to examine the presence, within this moment of the story, of the possible ambiguity on Persephone's part regarding her descent. Our interest is prompted by the fact that she reaches for a narcissus. When she reaches out, clearly desire is present, though it is not apparent where it will lead. While this movement, in the story, ultimately leads to transformation, a person who identifies with this particular aspect of Persephone might find herself locked in the landscape of narcissism. Indeed, the appearance of this particular archetypal moment in the life of a woman may be reflected in the ambiguity that is yet another characteristic of the dependent puella. Her own desires are generally well hidden, particularly from herself. She appears to be always ready to adapt to others, even to be the passive recipient of others' needs. Turning to others for meaning, she seeks their attention, yet remains unable to be nourished by it. Finding her definition through the presence of another, not from within herself, she learns to be vague in order to win attention from others. Identified with the archetypal energy of reaching out for the flower, she reaches out over and over, but she remains impenetrable. This moment is not unlike the moment when Narcissus falls in love with his image. In both stories, there is subsequent transformative movement. However, a human life may well remain within the grip of the dynamics this moment is symbolizing, caught in narcissistic defenses.

What Demeter may represent becomes clearer as the story proceeds. Returning to the myth, we hear the emotionality becoming yet more intense:

> Finding no trace of Persephone, in despair Demeter turned to Helios, the great sun god, who informed her that Hades, with Zeus'

permission, had abducted Persephone. Helios admonished Demeter to "stop your own great weeping. It does not fit you, this anger that's so vain and insatiate." At this point, in great grief, Demeter left Olympus and, disguising herself, chose servitude in a human household.

Here we see Demeter, launched into an affect-laden search. If a person becomes caught by the archetypal pattern portrayed in this particular part of the story, she will find herself locked into repetitive rounds of powerless and frustrated rage, accompanied by an inner sense of terrible shame. External voices telling her to "control herself" collude with an internal voice that has the archetypal power to dismiss her anger as "vain and insatiate." This person then lives with an inner shudder of shame about a relentless, pressing swamp of affect that she experiences as "always" rising up within her. Meanwhile, her focus tends to remain on the other who is perceived as being in power, as she tries again and again to plead with and/ or pound against this person in order to change the situation.

When Demeter disguised herself and chose servitude she did retreat, yet she did not withdraw and isolate. She stormed off and hid. She then sent out clues as to her real nature, clues that ultimately led to her being revealed as a goddess with, as we shall see, an unarguably renewed power. This pattern of retreat, disguise, and emergence also appears in the two fairy tales we have presented in our explorations of the seeking relational pattern. In the tale of Allerleirauh in Chapter 4, we see the girl fleeing into the forest, disguising herself as a wild animal. The young stepdaughter in Mother Holle is more subtly disguised as the overworked housemaid, similar to the well known Cinderella. Each of these young heroines, wrestling with loss and in disguise, seeks contact with another; by sending out messages, she lets others know that she is more than she seems. These tales are fundamentally different from those that portray the encapsulated person in the withdrawing relational pattern, tales about Snow White, Rapunzel, or Sleeping Beauty. In each of these stories the maiden is some-how encapsulated, but definitely not disguised, and the suitor has to find her, waken her, and release her. Not so with the seeking pattern; although disguised, these maidens want contact and their own actions lead to their being "revealed." Whether they reach out to the Prince or dive into the Underworld in search of the shuttle, they are searching as is their nature. In each of these tales, this search eventually leads to an emergence: ultimately the protagonist comes forth with a newly developed power well-rooted in the Self. Her plight is a terrible misfortune, while simultaneously it is a necessary step in her individuation. In her retreat, in effect she prepares to emerge with accrued strength.

When this story is manifesting itself in a human life, the process of retreat and disguise has a particularly strong tendency to take over a person's psyche and develop into an entrenched defense. In this case, in essence, the story stops right there; and we find a person with a dependent narcissistic character structure who has lost access to her soul, a person who is consequentially an underachiever, often bitter, blaming, and typically depressed. Like the disguised figures in the archetypal stories, a person with a dependent narcissistic character structure frequently hides her brilliance and power. Not laying claim to her authentic being, this "disguised" person may remain forever in the soot, suffering to no avail, suffering without redemption.

Demeter's retreat and disguise is paralleled by Persephone's immersion in the Underworld. Although we hear no description of Persephone's experience, we are informed that when she emerged she had become Queen of the Underworld. This transmutation from innocent maiden to Queen of the Dead tells us that her period of "retreat" was also deeply transformative. Yet just as a person may be caught by the archetypal power that is portrayed in the moment when Demeter is lost in her disguise, a person also may be caught by the archetypal energy portrayed as Persephone when she is Queen of the Underworld. The person identified with this aspect of the archetype may find herself immersed in mysterious and inexplicable realms of experience that defy explanation or analysis. Given that this myth revolves around intense affect, it is possible to imagine that this indescribable world encompasses unimagined, unembodied, raw archetypal affect. Immersion in this realm leads to several different forms of dependent narcissism. Common to each is the person's experience, conscious or not, that they have special contact with the other world, with dimensions of extraordinary and daunting depths, depths populated by indescribably intense feelings.

A person who finds herself caught by the archetypal energy portrayed in the myth as Persephone in the Underworld may experience this identification in either a deflated or inflated mode. With a deflated attitude, this person may experience her life as a more or less explicitly described, ongoing victimization. She may well be living, consciously or not, as if she had been chosen by the gods, by fate, or by a random accident to be uniquely tortured, more tortured than anyone else could possibly imagine. She may feel, in effect, that Hades, or a sense of "living hell," holds her in constant agony against her will, that this is simply her lot in life. Another person may live out the grip of this archetype more subtly by living in and conveying an illusive sense of being haunted by an indefinable sadness and sorrow; theirs is a life lived melancholically in the shadows, a life not truly lived.

In marked contrast, the person with an inflated attitude may find herself in the grip of this archetypal reality in her deeply held, conscious or unconscious conviction that she has been chosen by the gods to be uncommonly connected to profound emotional depths. Convinced at some level that she has access to realms that others fear to tread, she subtly projects an awesome familiarity about these dark turbulent waters. Mysterious powers and unutterable knowledge are hers. It is not uncommon for a therapist to be caught in this inflation, imagining that she can expertly and uniquely guide others into these realms. This therapist employs the power of the archetype defensively, deriving narcissistic gratification from its use. Wielding her uncommon assets, she enmeshes herself in the lives and hearts of others as a defense against a human life lived with limitation. Whether deflated or inflated, identification with these archetypal forces inhibits an authentic dialogue between a flexible, realistic ego and the Self and the person's psyche remains, to whatever degree, imbedded in the collective unconscious. This person lives in a sort of secret love/hate affair with Hades, suffering a descent with no return. Returning to the story once again:

> When Demeter's disguise was seen through, she dramatically resumed her divine form and demanded that a temple be built for her. Residing in it, she summoned an awesome resolve and determined that the earth would yield no further growth until her daughter was returned. Demeter remained unassailable as she gave vent to the awesome rage of the goddess of death: the earth dried up, the crops failed, men were starving and could find nothing to offer the gods.

Both the intensity and the utter necessity of rage in this myth can often be seen in the lives of people with dependent narcissistic character structures. We noted the intense rage in the case vignette about Mary. When she entered analysis, her rage was enacted in her determined searching, scanning, and invading her daughter's life. These infringements were killing off the human love between the two of them, simple care was drying up, the fields of connection were "lying fallow." It was as if the archetypal wrath of Demeter held sway. Mary's rage in and of itself was not the problem; the problem was that her grief about Lisa's separating had been defensively buried in depression and her rage had been directed against and acted out by Lisa. As our process progressed, Mary held herself in the temenos of analytic work, somewhat like Demeter installed herself in her temple, until she could tolerate contacting her own deeply hidden feelings and thus foster a reconnection to her split off bountiful self, to spring. Thus anchored, she was able to transform her rage into appropriate anger and employ it creatively in her relationships, enabling her to establish and hold effective boundaries with Lisa as well as with others.

Learning to say no is a critical moment in the life of a person with a dependent narcissistic character structure. For this person, engagement with another has typically become the principal defense against facing her own inner turmoil. Caught in an inflation with the life-giving aspect of the bounteous Great Mother or all providing Father, this person is compelled to provide, care for, and nourish to the point of self-denial. Extracting herself from this defensive inflation and the consequent enmeshments with and invasions of others is perhaps the most challenging task this person can undertake. The resource for this extraction lies in archetypal energies such as the fierceness that Demeter mobilized. The archetypal capacity to kill off life for the sake of initiating the seasons manifests itself in human life, when well mediated, as the capacity to say no to unconsciously compelled engagement. The essential role of rage in this process is unmistakably portrayed in Demeter's actions.

Yet the archetypal power of this rage can be employed by narcissistic defenses and thus robbed of its generative potential. Inflated by the rage and power of the death goddess, this rage tends to irrupt, or leak, into a person's life as narcissistic rage directed at others or herself. It serves to create chaos and entanglement rather than clarity and boundaries, death rather than life. Could it be this archetypal rage that is being referred to when we hear people say that anger is not good for us, not good for our immune systems? That it is abusive and damages our children's development. That it is not spiritually advanced. Indeed, when our defenses employ archetypal energies, our merely mortal lives and certainly our mental and spiritual health are at risk. Nevertheless, it is this very energy, when well mediated by an active dialogue between the ego and the Self that can bring us wholeness and the capacity to relate to others with boundaries and love.

> Demeter's rage was eventually heard. The gods responded and Hermes was sent to the Underworld to retrieve Persephone. When Demeter saw her daughter's beautiful face she quickly recognized that Persephone had eaten several fateful pomegranate seeds "slipped" to her by Hades and would have to spend a part of each year in the Underworld. Nevertheless, joy dispelled grief in Demeter's great heart and she agreed to teach men the ministry of her rites and the beauty of her mysteries. When Persephone returns, spring arrives; when she descends, the crops wither. Thus the eternal cycles of nature revolve, as death follows life, and life follows death.

The myth presents us with an image of separation, descent, and differentiated reunion. This process of differentiated reunion is of paramount value for the person with a dependent narcissistic character structure whose defenses pull towards enmeshed attachments. For this person, learning the art of letting go and reconnecting is a great achievement. We saw in several of our cases that the emergence of this capacity appeared both interpersonally and intrapsychically as the person learned how to effectively separate from and reconnect more constructively with others as well as with parts of themselves. In effect, both they and the other people in their lives were freer to engage in the next steps of their individuation process. The dependent narcissist may develop an increasingly flexible and resilient ego and she may be able to participate in increasingly constructive and fulfilling relationships. However, as the flexibility of her ego invites further relationship with the Self, she will undoubtedly find herself challenged again by a descent into the underworld. She may be able to remind herself that these cyclic descents in fact renew and revivify life even though they feel like torment and death, but she will not be released from the process. It is her nature to be asked to cyclically follow the steps of Persephone into the Underworld and the steps of Demeter through her affective trials.

Final thoughts

We have retold and explored the story of Demeter and Persephone, along with the other stories and cases in this chapter, in order to amplify and thus breathe life into the term dependent narcissism. Now when you see this term, we hope it leads you into imagining the fairy-tale meadow at the bottom of the well, the yearnings of Ophelia for Hamlet, and the moment when Persephone is abducted and Demeter falls into her despair and rage. We also hope it leads you into reflections about yourself and others in your life and that these reflections include appreciation of the many gifts that can emerge from the wounds that lie behind this structure.

When a person with a dependent narcissistic character structure consciously learns how to be informed by, rather than unconsciously possessed by, archetypal affects she has an unusually powerful capacity to bring delight, warmth, and empathy into her life, including into relationships. Her developed and reflective use of affect enables these forces to be woven into her ever so human life in an inspiring rather than a destructive manner. Aware that affective energy informs the authenticity of her being, she is ever mindful to return to this source, honoring its depth and beauty. In creative dialogue with the Self, that is, initiated into the mysteries, the dependent narcissist has the capacity to weave the affective truths of the deep, dark mists of the Underworld into the fabric of everyday life, symbolically showering the lives of those around her, as well as herself, with gold.

Notes

1 We would like to thank Deanne Newman for conversations some years ago that shed light on these particular dynamics and images that supported their transformation.
2 This version of the story is an adaptation of story number 24, "Mother Holle," in *The Complete Grimm's Fairytales* (1972: 133–6).
3 At the same time I was working with Paul, whose dependent narcissistic dynamics were inspired by the archetype of the puer, I was also seeing another man, Robert, a gentleman in his sixties, whose dependent narcissistic dynamics were just as clearly inspired by the senex. Sharing the same underlying character structure, these two men represented different poles of the puer–senex archetype. Robert,

the acknowledged "patron" of his immediate and extended family, was known to be generous and good-of-heart. He couldn't understand why, now, he wasn't receiving the respect and obedience he deserved from his wife, children, friends and colleagues. As our work unfolded, it slowly became apparent to Robert that his need for contact with others had been expressed through constant controlling. He was an emotional tyrant: he had laid down the laws and enforced them with easily ignited, intense rage. He had defined the experience of those around him so that he would feel loved, admired, and cared for. But the inherently invasive nature of his controlling maneuvers actually drove everyone away from any satisfying personal contact. Here we see not only how hunger for the other's attention can manifest as Saturnal control but also how this control, as yet another expression of seeking to find meaning in the other's loving glance, is ultimately unsatisfying.

4 This story is retold, in sections, based on "The Hymm To Demeter (I)" in *The Homeric Hymns*, translated by Boer (1970: 89–135).

Chapter 6

Hysteric character structure

The golden promise

Alice's world

"I'm late, I'm late, I'm late!" cries the White Rabbit, and Alice follows him into a wonderland of exaggeration, animation, hilarity, and impotent rage: a world beriddled by the dynamics of disbelief. Intense but shallow affect, a quickly changing, seductive emotional tenor, and the shimmer of archetypal affect announce the presence of the hysteric.

Lewis Carroll's *Alice in Wonderland* symbolically amplifies many of the dynamics that are typical of the hysteric character style. In this well-loved story, a proper English girl is tempted by her curiosity to follow an odd white rabbit in a waistcoat. Leaving her proper English world, she follows the rabbit into a wonderland that is topsey turvey and upside down. In this not-so-proper world, size fluctuates incomprehensibly, Alice nearly drowns

in her tears, the animals talk, the tea party is preposterous, events are unpredictable, the rabbit rushes by, "Oh dear! Oh dear! I shall be too late!" Classically, hysteria is characterized by a shifting and fickle pattern of emotion, by a lack of fidelity and loyalty, by a need for constantly replenished stimulation and attention resulting in a seductive drama of capricious relationships. Dramatic and capricious, what could be more descriptive of the Wonderland into which the White Rabbit leads Alice!

In the previous two chapters, we have told stories of distressed maidens who are driven or forced into their descents. Allerleirauh flees into the dark forest to avoid the advances of her incestuous father, while the maiden in "Mother Holle" is forced by her stepmother to go down the well. In *Alice in Wonderland*, the rabbit's appearance is inviting and she chooses to follow him down the rabbit hole. In each story, a threshold is crossed, the unconscious is entered, and archetypal realms are revealed. The revelations, experience, and establishment of contact with these realms serve to animate, differentiate, and potentially integrate the psyche. Allerleirauh cloaks herself in animal skins and covers herself in soot to disguise and protect herself until she is safe enough to reach out. The maiden in "Mother Holle" meets and serves the Great Mother with genuine respect. Alice's underground is not unlike the meadow that opened at the bottom of the well for the maiden who meets Mother Holle. However, Alice not only has more choice about getting there, she also has more room to play. Not incidentally, she is faced with numerous relationships. No longer safely at home, Alice is required to navigate an increasingly complex world. In this world there is room for play, along with earnest encounters.

While in this descent, Alice meets one hysteric figure after another. In each encounter she learns more and more about herself. At the bottom of the rabbit hole, stuck in a long hall with locked doors, confused and distressed by the drastic changes in her body, she ends up swimming in a pond of her own tears. She meets the stoned caterpillar, philosophizes with him, and garners meaning. She attends a timeless, chaotic tea party at which she sets the limits. She encounters the blustering Queen and, standing up to this two dimensional witch, she expresses her own personal integrity.

Wonderland vividly portrays hysteric defenses, including dissociation and undoing, taking it all back and forgetting, and the distracting scatter of information that hides unaccountability. Alice has to acquaint herself with and extract herself from these defenses in order to develop her individuality. Her journey maps the steps through which an analytic process with a patient with a hysteric character structure might, at its best, proceed. Alice's descent into this underground realm evocatively describes the regression into borderline chaos that a person with an hysteric character structure may have to undergo in order to reestablish contact with the Self. Wonderland represents the wealth as well as the poverty, the beauty as well as the treacherous temptations of this archetypal landscape. Wonderland in dialogue with a strong and flexible ego can bring joy, delight, and transformation into the world; consciously contained, it offers wit, vivacious play, poetic imagination, and spontaneity.

An introduction to the hysteric character structure

The hysteric patient sits on your couch, legs crossed, skirt above her knees, skillfully charming you. Witty, seductive, and fast-paced, her vulnerability is part of the charm with which she seeks your attention. Her flirtatious, intense affect is punctuated by quick, skittish retreats. She knows more about you than she does about herself. A direct question about her inner life is met with myriad distractions and any mirroring of her presence is discounted. Meanwhile, she courts your admiration.

The child who develops a hysteric character structure enters the pre-neurotic phase of development able to entertain leaving the primary dyadic relationship with mother and focusing on triadic dynamics. Having negotiated the developmental challenges of the primal and narcissistic phases, she can now turn towards the larger world, supported by an ego that is relatively differentiated from the unconscious. The young girl ventures out into the wider world of the father using her girlish charms to negotiate that world. Without committing herself to rivalry with her mother, she begins to focus on winning her father's attention. Her adventures are outside the world of the mother, but not yet into daddy's lap. The young boy similarly begins his battle to wrest himself from the mother's arms and enter the world of the father. But not yet fully out of his mother's arms, he too is in a tenuous in-between space. Caught between a desire for connectedness and a longing for autonomy, the hysteric is confronted with desire, competition, and guilt as he proceeds to take on the challenges of triadic relatedness and budding but immature sexuality.

At this pre-neurotic phase, the person employs relatively mature ego defenses of denial, repression, rationalization, undoing, turning against one's self, displacement, and compartmentalization. The hysteric, employing archetypal affect, defensively resorts to immature seductive behaviors, exaggerated emotionality, and inconstancy that she denies and undoes. Any confrontation of these defenses threatens to evoke a descent into the affective chaos that underlies this relational pattern and is strongly resisted.

Case vignette: Kayla, without a clue

When Kayla first called to ask for an appointment, she wanted to come see me because of a disturbing dream and she gathered I worked with dreams. Kayla was a 28-year-old kindergarten teacher, married without children. She expressed pleasure and satisfaction in her relationship and in her work.

Elegant and lively, in sessions she was rather distracted. With great animation, she told me her dream but then resisted exploring it. It took her some time to let me know that what she was actually disturbed about was a situation at work. In bits and pieces, she described how her interactions with the principal of her school were becoming increasingly threatening. What had begun as professional cooperation seemed to be turning into sexually charged encounters, and Kayla could not understand why. She felt terribly guilty and was extremely worried her husband would find out. She was also concerned that the principal would blame and punish her for the direction their relationship was taking. "Curiouser and curiouser," she didn't have a clue why the principal was interested in her.

The clues, however, were quite apparent to me. She was far more flirtatious than she realized. She typically wore a long red scarf, flamboyantly thrown around her neck. Her skirts were short, her necklines cut low. Her vivacious affect soared up and swooped down, as if it knew no bounds. Her enthusiasms had ample room for play in the classroom; she would describe without inhibition how carried away she could get with the kids. She was exaggeratedly irritated with the principal and his obviously overactive male drives. She considered herself to be a skilled feminist, asserting that her sexuality was well contained within politically correct parameters. Not only was she disturbed by the principal's interest in her, she was also upset that so many of the other female teachers dismissed her as naive. They either treated her like a kid or made sniping, competitive attacks to her face and bitchy slurs behind her back. She resented the fact that these women, who seemed uptight to Kayla, were so obviously judgmental of her vivacious enthusiasm. There was simply nowhere in school where she felt safe.

With little insight into her behavior and its impact on others, Kayla remained perplexed by the responses she provoked. Lack of insight into a highly sexualized self-presentation is the hallmark of a hysteric character structure. Denying her ongoing needs for connection with her mother, the hysteric courts the intimacy that she both wants and fears with her father. Yet she then quickly undoes this self-assertion. She therefore often throws herself into the middle of the action in order to get attention, but then quickly flees. With little sense of herself, she seeks the approval of others. Employing archetypal affect defensively, she displays what appear to be intense emotions but they do not remain constant since they are not authentic expressions of her true self. Indeed, her exaggerated emotions frequently serve to ward off the contact she both desires and dreads. Thus, to herself and others she may seem fickle and insincere. These behavior patterns were all amply apparent in Kayla's life.

Once we developed a sufficient amount of trust in our relationship, Kayla was able to begin to explore how her behaviors and her intentions were out of synch. Ultimately, she acquired an understanding of how essential it was for her to become conscious of the archetypal affects that informed her personality. While her beleaguered ego had previously employed undiffer- entiated and unconscious affect defensively, Kayla eventually developed sufficient ego strength to become consciously engaged with and find human expression for this wellspring of her being. Her process exemplifies how essential it is to recognize and value one's character structure, how we individuate through our character structures, not in spite of them. As Kayla gradually developed more capacity to relate to and find conscious expression of the archetypal realms of Aphrodite, the issues with the school principal dissipated. She had learned to take herself seriously, and as she did so she began to be taken seriously by others.

Theoretical considerations

Hysteria is as illusive a category as borderline, if not more so; and it similarly evokes and provokes controversy. As a further development in the seeking relational pattern, hysteric character structures are directly related to dependent narcissism and borderline character structures. At the pre- neurotic developmental phase, a person with a hysteric structure is faced with the complications and challenges of triadic relatedness. With somewhat more developed ego consciousness and access to more mature defenses, archetypal reality is less overwhelming. However, fears about separation and retaliation from the mother, intensified by increasing needs for auto- nomy, and guilt about emerging desires generate new conflicts.

Historical perspective

The fact that "hysteria" has been with us, as a description or diagnosis, since Egyptian and Greek times, across cultural contexts and historical periods, hints at its archetypal nature. Borossa (2001: 3–71), Millon and Davis (1996: 244–60), and Schapira (1988: 37–58) all present extended reviews of this history. At times seen as an illness, at other times as an emotional maladjustment, hysteria has been generally associated with demonic possession, ecstatic states, seductiveness, wanting things in excess, and a propensity to lie and manipulate. Etiologically, *hysteria* is derived from "wandering womb," suggesting that the womb detached, wandered through the body, settled in the brain and produced the wild emotion and excessive lust characteristic of hysteria. With this connotation, hysteria has been seen as inextricably related to women's bodies and dissatisfactions. To control their archetypally driven hysteric outbursts, different cultures have kept their women veiled, separated in places of worship, commanded to silence. In western culture, hysterical symptoms became regarded as evi- dence of witchcraft and early medical interventions were replaced by religiously mandated punishments, including burnings at the stake. Later, with advances in biological knowledge from the seventeenth century on, hysteric forms of behavior became progressively remedicalized and more generally diagnosed as related to the brain and nervous system than to the womb. The diagnosis then became applicable also to men, though it has never really lost its association with the feminine and with "bad" behavior. By the mid-nineteenth century the stage was set for hysteria to become "the disease of the moment," identified by "flirtatiousness, deceitfulness, exaggerated gestures, unseemly displays of emotion, excessive wants or dislikes, overt sexual behavior or the ostentatious refusal of sex" (Borossa 2001: 12). Emerging notions of an irrational "other within," a "doppel-ganger," combined with observations of the suggestibility of the hysteric, encouraged Charcot and Janet to effectively employ hypnosis to explore hysteria.

Freud combined these efforts with a conviction that hysteric symptoms made sense as psychic expressions of trauma based on thwarted libidinal impulses. He concluded that the trauma could be accessed and transformed through remembrance and catharsis. Surmising that his patients' stories were the key to a cure of the symptoms, Freud learned not only to encourage the patient to construct coherent stories about her trauma but also to listen to these stories attentively and with respect. Eventually, Freud shifted his position, concluding that patients' stories about trauma, typically about childhood sexual abuse, were not located in historical truth, but internally in the person's own desires and fantasy life.

Freud's "abandonment" of the seduction theory, his original idea that the child had been abused, has created volumes of analysis and debate. We want to suggest that, symbolically, the pre-Freudian and Freudian theoretical reformulations can be seen as manifestations of hysteric dynamics. These hysteric dynamics of shifting realities and disbelief appear as numerous questions within the discussions about hysteria: What is truth? Who is to be believed? Who is the seductress? Who is seduced? Is her behavior erotic or is it not? Is it manipulative or is it an expression of her deepest desire? Who is in power? As Jungians, we surmise that the dynamics at play in all these questions arise from both human relationships and archetypal patterns. They are akin to the dynamics we glimpsed in Alice's adventures and, as we will see, they also find their expression in the mythic story of Cassandra and the glorious and awesome presence of Aphrodite.

In the developing world of psychoanalysis, while Freud concentrated upon sexual and aggressive drives and their repression, Jung investigated the dissociability of the psyche. He reasoned that traumatic experiences in childhood induced the formation of complexes that became autonomous splinter psyches (Jung 1960). In a recent review of Jung's ideas about dissociation, Wilkinson points out that, in a similar shift to Freud's, Jung also moved away from attributing these defensive maneuvers to developmental experiences and he too produced an explanatory hypothesis emphasizing intrapsychic dynamics. Nevertheless, during the ensuing years, particularly the last half of the twentieth century, clinical interest has swung back towards Jung's initial idea that real, traumatic events lead to a dissociative process in the psyche (Wilkinson 2005).

Jung's theory of dissociation and formation of complexes is a general theory about the psyche and relevant to all character structures, not hysteria alone. As we have explored, when rigidly employed, defensive processes interrupt the emergence of a dialogic ego–Self axis. In this process, a vital aspect of a person's "true self" (Winnicott 1960) or "personal spirit" (Kalsched 1996) is left behind, hidden and protected, in the unconscious. Using the terminology of Jung's theory of dissociability, we could say that a central splinter psyche has been dissociated. With an emphasis on the unpredictable eruptions of highly charged affect, the theory of dissociability and the subsequent formation of unconscious splinter psyches seems most directly applicable to the character styles in the seeking relational pattern. Clearly, we can observe dissociative processes behind the sexually provocative, egocentric, emotional labile, and self-undermining behaviors of the hysteric. However, dissociation can also be at work in the encapsulation of the withdrawing pattern and the ruthless acting out of dominance in the antagonistic pattern.

Psychodynamically, insufficiently met oral needs have been seen as central in the formation of hysterical symptoms, though it has also been suggested that there may be a spectrum running from orally fixated to Oedipally fixated hysterics (Millon and Davis 1996: 248–9). Bollas suggests that hysteria reflects a fundamental disruption of the maternal relationship in response to the mother's early rejection of the child's sexuality. The child develops a false self that she offers to the father, though she maintains a pervasive desire to return to pre-Oedipal states of desire for the mother. Consequently she not only tends to confer desire and anti-desire at the same time, but she also begrudges maturation (Bollas 2000: 92, 103–4). Mogenson argues that by linking hysteria to Oedipal desire and a wish to regress to the womb, Bollas has reduced psyche's ills at the expense of its mystery. Proposing that hysteria is the unfolding manifestation of the anima (which we would call soul), he imagines that this timeless figure can lead us to the space between the two worlds of reality and dream, truly psychological space where personal concerns have not only external referents but are also radically interiorized (Mogenson 2003).

The obvious gender bias and apparent fear of women in the history of hysteria is amply apparent. This is abundantly clear in the etiology of *hysteria* which, as mentioned, is derived from "wandering womb." As Millon and Davis point out (1996: 245): "Strangely, history holds no such member that might become detached, take up residency in the brain, and distort perception in order to explain antisocial behavior among males." Commenting on the shift from "the ancient superstition called possession" to "the modern superstition called hysteria," Hillman concludes: "The witch is now a poor patient – not evil, but sick . . . The misogyny does not change; it appears in a new form. The woman is still to blame" (Hillman 1972: 254). An attempt to correct this blatant gender bias led to the use of the term "histrionic" in place of hysteric, in order to highlight the attention-seeking, performance-driven aspects of this character structure. However, this suggestion has only slightly amended the controversy surrounding the term. Although clinicians are occasionally reminded that this clinical profile is found among both women and men, it is frequently overlooked or misdiagnosed among men. Attempting to rectify this blind spot, Horowitz emphasizes that "a failure of a firm sexual identity is always part of a hysterical structure," and both male and female hysterics present a "caricature" of a sex role. While women tend to express this undeveloped sexual identity as hyperfeminism, they can also adopt an antithetical hypofeminism. Hysteric men tend to express this identity issue in either an effeminate, hypomasculine or an assertive hypermasculine manner (Horowitz 1991: 46–7).

Hysteria as a diagnosis lost its preeminence during the twentieth century, yet the issues these dynamics generate remain at the heart of many current debates in psychoanalysis. We continue to grapple with how to understand historical truth as related to the symbolic nature and curative power of narrative truth. (In Chapter 4, we presented the way Rachel wrestled with this dilemma in her treatment.) We continue to consider how, and why, different sectors of the psyche seem to take on autonomous realities, and wander into hidden places, yet now we talk of horizontal splitting (repression) and vertical splitting (dissociation). Naturally, we continue to debate the desirability of and how to handle intense affect, especially sexualized affect, in treatment. While the debates remain familiar, the "name" for these phenomena has varied widely. At this point, the word "trauma" itself stimulates animated conversations about the degree to which trauma is generated in literal history or imaginally amplified "memories." These conversations might well have been about "hysteria" some years ago. Furthermore, the behaviors and psychological dynamics that were descriptive of classical hysteria are inherent in many of the disorders receiving abundant clinical attention these days: eating disorders, multiple personality disorder/dissociative identity disorder and the frequently misapplied diagnosis of borderline personality disorder.

Bollas argues that the overuse of borderline as a diagnosis shoved hysteria off the stage for some time, but that now "the colorful garments of the hysteric" are reappearing, compelling us "to think them again and again" (Bollas 2000: 179). In a somewhat similar vein, the argument has been made that hysteria appears today in "epidemics" such as chronic fatigue, recovered memory, Gulf War syndrome, satanic abuse, and alien abduction (Showalter 1998). This author points out that, as in classic hysteria, each of these ailments is experienced as painful and is amenable to charismatic healing while its objective reality is collectively doubted or disbelieved.

In conclusion, we see that the archetypal landscape of hysteria tends towards abundant, quixotic, sexualized interactions, creating a rapidly fluctuating, affectively charged plethora of near-but-missed contacts. Both the diagnosis and the person diagnosed are always a little hard to define, a little hard to get hold of; they each remain tempting but elusive.

The dynamics of hysteric character structures

As mentioned above, a person with a hysteric character structure employs more mature defenses than the dependent narcissist. In the pre-neurotic phase, the ego is relatively differentiated from the Self and its defensive processes serve to protect its relatively new independence. These ego defenses tend to rigidify the differentiation of the ego from the Self and as archetypal affects that are characteristic of this relational pattern are repeatedly repressed, the flow of energy along the ego–Self axis is obstructed. The hysteric then, confident of her conscious position, finds herself moving into life and love as if she knows what she wants and knows what she's doing. However, her disowned affects threaten to, and often do, break through with wildly contradictory messages. Thus she seduces and then withholds, excites and disappoints, both others and herself. The battle between the ego and the unconscious develops in tandem with the child's movement towards the opposite sex parent and since in this relational pattern affect is at the steering wheel, expressions of the newly activated battle frequently occur in highly emotional and frequently sexualized terms.

Our culture amply rewards and encourages the young hysteric woman who is flirtatious and charming, as it does the generously adaptive dependent narcissistic. Yet, in a cruel enantiodromia, "we" essentially revile the older hysteric woman, seeing her as a pathetic embarrassment. Her irrelevance can drive her straight into an intense addiction, typically alcoholism. Quite probably each of us has known someone we felt was like Mrs. Robinson in the classic film from the 1970s, *The Graduate*. This is a woman who desperately needs to remain attractive in order to support her inner coherence. Cosmetic and surgical industries ply upon her insecurity. Meanwhile, some male hysterics are also amply rewarded, though neither they nor our culture tends to see them as hysteric. Let's consider the Marlboro man, the handsome, tough macho guy to whom so many women are drawn. He may swagger instead of mince, look her straight in the eye with a wink instead of casting a sidewise sultry glance, but his flirtations are spiced with a similar sensuality with that unmistakable mixture of beckoning and rejecting. His seductive, immature sexuality is not likely to be around for the long haul. Then we also find the gay man who has a hysteric character structure. Some gay subcultures tend to reinforce affect-laden, intense flirtations combined with a lack of substantial related intention. Whatever gender marked cultural overlay is adopted, the hysteric pattern remains dynamically the same dramatic attempt to appeal in order to receive the attention that does not satisfy the other or herself.

Hysteric character structure as distinct from the other character structures

A person with a dependent narcissistic character structure or a borderline character structure looks and behaves differently from a hysteric even though each is informed by archetypal affect. A person with a borderline character structure lives at the mercy of these archetypal dynamics, while a person with a dependent narcissistic character is inflated by them. In contrast to both of these configurations, a person with a hysteric character structure defends against these affects while their every move, internally and externally, remains thickly imbued by them. Far removed from the Self, this person is bereft of an authentic connection to his desires. Faced with multiple relationships, he feels excited but quite at sea. The intrigues, betrayals, and dramatic suffering that the hysteric throws himself into manifest and consolidate the ego defenses which protect him from a fearful regression into the terrifying chaos of borderline reality. It is possible that the crises in his life will accumulate to the point where a regression into raw and chaotic borderline dynamics will be required in order for the person to reemerge with a sufficiently flexible ego to maintain a creative and rewarding life.[1]

Intense, affect-loaded entanglements differentiate a person in the seeking relational pattern from people in the withdrawing or antagonistic patterns. This is naturally as true in the pre-neurotic phase as it is in the primal and narcissistic phases. The basic underlying ground of archetypal affect propels a hysteric into the arms of others. Meanwhile, the obsessive-compulsive tries to stay as removed as possible, with dignity, though he may unconsciously long for contact. The passive-aggressive unconsciously attacks the very one he wants to be with. Remembering that the relational patterns that are "other" hold the shadow elements that bear the fruit of wholeness, we can imagine that the hysteric would do well to seek some soothing encapsulation. She might discover that developing a meditation practice, a singular sport such as track, or merely long hikes in the woods alone could support a sense of containment that would balance her naturally engaging impulses. Certainly she could afford a conscious dose of antagonism to balance the internal sense that all value lies in the other.

Cassandra: gifted and cursed

What is truth? Who is to be believed? Who is the seductress? Who is seduced? Who is in power? These questions are dramatically woven into the story of Cassandra. Daughter of the King and Queen of Troy, Cassandra was gifted the powers of prophecy by Apollo. It is said that one day when Cassandra was in Apollo's temple, this great god appeared and promised to teach her the art of prophecy if she would lie with him. Cassandra agreed, accepted his gift, but then "went back on the bargain," refusing his advances. Apollo begged her to give him just one kiss and, as she did, he spat into her mouth, thus ensuring that no one would believe the prophesies that she would utter. Cassandra did indeed foretell many dreadful events of the Trojan war, though she was dismissed as mad and disbelieved by all. When Troy fell, Cassandra was awarded as a spoil of war to Agamemnon who took her to his home in Greece where his revengeful wife Clytemnestra promptly killed them both, just as Cassandra had foreseen (Hamilton 1940: 252–4; Graves 1955: 263–4, 338).

This mythological story evocatively amplifies the dynamics of hysteric reality. Being playful and flirtatious, receptive and naive, as well as easily alarmed and propelled into flight, the hysteric is generally not believed or taken seriously. Emanating a mysterious magnetic allure, she is chosen and desired, receives the attention and gifts offered, but then in one way or another she does not hold up her side of the relationship. This tends to evoke retaliation and curse from the other.

In an extended presentation and analysis of this story, Schapira suggests that one way to understand Cassandra is to imagine that she did not have sufficient ego strength to confront Apollo consciously and directly. Schapira suggests that Cassandra had not only a powerful mother complex that left her without sufficient grounding in the feminine matrix, but also an animus dominated ego. Thus, Cassandra was cursed with a character flaw that ensured tragedy (Schapira 1988: 10–17).

Bearing both a gift and a curse are the elements of Cassandra's fate, as is generally true for a hysteric. Blessed with gifts of brilliant insight, she is cursed with an inability to express the shadowy truths she sees in a way that is believed, even by herself. As is characteristic of the medial woman, she has unusual access to the collective unconscious, yet she has insufficient capacity to express what she sees (Schapira 1988: 53). Vivacious and enter-taining, but also flighty and ungrounded, she is perceived as superficial and is readily dismissed.

In this mythic story, we find an evocative archetypal portrait of the dynamics that we have considered above. With a name that means "she who entangles men" (Graves 1955: 385), Cassandra is an apt representative of the seeking relational pattern. While each of the character structures within this pattern create entangled enmeshments, the hysteric does so with the added twist of sexuality. Like Cassandra, the hysteric woman tends to be desired by men but isolated from women and cut off from authentic contact with herself.

Jason: developing a personal connection to feelings

I worked with Jason during two different periods of his life. He first came into analysis when he was 28 years old and in crisis following the stormy collapse of a relationship. We worked for barely one year, at which point he began another relationship and terminated treatment. Ten years later, he contacted me again and this time we entered a process that lasted for a number of years.

The first year of therapy

At the age of 20, Jason had left a college life dominated by drinking and partying. Feeling bored with his classes, he was able to squeeze by academically, but he had become more and more restless. He decided to set off for a number of romantic adventures. Living on a generous allowance from his father, he had wandered the world, joined an ashram, performed with a theatrical company, worked as a chef, and gone to an art school in Rome. While he was in art school, he had fallen in love with his Italian instructor. He was a flirt and so was she. His hours in the studio extended themselves into long intimate evenings with her. He was devastated months later to discover that his lover was married. After she ended this relationship, and somewhat surprising to him, he frequently fantasized about defeating her husband and winning her back. These fantasies haunted his next few love affairs but, diluted by these new interests, the fantasies eventually receded.

Jason acknowledged that "love affairs" were probably not quite the right words for his numerous relationships during these years, because he recognized that he had plunged into and out of each of them with a kind of abandonment that left him paradoxically outside of honest relatedness. Honing his image as a dashing, sensitive, hip young man, he developed what he himself called "an alternative macho charisma" that was quite irresistible for many young women. Swaggering and proud of his proficiency as a lover and playmate, Jason skated through several more years of his life.

He moved to my community with the intention to "get his life together." He wanted to develop a profession and he had decided on a specialization in physical therapy, with a concentration on Rolfing. While in school, he met another student, Robin, who "won his heart." The next night, she moved into his apartment. Like him, she had spent her twenties on the road. She was rougher and more streetwise than anyone he had been with before. Her appetite for exotic clothes and drugs increased as time went on. What at first seemed exciting to Jason began to appear as dangerous and expensive. When she realized that his finances could not supply the increasing demands of her habits, she turned to a richer and older man. Jason was distraught, and yet also relieved. The drug-heightened excitement of their sexuality had begun to frighten him. He turned his energy to completing school – and an occasional affair.

Having graduated, Jason discovered how complicated it was to do bodywork. He received a choice internship at a local clinic but was disheartened to discover that he was expected to work hard at low pay. Soon he decided to set up a private practice, but he was dismayed by just how much was involved. He was intimidated, not only by the details of running a business, but even more so by the multilayered interactions with his clients. He found himself involved in interactions that required him to deal with the sexuality of others on a regular basis. He was surprised that these interactions created so much confusion and distress for him. He thought he had his sexuality perfected and in control. However, numbers of his clients either let him know that they thought he was inappropriately flirtatious, or they themselves were inappropriate with him. The realization that his career choice appeared to be insurmountably challenging threw him into rounds of anxiety that he was unequipped to handle. He began to get terrible headaches. He called me for an appointment.

So we began our work. In our very first few sessions, he laid out his life story. His father was a self-made, highly successful insurance broker. He was noted in the community for his expert customer service, impeccable management skills, and prosperity. He was disciplined, hard working, ambitious, and emotionally unavailable. Jason's mother's warmth and generosity complemented her husband's cool precision; her social skills contributed substantially to her husband's success. Their first child was a son who resembled the father and was his father's prince. Jason, who had his mother's blue eyes, arrived as a surprise six years later. He fondly remembers being cradled in his mother's arms; he remembers her building his red wagon; he remembers her smile.

Jason was sent off to his paternal grandparents' farm each summer. Many of his most vivid memories were of his time on their farm. His experiences there had both fascinated and scared him. The rawness of farm life, the explicit exposure to farm animals and the realities of sexuality, birth, and death all created lasting, haunting images. Jason found that now as a young man he often thought, uneasily, of the men who worked the farm. He recognized that as a kid he had practiced being like them, wearing cowboy boots and a Western hat, swaggering and looking tough. Now he found himself reliving the details of the moments back on his grandparents' farm, when these men were rough and joking with him, and he had felt so terrified.

In the first months of treatment, we focused on Jason's experiences in his work. He did not want the inconsistency of another career change in his life. However, it was becoming clear just how uncomfortable he was in this work. As we talked about the sexually charged encounters with several of his patients, he began to conclude that he was simply in over his head. In our sessions, as I encouraged him to stay with his feelings, he eventually turned inward towards his inner turmoil. Extracted from the drama of his outer life, for at least brief periods, his distress tumbled out.

Previously, the primary feelings that Jason had expressed about the end of his relationship with Robin were relief. Now he confessed that it was really far more complex than that. He described how he couldn't quit thinking about the two of them together, especially when he was alone in his apartment at night. Wrestling hard with his intense guilt that periodically silenced him, he was finally able to tell me what he'd been up to. Not infrequently, he had been driving over to the house where Robin was living with her new man and parking outside to wait to see them. He'd even followed them at times when they came out and went somewhere. He had made numerous calls in the middle of the night and had tried to find out everything he could about this man's business.

One night, feeling particularly disturbed about Robin, he went to their favorite theater. In the lobby, he ran into her with her new man. They exchanged chilly but loaded greetings and he watched as her new lover triumphantly escorted her to the door of the front box seats. Jason was enraged and overcome with jealousy and fantasies of revenge. Following an uncontrollable urge, he ordered drinks sent to their box with a note which said, "I know the kind of shady life you two are living; one day I'll turn you in." Once the note was handed to the attendant, Jason was filled with guilt, terror, and inadequacy and quickly fled.

Jason was anxious to work on all this; he wanted relief. His headaches were becoming unremittingly intense migraines. He was just beginning to become aware of his anxiety about acting out, to manage it, and begin to develop a therapeutic alliance with me when he met a wealthy, charming, well-established, local businesswoman named Joan. She was immediately taken with his vivacity, youth, and flamboyance. Jason quite quickly felt better about everything. The day after Joan accepted his proposal that they marry, he let me know that he thought our work together had been a success, and he left treatment.

Initial reflections

Jason's life was being tossed and turned by the capricious dynamics of hysteria. As a young child, he had adopted the persona of a tough farm-hand to manage his vulnerable, emotional nature. As a college student, his persistent choice to party and drink reflected the extent to which he could not take himself and his life seriously. Clearly not able to set and stay committed to long-term goals, this revelry was a way that Jason, as a young man, could immerse himself in emotionally charged apparently intimate encounters. Using this context as an acceptable, macho expression of his highly affective nature, Jason began to rely on arousing adventures. He experienced his sexual escapades as easy and entertaining, yet he was unable to manage his own or others' aggression. These impulses fascinated him, as was evident in his interest in Robin, while they also overpowered him. The repressed rage and sexualized aggression that are embedded in hysteric character structure were putting pressure on his ego. Striking out with an empty threat, in a classic hysteric touch-and-go manner, Jason attempted to assert himself but did so ineffectually. His intense, regressive behavior in the theater scared him and he fled into a restoration of his persona: another successful seduction. He hoped he could settle down in this one. His rather superficial conclusion that our work had been "successful" exemplifies the defensively motivated, shallow behaviors that are commonly seen as characteristic of a hysteric person.

Ten years later

When Jason called this time, he was again in the midst of turmoil and he was having periodic anxiety attacks that he felt at the mercy of. He remembered that he had felt calmed by our sessions and he hoped for immediate relief. As we explored his current life circumstance, the reasons for his anxiety emerged. While his marriage had had a stabilizing effect on his life, emotionally and sexually, he had been deeply disappointed by it. He was finding it harder and harder to remain loyal to Joan, his wife. There was a young woman in the clinic where he now worked who was clearly interested in him and he had begun to return her flirtations. Jason had by now developed quite a flamboyant persona. His long, thick hair pulled back in a handsome ponytail, his casual but impeccably classy and form-fitting clothes, and his poetically cocky manner had brought to near perfection his "alternative macho charisma," as he was still proud to call it.

As our work progressed, Jason shared that he was distressed that he wasn't finding sex satisfying any longer, in fact, he was often impotent. Whereas he had thought his anxiety was about his disappointment in the marriage and his flirtations, he came to see that he was far more anxious that Joan was getting bored with him. He imagined that she was interested in several other men at their tennis club. He began to find his evenings filled with distressing fantasies, not unlike years before with Robin. He imagined that Joan was in bed with one of these men, and he imagined himself confronting her lover and then weakly retreating in both guilt and defeat. Recognizing that he had acted out this fantasy once before, he found its reappearance extremely disturbing. In addition, he did not want Joan to leave him. He thought he genuinely loved her and he could feel how much he needed her.

As we worked with Jason's aggressive but impotent fantasies, images of his father began to appear. He began to face how little his father had given him and how this had been underscored by his father's favoritism towards his older brother. A series of dreams arrived depicting his father's cold-hearted distance and Jason's broken heart. Experiencing anger directly at his father and brother enlivened and strengthened him. He then realized that the aggression of the men on the farm scared him because he had such intense but repressed rage at his father. He found it moving to see that he had identified with these men, adopting their swagger not only to cover his vulnerability but also to ward off his own real aggression. He then began to associate this childhood anger with the anger he felt towards the other men in his lovers' lives and the general disdain he felt towards conservative, typical masculinity. He felt interested in how he had adopted the male swagger, interpreted in his own way; and he began, tentatively, to be curious about his sensitive, emotional nature.

With this clarity and consolidation, Jason could turn towards the exploration of his early memories of his mother. His fond memories of being warmly held and played with began to give way to feelings of being teased and seduced. With the help of his dreams, he felt the awakening of his sexual feelings towards her. These feelings confused him immensely and he retreated from this process any number of times. Nevertheless, memories of and feelings towards his mother persistently found their way back into the room. At times, he was drawn into her embrace, into the thrill of her building the red wagon; at other times he was enraged, telling her to back off, go away, let go! Although she had died some years previously, he wrote her a number of letters. Eventually he saw how seductive and unboundaried she had been, how much she had sought to get her emotional needs satisfied with him. He found himself on a see-saw between rage at her narcissistic use of him and grief about his loss of a well-related mother.

In the midst of the intensity of this work, it became evident how both Jason's sexuality and his aggression were at play in our relationship. When I offered such an observation, he typically took a step back, in denial. But then, often rather quickly, he'd return to the issue, generally with heated affect, followed by guilt and severe self-recriminations. In this manner, we explored how his subtle disdain and flippant, cocky humor were manifestations of his disowned anger, and how he employed his boastful seductions to keep me interested and present. These explorations between us led him to an increased appreciation of the creative potential and boundary-setting capacities that arise from his expressions of anger. They also enabled him to experience me as consistently present, caring for him, without his having to win my attention. He began to take not only his feelings but himself progressively more seriously. Naturally, this work had a profound effect on his relationship with Joan. His distrust of her love and loyalty abated; and, quite to his delight, his sexual interest in her reappeared in a new, grounded, and fully felt way.

Jason terminated our work unusually slowly, continuing to come off and on for several years, resisting his old pattern of "here today – gone tomorrow." Over these years, he became professionally more accomplished; not only did his private practice do very well, but he also joined the faculty of a training institute. Respected by others and himself for his balance between sensitivity and masculine strength, he enjoyed his life.

Additional reflections

In Jason's life, archetypal affect was tenaciously employed as a defense against authentic feelings. His professed desire, his provocative and seductive masculinity, and his entangled relationships all wore the cloak of intense feeling while they masked his disowned heartfelt sexuality and his roaring rage. Identifying himself as a skilled, macho lover, Jason adopted this archetypal form and thus protected himself from his personal connection to feeling. In the patient reworking of his feelings towards both his mother and his father, towards me and others, Jason claimed his individuality.

Transference and counter-transference

Like all pre-Oedipal transferences, the transference for the pre-neurotic hysteric is not clearly contoured. In analytic work with a neurotic patient, a therapist would expect to find well-developed historic figures, whole objects appearing in the transference. The patient might experience the therapist as an abandoning yet critical mother or as an exciting and alluring father. However, for the person with a pre-neurotic hysteric structure, while the therapist may be experienced by the patient as critical or alluring, it takes a considerable amount of work to consolidate and ground these projected affective states into whole object relating. The benefit of staying close to and developing feelings is that this supports the emergence of genuine relatedness. In the midst of this process, the hysteric patient tends to act out his ambivalent desires for contact and autonomy within the transference. Denying his unmet needs, he may be rejecting and dismissive, although his intense desire for contact, to whatever degree it is sexualized, may propel him into flirtatious seductions.

Counter-transferentially, it is hard not to respond to the hysteric. His engaging charm, though defensive in purpose, is often charismatic and appealing. The pyrotechnics that are part and parcel of the hysteric defense are a challenge to relate to without getting drawn into the drama. Threatened by the amount of affect in the room, a therapist may resort to distancing. Excited by the amount of affect in the room, a therapist may join into the play unconsciously, courting and cavorting in lieu of analyzing. The therapist may also be tempted to voice the critical, even patronizing parent. A measured amount of affect and structure, play and reflection, may allow the patient access to his affect and creativity without leaving him in continued danger of being possessed by it.

Aphrodite: the golden goddess

Known as the "irresistible goddess who stole away even the wits of the wise" (Hamilton 1940: 32), Aphrodite is certainly an apt presence to turn to as we continue to explore the dynamics of hysteric character structure. In her stories we find the elements of seduction, possession, enthrallment, betrayal, and the traits of mutability that we have seen at play in hysteric lives. She evocatively portrays the powerful archetypal landscape that underlies these dynamics. Let's turn to her stories, to her irresistible glimmer.

Aphrodite, the Greek goddess of love and beauty, is also known by many as Venus, a later Roman embodiment of this goddess who was in truth as old as time. Descending primarily from the Mesopotamian goddess Inanna-Ishtar (Baring and Cashford 1991: 352–9), we see Aphrodite's ancient essence reflected in the tale of her birth that reveals her emerging from the foams of the sea. It is said that Uranus/Heaven would not let Gaia/Earth nor their children see the light. Chronos, their son, armed with a sickle given him by his mother, "harvests" his father's genitals, throws them into the sea, and thus slices heaven from earth. As time passed, this immortal flesh gathered foam around it and this foam came forth from the sea as a goddess, beautiful and feared. Here Aphrodite is acknowledged as an essential force in the very essence of the creation of the world. Her arrival heralds the birth of light, symbolically the birth of consciousness.

Acknowledged as the one who awakens desire in the hearts of gods and men alike, Aphrodite wields love not only to create but also to destroy. We see this in the stories of Aphrodite's impact on the lives of others, as well as in her own affairs. When she is not properly honored, she drives her victim into sexual alliances that break boundaries and hearts. For example, in the story of Hippolytus, Aphrodite was affronted by Hippolytus' rejection of her advances. In order to punish the lad, Aphrodite created an elaborate intrigue in which she instilled an all consuming love for him in his stepmother's heart which ultimately sent them both into the arms of death. In another story, affronted by the beauty of a young mortal, Myrrha, Aphrodite drove her into an incestuous embrace with her father who then turned on his daughter murderously.

The archetypal energy of Aphrodite can inspire complicated and enormously destructive dynamics in our merely mortal lives. If this archetypal energy is not respected, if it is not consciously woven into our being through spontaneous, loving, and joyful unions, we leave ourselves in danger of being driven into chaotic and destructive unions. In the stories of Hippolytus and Myrrha, we see how the wildness of hysteric patterns, the over-sexualized, constantly seeking yet never gratified, hungry and fickle – and sometimes even incestuous – chaos is stirred by the goddess herself if she is not respected by consciousness. In effect, if the ego maintains a relationship with this archetypal force, love and beauty can grace one's life; but if access to her is unavailable to consciousness, she arrives in any case, creating destruction and chaos.

Aphrodite's webs of erotic madness pervade her stories. Frequently unfaithful to her lame, misshapen mate, Hephaestus, Aphrodite had dramatic liaisons with Ares, the great god of war, and a more tender, cyclic affair with Adonis, her adored son-lover. The startling limitations of the union between Aphrodite and Hephaestus may represent the elusive nature of Aphrodite's love, a love that tolerates no boundaries and is ever changing, ephemeral and never to be counted on. It is said that Hephaestus forged a net of chains to trap Aphrodite and Ares in adulterous union. When he had ensnared the faithless couple, the many gods assembled and only a humorous remark from Hermes released the tension of the scene. Although Aphrodite flees from this crude exposure to her sanctuary to be restored, naturally she soon continues her beguiling ways for fidelity is simply not her nature.

Ginette Paris remarks that it is part of Aphrodite's myth that love gives itself as eternal and yet it departs. "Anyone who catches a glimpse of Aphrodite soon learns that she holds no promise of eternal love" (Paris 1986: 65). She concludes that Aphrodite simply cannot accommodate herself to "truth" as defined by Apollo or Zeus. Here we find the suggestion that while Aphrodite embodies her own noble truths, these are not seen as noble from a logical and social/ethical perspective. Thus enters the quixotic reality of the hysteric: Is she telling the truth? Whose truth? The debates that pervade clinical discussions about hysteria apparently have deep roots in this archetypal reality.

Aphrodite's passion for her various lovers sheds light on hysteric dynamics. In her love for Ares we see the attraction of opposites, peace and war, desire and aggression. Noting that the union of the hyperfemininity of Aphrodite and the hypermasculinity of Ares produces a child, Harmony, we might consider the possibility that, psychologically, we cannot have love (pleasure, sexuality, laughter, and joy) without hate (rage and aggression) (Paris 1986: 80–1). In this case, hyperfemininity and hypermasculinity describe characteristic sets of behaviors as not only lacking in development, but also having archetypal meaning. Indeed when Bolen describes Ares as having a "swagger-braggart machismo" (Bolen 1984: 249), we see how this archetypal energy informs the hysteric profile of the hypermasculine patient that we described above. In her rhythmic reunion with Adonis we find

Aphrodite drawn to a delicate, sensitive, and young lover. Far from the embattlements with Ares, here Aphrodite enters into a romantic sweetness. Yet this love is poignantly ephemeral. It is not meant to last, for at the end of summer the young son-lover dies, descending into the Underworld for part of each year. He not only "dies" each season, but he eventually dies when hunting. Aphrodite is thrown into grief, and cries inconsolably. Aphrodite's vulnerability to the pain that love contains testifies to her own capacity to endure love in its essential ephemeral nature. She turns towards love, knowing that her lover will leave. Suffering the finitude of love, she accepts transience – and his repetitive death.

Aphrodite, like Dionysus, is a "hot-headed" divinity who lacks the self-control of Apollo and Athena (Paris 1986: 82–3). As the founts of desire and madness, these divinities challenge the fabric of human lives. In Chapter 4, we have described how Dionysus fuels the chaos underlying borderline reality. Aphrodite carries this intensity of affect into the hysteric character structure. It is archetypal affect inspired by Aphrodite that inspires and conspires in the life of the hysteric.

Described as the lover of laughter, Aphrodite, whose seductions no one can escape (Boer 1970: 70–1) is an archetypal force that requires dialogue with a strong and flexible ego. In human lives, this golden goddess can bring the freshness of spring and the delight of shimmering romance, yet she also can bring seductive, boundary-breaking escapades that leave the person and others in terrible pain. Left to govern the psyche, Aphrodite will no doubt have her way, creating a multitude of indiscriminate affairs. Her dark side can create strife, distrust, and even violence in relationships. With no respect for boundaries, she drives the gods and goddesses as well as mortals into frenzied, incestuous chaos as it suits her. When these archetypal forces overpower the ego, they can propel a person into impulsive behaviors that leave one racked with guilt.

In the sense that Aphrodite insists that we seek love, she is the consummate goddess of the seeking relational pattern. As Downing concludes, for Aphrodite "reaching towards the other is an essential act of the self . . . you [Aphrodite] need to be turning towards others to be yourself. . . . We may learn from you a way of knowing ourselves and the world that comes only through turning in love toward another" (Downing 1987: 201–2). In Aphrodite's realms, it is through turning towards others, that one discovers oneself.

It is Aphrodite's gift to teach us of love and relationship. This love can lead us to a lyric consciousness, a delicate, attentive, detailed consciousness, colored by the rosy light of dawn and dusk; a "being conscious in relationship" as distinct from an Apollonic "being conscious of relationship" (Downing 1987: 206–7).[2] Being conscious in relationship is clearly the prospective intent of the seeking-of-others that pervades the lives of people with this character structure. For this person, guided by Aphrodite, it is in the creation of relationship that meaning arrives. This capacity for relationship is simultaneously intrapsychic and interpersonal. Just as one discovers oneself through turning to others, it is also true that when one can bring the awesome presence of Aphrodite into relationship with consciousness, love can infuse her entire being. This is a love that honors not only beauty and union, but also finitude, loss, and grief. In essence, if the ego creates a dialogue with her, love, joy, and a capacity to live in the ever-changing reality of relationship can bless one's life.

Summary of the seeking relational pattern

As with the withdrawing pattern, each of the character styles within the seeking pattern has a similar "feel" to it. Allerleirauh smeared in ash, living in desperate torment, continues to reach out for connection. In "Mother Holle," the unloved and envied stepchild continues through her industriousness to maintain a connection with her caretakers. Meanwhile, the girlish Alice's astounding adventures in Wonderland portray determined engagements with one character after another. The seeking and enmeshment never stop. In this relational pattern, archetypal affect is used as a defense against the development, differentiation, and expression of individual feelings. One's source of survival, satisfaction, meaning, and personal coherence is experienced as residing in another, whether in another part of the psyche or another person, and it is constantly sought. The seeking person tends to estrange the very people with whom she hopes to connect. The string of disappointments and broken relationships continues to create an external picture of chaos that mirrors her internal experience of chaos. Dominated by archetypal affect, she has limited access to the clarity and inspiration of mind and imagination, as well as to the sturdy embodiment provided by the physical vitality characteristic of the antagonistic pattern.

The relentless assaults of the affective unconscious may leave the person in endless chaos, yet this aspect of the collective unconscious may also be the fount of a passionate, full hearted, engaged, rather than enmeshed, life. The person who is consciously informed by, rather than possessed by, the affective unconscious may call upon her access to the affective realms to facilitate her emergence as an unusually empathic, generous, engaged, warm, and loving soul. The seeking person has a remarkable talent for creating moments of ecstasy and magic. Her spiritual experience may emphasize union with God, at times through union with another.

Notes

1 Clinicians at times refer to one character structure having features of another: e.g. an "hysteric with borderline features." We see this as referring to what we

describe here as the dynamic process of regression that an hysteric will naturally move into under stress or in development.

2 Downing finds the roots of *conscious loving* in Aphrodite's nature itself yet it can also be seen as arising out of Psyche's love of Eros and her courageous responses to Aphrodite's cruel demands.

Part III

The antagonistic pattern

Chapter 7

Psychopathic character structure

Culling the herd, dominance, control, and predation

The avid fascination in our culture with psychopathy is undeniable. Novels and movies about killers, rapists, and shrewd and ruthless law-breakers spin to the top of the charts; headlines about such events hold us rapt. We cannot ignore the immensity of the psychic energy in all this. It is our responsibility to try to understand the psychological dynamics which are involved in our cultural fascination with psychopathic personalities, as well as the dynamics which lie behind our individual attraction to and/or repulsion from these controversial but intensely energetic individuals.

Many modern films present us with the raw experience of violence, or domination, or gratuitous sexuality. These films offer a discouraging but not unrealistic prognosis for the psychopath who has little hope of release from this pathology. Our hunger for these films provides ample evidence to support the disturbing hypothesis that as viewers, we are living these thrills vicariously or, even worse, we are being desensitized and presented with compelling models of violence. Beyond these bleak possibilities, there are films, which offer stories and images of how transformation may appear.

For example, the film *Girl Interrupted*, based on an autobiography by Susanna Kaysen, presents these dynamics in a sophisticated, personally engaging, and to some degree redemptive movie. The protagonist Susanna, having been handed a bewildering diagnosis of "borderline" at age 17, is sent off to a treatment center. There she encounters another inpatient, Lisa, whom we quickly realize is psychopathic. Bold, daring, adept at manipulating the system and flaunting her victories, this disturbingly entrancing young woman is hell-bent for a good time and for trouble. Played by Angelina Jolie in an Academy Award winning performance, Lisa struts on to the scene dressed in tight jeans, cowboy boots, and with an attitude that commands our immediate attention. We see how her cunning ensures her domination over the rather motley group of inmates; without a doubt, she rules. She charms, seduces, baits, scorns, tricks, and lies to secure her power; and she does all this with astonishing charisma. This is an apt portrayal of an intelligent, young, still vibrant psychopath.

Now the question arises: How are we drawn into her spell? Why are we fascinated? Whenever we become fascinated with another person, or a story, one analytic hypothesis is that the fascinating other is carrying or representing a part of ourselves. Their magnetism, positive or negative, whether they are idealized or scorned, measures how intensely we have split off this aspect of ourselves and projected it on to others.

Girl Interrupted vividly portrays this process as we watch the unfolding of the relationship between Susannah and Lisa. Susanna becomes intrigued by Lisa and follows her through a series of wildly intoxicating adventures, which Susanna's inhibitions would have prevented her from experiencing. We can see that Susanna becomes drawn in and fascinated by aspects of Lisa's character to which she herself had little access. Susanna's split off impulses are projected on to Lisa.

The key to the redemptive value of this story lies in the fact that Susanna's life was enriched and widened by her associations with Lisa, once the grip of her fascination was loosened. The turning point came when Susanna was confronted irrefutably and agonizingly with the vicious and predatory side of Lisa. When Lisa's drive for adventure turned to merciless tormenting and unconscionable aggression, Susanna was able to free herself from the entrancement and differentiate herself from Lisa. Susanna was able to use her experiences with Lisa to outgrow her own constricting fears and defenses. She was able to withdraw her projections and thus return to life a fuller, more complete woman. Having experienced and integrated the cunning energy of Lisa, Susannah manages to move along her own path of individuation. Susanna was able to creatively and constructively use her experiences with this wild child.

But what of Lisa? The film leaves one with the feeling that it would be close to a miracle if she were touched deeply enough to be able to wrench herself from the constraints of her character pathology. At the movie's end, we see her captured and confined once again. A poignant image, this is a fitting portrait of the psychopath because, even when triumphant, she is possessed by a raw archetypal energy which thrusts her into another round of action. She has little conscious capacity for mediating these forces. Driven to dominate, she remains ironically and tragically dominated by her own character structure. The prognosis remains poor. Both the nursing staff and Susanna wonder if Lisa will remain "dead inside." We will continue to explore in this chapter how an experience of deadness occurs for the psychopathic patient. We will explore the possibility of redemption for the psychopath herself as we proceed.

In review, when the film began, Susanna had not tasted her own passions and waywardness. Thus impoverished, without access to the enlivening energy of her own sense of power and adventure, an inhibited and reserved Susanna was enticed by this energy in Lisa. Susanna projected her unconscious shadow on to Lisa. Fascinated, Susanna rose to explore these dread but intriguing dynamics in herself. Over the course of the story, Susanna was able to withdraw her projection from Lisa and expand the context of her life.

We might extend this analytic paradigm to ourselves, the general audience of this film. From this perspective, we have an opportunity in viewing the film to intensify, differentiate, and attempt to integrate potentially creative psychic energy bound up with our own psychopathic shadows. We will return to the dynamics of how we might make use of our own psychopathic complexes in service of individuation at the end of this chapter.[1]

While an individual may have a psychopathic character disorder, like all of the character structures that we have discussed, psychopathy may also appear as an underlying structure in a person with a more developed and flexible ego. Such a person is more functional, personally and socially. Yet, the elements of seductive charm, risk taking, deceit, disregard for others, and an ambient promise of wild sex as well as violence, still charge this person's interactions. She may contribute an exciting and adventurous element to the group, playing well enough within the rules to get by with it all. Meanwhile, her underlying psychopathic character structure can remain unrecognized and unnamed. For the clinician working with this person, the underlying character structure is possible to miss or overlook, because we tend to react to these dynamics with naivety or as starkly pathological and "other."

While movies and the media offer us rich contemporary images with which to explore psychopathy, psychopathy itself is archetypal and eternal and surfaces in characters in myths and fairy tales. No one would quickly associate the character of Lisa from the movie *Girl Interrupted* with a classic fairy-tale princess, though such a princess does exist. The cruelest princess we might conjure up is one who would shun her suitors or subject them to multiple strenuous tests. But what sort of princess actually cuts off the heads of 97 suitors and mounts them with delight on 97 posts at the foot of her castle walls? The Brothers Grimm portray such a princess and we will meet her extensively later in this chapter. The Sea-Hare Princess lives a lifestyle of violence, domination, and control (Grimm 1972: 769). The princess in this story is determined to rule over her kingdom, alone. She does not want help. She does not seek a partner. She fears nothing.

And she may well be sitting across from you in your office. Some of us have court-ordered psychopaths in our caseloads; many of us no doubt have more sophisticated and therefore more disguised psychopathic patients. Every interaction tends to be a sparring, a challenge, a con. Information is only given if a patient thinks he can use it to further his case, with you or in court. You may feel merely wary or even defeated; you may feel a level of fear that makes no understandable sense in the moment. You may feel intruded upon and unsettled by an aggressively sexual interest that is unspoken but palpable in the room.

We will consider in this chapter how the extreme nature of attachment disorders of psychopathically structured individuals preclude the further development of emotional attachments and work towards limiting inter-actions with others to sadomasochistic exchanges based on power. As a consequence of an excessive need and quest for stimulation, malicious interactions serve to alleviate frequent periods of boredom (Widiger and Lynam 1998). With little differentiation of ego from the unconscious and possessed by ruthless archetypal impulses towards aggressive action, psychopathic acts of dominance are highly gratifying and strengthened as the individual becomes sadistically aroused and excited by the hunt and the kill.

Psychopathy, sociopathy, antisocial personality disorder

Along with several other theorists, in this work we choose to use the term psychopath rather than sociopath or antisocial personality disorder (Cleckly 1976; Meloy 1988, 2001; Widiger and Lynam 1998; Gabbard 2005). The term psychopath directs our attention towards intrapsychic, interpersonal, and developmental dynamics rather than solely emphasizing social and behavioral factors. In addition, we want to highlight how early failures of attachment contribute to neurodevelopmental impairments in this character structure in the first year of life (Reid et al. 1986; Hare and Hart 1998; Schore 2003b). Furthermore, antisocial behaviors occur across a spectrum of personality disorders, most particularly in the borderline, hysteric, and paranoid structures (Millon 2000; Gabbard 2005). Finally, our Matrix allows a precision in differentiating psychopathy from alpha narcissism, which we will explore in more depth in the next chapter.

In a classic comprehensive work on psychopathy, Herbert Cleckly presented a comprehensive diagnostic behavioral measure in a field that was more accustomed to moral condemnation than objective analytic criteria (1976). He observed that a concealed psychosis lies beneath the psychopath's adaptation and behavior. The book's title, *The Mask of Sanity*, refers to the psychopath's strong but cool aggressive stance. This "mask" shrouds the disorganized nature of their inner world, which is chaotic and poorly attuned to the demands of reality and society. In this regard, he noted that the psychopathic person can only relate superficially to others, is unable to have regard for the feelings or safety of others, and thus can be highly irresponsible in relationships. Karen Horney (1945) focused on the psychopath's fixed pattern of interpersonal exploitation. Otto Fenichel, addressing intrapsychic and developmental dynamics, outlined the psychopath's inconstant experience of the object and subsequent failures of internalization (Fenichel 1945).

Theodore Reich contributed to this dialogue by including the psychopathic personality within his conceptualization of phallic-narcissism (Reich 1949). Kernberg as well designates the psychopathic personality as a "severe" variant of the narcissistic personality disorder (Kernberg 1975). While we have observed an antagonistic relational pattern and antisocial behaviors in patients that Reich would describe as phallic narcissists and that Kernberg would diagnose as malignant narcissists, we differentiate narcissistic disorders from a psychopathic character structure, whose development is most strongly marked by its severe trauma in the first year of life, the primal phase of development. There is precedent for distinguishing psychopathy from antisocial forms of narcissism, which we will explore in more depth in Chapter 8 on alpha narcissism (Gabbard 2005).

Evolution of a descriptive definition

The advent of the development of the American Psychiatric Association's *Diagnostic and Statistical Manual of Mental Disorders* has heavily influenced terminology in our field. The *DSM* has had, and continues to have, an impact on the nomenclature of psychopathy. In an attempt to establish some distance from the morally judgmental descriptions present in eighteenth- and nineteenth-century psychology, diagnostic descriptions in the development of the *DSM* have consistently moved to a behavioral focus (see Gabbard 2005: 514). In the seemingly well-intentioned movement towards using behavioral terminology, valuable information about intrapsychic, interpersonal and developmental dynamics is lost. As noted above, antisocial behaviors can be applied to a broad spectrum of patients with many character structures. Yet people who are not psychopaths behave antisocially for different dynamic reasons and can have different relational styles and a different prognosis. These differences necessarily affect decisions about treatability, appropriate modes of treatment and psychotherapeutic goals. Perhaps most importantly, these distinctions have implications for how we can most effectively relate to our patients.

Alongside the developing behavioral focus of the *DSM*, in a period of increased social awareness in the 1960s a trend developed preferring the term sociopath to psychopath for several reasons. The term *sociopathy* expressed yet another attempt to remove the moral stigma associated with the term psychopath and to express the intention to refer directly to the social origins of these patients' difficulties. In *DSM II*, published in 1968, antisocial personality became the preferred terminology by its editorial board. By 1980, in the *DSM III*, the changing extensive diagnostic criteria for antisocial personality disorder had altered Cleckly's original clinical description of the psychological dynamics of psychopathy, so that the *DSMIV-TR* criteria describe a criminal population who most often come from oppressed, disadvantaged, or lower socioeconomic groups (Halleck 1981; Modlin 1983).

Currently, the term psychopathy is again gaining popularity in clinical and research settings as it implies both intrapsychic and interpersonal characteristics as well as biological features not captured in the *DSM-IV-TR* (2000) usage of antisocial personality disorder. Psychopathy implies a more severe variant of character structure than antisocial personality disorder. As we have outlined, there are individuals who commit antisocial acts who are not psychopaths and there are psychopaths who do not fit the criteria for antisocial personality disorder. To summarize, a psychopathically structured person is someone who suffered a massive failure of human attachment and, as a result, has been unable to incorporate objects into their inner world. Subsequently this person insists upon and relies on the omnipotent control of others. The organizing preoccupation of the psychopathic patient is domination, getting it over on or consciously manipulating others (Bursten 1972). Psychodynamically, it is generally agreed that the psychopath uses the primitive defensive operations of projective identification and numerous forms of dissociation.

A Jungian theoretical perspective

Amplified from a Jungian perspective, Neumann describes for us how the unconscious might appear to an undeveloped ego:

> This primitive state belongs to a consciousness and an ego that are still incapable of differentiation. Represented in our imagination, the images emerge as monstrous and inhuman. This is the phase of the chimerical creatures composed of different animals or of animal and man – the griffins, sphinxes, and harpies, for example – and also of such

monstrosities as phallic and bearded mothers. It is only when consciousness learns to look at phenomena from a certain distance, to react
more subtly . . . that the mixture of prevailing symbols separate into the
groups of symbols characteristic of a single archetype or of a group of
related archetypes.

(Neumann 1963: 12–13)

Opposites that are clearly perceived as separate to a more developed
consciousness commingle in the timeless eternal reality of the unconscious
of a person with a psychopathic structure and remain undifferentiated into
adulthood. So for instance, the opposites of good and bad, right and wrong,
self and other remain relatively undifferentiated. One way to imagine the
psychopath's participation in this chaotic unconscious mixture is to consider
that the psychopath is not immoral, but amoral. He is not interpersonally
exploitive, but rather embodying the role of predator in the great round of
nature. Perhaps the most challenging conundrum to comprehend in the
psychopath is the commingling of sexuality and aggression. Arrest at a
psychopathic stage of development occurs before a developing consciousness could have a differentiating effect on sexuality and aggression. This
primitive undifferentiation, fueled by the energetic action-oriented reality
of this relational pattern, may give rise to sadomasochistic sexuality, or,
even more darkly, to the acts of rape, torture, and sadistic coercion of
which some psychopaths may be capable. However, with a highly developed
ego and an underlying psychopathic structure, commingled sexuality and
aggression may find their characteristic expression in more familiar forms:
a charming seductive salesman, an erotic manipulative hairdresser, or a
powerfully ambitious and successful medical director.

Origins of psychopathy in the antagonistic relational pattern

Without an environment in place that would attract a developing infant's
consciousness towards seeking or withdrawing styles of relating, all relating
both inner and outer, is guarded against. For the child in the antagonistic
pattern, survival, integration, and meaning are maintained by acts of
domination, manipulation, and control. Driven to fight for power over, it is
literally me against the world. The antagonistic person is fed by defensively
employed aggression, with little access to the clarity and inspiration of the
imagination, as well as limited access to the emotional wealth and glue of
the affective unconscious. Like Bluebeard and the Sea-Hare Princess, the
antagonistic person remains isolated in their world of impulsive action.

As we reviewed in the work of Neumann above, when consciousness is
thwarted from developing out of the unconscious as a result of hostile or
hostilely indifferent interactions between caretaker and child, the child's
original primary immersion of consciousness in the unconscious continues

in a profound manner. Intrapsychically, in this state of immersion, opposites remain undifferentiated in the unconscious. As a result, the child who is predisposed to psychopathy is unable to identify with either a differentiated good or bad object. Notably, the undifferentiated dynamics of sexuality and aggression remain commingled, so their conscious differentiated expression is crippled. Dramatically, this child's energetic biological temperament, early experience of a hostile environment, and consequent intrapsychic undifferentiation contribute to the ascendancy of an extremely malicious and primitive inner archetypal figure. This child becomes identified with and possessed by the archetype of the stranger.

In a normal developmental sequence, "stranger anxiety" is an internally generated fantasy, which arises at about nine months of age (Schore 2003b: 159, 2003c). This fantasy is thought to help an infant anticipate the presence of the predator in the external world. Around this time, an infant becomes noticeably distressed in the presence of others whom he does not recognize. Deprived of the felt experience of safe and familiar caretakers, the child in the antagonistic pattern identifies with what has been called "a stranger selfobject," experienced as predatory (Grotstein 1982). Grotstein viewed this selfobject as an a priori representation that designates the unconscious pre-awareness of the enemy which is believed to be both within ourselves and to have an external counterpart. "[For a child who will develop a psychopathic structure] the predator selfobject becomes the predominant archetypal internalization of the infant" (Meloy 1988: 46). The availability of this predatory archetypal figure allows the child to form a defensive identity with a numinous archetypal image. In human terms, people with character structures formed in the antagonistic relational pattern live with a relatively undeveloped ego, an inability to form human attachments, plus the power of this archetypal identity renders them virtually inaccessible to psychic growth or transformation. With this archetypal identity intact, identifying with either a differentiated good or bad object is pointless. Metaphorically stated, "I am not a sinner or a Good Samaritan; I am the vengeful God who rules!"

Early identity with the archetypal predator is a major contributing factor to a severely underdeveloped superego. Without a functioning superego, the projection of blame, lack of moral constraints, and the inadequate impulse control that is evident in this relational pattern has sovereignty. Immersed in an identity with this awesome aspect of the unconscious, it is as if a shroud of unconsciousness is wrapped around the person. This generates a powerful archetypal charisma, and often creates an uncanny fear in others. The object of a predatory identification is not human it is eternal. We will explore the dynamics and consequences of this archetypal constellation throughout the character structures in the antagonistic relational pattern. The specific effects of these powerful unconscious dynamics on psychopathic, paranoid, alpha narcissistic and passive-aggressive character structures will be discussed in each respective chapter in the antagonistic relational pattern.

Archetypal dynamics in the analytic relationship: the risk of a naive assessment

As a beginning therapist, one of us worked with a woman, Sue, who had a complicated and desperate story. We will present this case below in further detail; for now, a brief introduction helps to illustrate these dynamics. Addicted to drugs, with a lien on her home, she dramatically pledged herself to individuation while she spent every ounce of her creative energy focused on her next investment scheme, the one that would be the jackpot. At times, it looked like she was working on developing an appropriately ego-based approach towards resolving her chaotic problems. It later became apparent that the elaborate plans were part of her psychopathic character structure. My supporting her problem-solving techniques, which were in fact frauds, was actually supporting her defenses. My attachment to being empathic and helpful masked the reality that I had been seduced and repetitively conned.

As a result of attachment failures in the first year of life, there are no internalized objects to transfer on to a therapist so the development of a personal transference is not possible. Archetypally, a therapist can be seen as either the rival predator or an object of prey. Given this, the prospect of any significant change remains very unlikely, since it is only by means of a human relationship and the subsequent development of transference that there is a possibility that this archetypal pattern can be broken. We can, however, accurately discuss counter-transference. The therapist may feel angry: angry at being challenged and manipulated; angry at being seduced; angry at being bound by the domination; angry at being powerless in the face of entrenched pathology; angry at being the target of relentless aggression. Indeed, the therapist may feel that she is being treated like prey – stalked, outsmarted, and attacked. Such entangling interactions may leave her feeling "both violated and soiled" (Meloy 1988: 72). Notice in this observation by forensic psychologist Meloy, how undifferentiated sexuality and aggression function in the dynamics of psychopathy.

Carrying the psychopath's tenaciously disowned vulnerability leaves the therapist in a tricky position. The projection of this vulnerability must be withdrawn, yet this is the last thing on earth that the psychopathic patient can afford to do. Their entire identity is based on being invulnerable; a chink in this adaptation could result in a psychotic decompensation.

There are a number of recurrent predatory figures from the archetypal realm that frequently appear in relation to psychopathic dynamics. We have mentioned Bluebeard in passing and the Sea-Hare Princess. One particularly enigmatic figure is that of the vampire. This otherworldly predator lives parasitically off the lifeblood of others. This immortal being, who is neither wholly alive nor dead, exists in a twilight realm and is driven to take lives. When a child identifies with this fearsome figure, they commit to being one of the living dead, living a dead life without much access to the multilayered and meaningful experience of a developed emotional life. In fact, it is the absence of an active emotional life that creates the boredom which occasions recreational manipulation and sadomasochistic acting out on others.

In summary, the psychopathic person lives with three powerful dynamics that actively work against the development of consciousness. Characteristic of individuals in the antagonistic relational pattern, the opposites in the unconscious remain undifferentiated. A very nascent individual consciousness early on develops an identity with the archetypal stranger during the critical period of a normal nine-month-old child's experience of stranger anxiety, which shuts down crucial development. This non-human identity inhibits effective human interaction and casts a shroud over consciousness. Furthermore, the inadequate differentiation of the ego from the unconscious that is prevalent in the first year of life continues throughout a lifetime for the psychopathic person.

A poverty of attachments and consequent neurological deficits

As we have previously discussed, emotional and neurological development cannot proceed without the bonds of human attachment. In an ideal development in the first year of life, experience-dependent neural structures develop through sequential build-up of progressive attachment experience between mother and infant that light up or activate neural connections between the brain stem and the limbic structures. However, when emergent consciousness with a particular temperament and genetic predisposition is met by a hostile and dangerous environment or caretakers, a predisposition towards violence emerges (Cleckly 1976; Millon 1981; Schore 2003c). Hostile or dangerously neglectful caretakers can be a source of trauma, the ripples of which reverberate through generations of children. In the events of their traumatization can grow "a solitude imbued with hate and fear and shame and despair . . . that must remain invisible to others, and most centrally, to themselves" (Grand 2000: 4).

When a robust infant meets threatening caretakers, the necessary attachment bonds that contribute to emotional growth and subsequent neural maturity cannot develop. The child misses this critical window of development and as a result of underuse, neural networks that could have developed and connected structures in the brain stem with the limbic system, which generates and regulates emotional life, are pruned. Cells that are not activated by attachment bonds are pruned. In other words, the plethora of axonal neurons available to the child are not utilized and they atrophy. The end result is that while activated brain stem structures have come online they remain to some degree unrelated to the limbic structures of the brain (Schore 2003b; Siegel 2003). With this severe lack of connectedness intact, an antagonistic relational pattern develops.

So, in an ideal development, one might be flooded by fear in dangerous situations, loaded with anxiety while lying, or averted from pulling off an exploitive fraud by appropriate shame or guilt. However, for people with antagonistic origins, their emotional underdevelopment allows predatory actions to be enacted without suffering affective pressures. Psychopathic and alpha narcissistic structured individuals experience normal or higher than normal levels of activity in the brain stem and lower than average activity in the underdeveloped limbic neural connections. As we will continue to explore, failures of attachment contribute to failures of internalization, which contribute to subsequent failure of superego development. Absence of superego functioning, which Kernberg refers to as "superego pathology", contributes to the capacity for manipulative or exploitive behaviors to occur without guilt or remorse (Kernberg 1975).

This complex interplay of nature and nurture ultimately negatively affects neurobiological growth. We have discussed the process of how individuals with a psychopathic character disorder have experienced a pruned connectivity to their limbic systems. Most startling perhaps is that in the psychopathically disordered population there is a lower overall percentage of development brain mass (Raine 2000). One consistent clinical observation of this patient population is the affective quality of their gaze:

> The reptilian, predatory eyes [of the psychopath] are, in a sense, the antithesis of the affectionate mirroring of the infant in the eyes of mother. The nascent self is reflected as an object of prey, rather than an object of love. The fixated stare of the psychopath is a prelude to instinctual gratification rather than empathic caring. The interaction is socially defined by the parameters of power rather than attachment.
>
> (Meloy 1988: 71)

Differentiating affective and predatory aggression

Individuals with a psychopathic disorder are most apt to react with *cold-blooded* predatory, rather than *hot-blooded* affective, acts of aggression that we see in other relational patterns (Meloy 1988; Schore 2003c). These two discrete categories of aggression have distinct neuroanatomical pathways. Predatory aggression seeks, waits, stalks, and then seizes the object of prey, intending to destroy it. In the hushed breath and quiet step of the predator, we can observe a low level of affective and physiological arousal. Affective aggression arises as a result of the occurrence of an internal or externally perceived threat. This threat results in an intense activation of the auto-nomic nervous system, accompanied by an attacking or defending posture. The heart of an animal of prey races, their breath is short, anxiety is intense. "Predatory aggression is the hallmark of the psychopathic indi-vidual, whether it is a primitive act of violence against a stranger or a technically sophisticated act of revenge against a business associate" (Meloy 1988: 25).

One behavioral consequence of these interpersonal and neuro-psychobiological dynamics is that the antagonistic individual employs a manipulative cycle of defense to maintain the dominace that is psycho-logically and archetypally necessary. Bursten describes this manipulative cycle as one of interpersonal exploitation, an ongoing need to "put some-thing over on someone," with the concomitant experience of contemptuous delight when victory is perceived (Bursten 1972, as cited in Meloy 1988). This manipulative cycle and its inherent gratification illustrate how the central dynamic of power and control, rather than attachment and bonding is acted out in the antagonistic pattern. It is important to notice here that manipulation is used differently than in other relational patterns. The aim of manipulation in the seeking pattern is to acquire affective proximity. The aim in the withdrawing pattern is to maintain distance. The aim in the antagonistic pattern is dominance and predation.

Treatability and assesssment

While the task of diagnosis and assessment of psychopathy are critical steps, they are followed by the imperative need to acquire the specific technical skills that can be effective. The psychopathic patient's incapacity to relate and make use of interpersonal interactions to build self structures creates extremely complicating factors in their treatment. Some people consider the psychopath untreatable; many are. Skills needed in this work are specific and don't come easily to many clinicians. When a patient is assessed as treatable, the analytically oriented therapist would ordinarily aim towards the establishment of a human relationship and the subsequent development of transference in order to mediate archetypal energy. How-ever, the drive for dominance, which is inherent in this patterning, makes the development of a therapeutic alliance extraordinarily difficult. Profes-sionals who have success with treating psychopaths share a seemingly paradoxical treatment technique. The key is that a therapist needs to have no investment in change. The therapist must disidentify with the role of being the healing agent and/or the rescuer. Empathy is ineffective and is interpreted by the patient as a weak display of feelings, which only increase the psychopath's contempt of the other. This is a heavy demand for therapists who entered their profession with the intention of healing and caring about others. This patient's interest can be peaked when the therapist demonstrates that she may know what is in the patient's self-interest. It is only through the therapist's constancy, her consistent use of firm boundaries and manifest integrity that the patient may eventually begin to see that the therapist has something to offer him beyond filling his predatory needs. The therapist's honesty with and respect for the patient may enable the development of a human relationship over time and thus facilitate an initial development of transference. Any therapeutic change with a patient with a psychopathic personality disorder is hard won and extraordinarily rare. The more developed patient with an underlying psychopathic character structure may have some degree of capacity for relationship and therefore for development. Transformation may only be possible when the patient, forced by life circumstances, is able to submit to and suffer through a serious depression, perhaps of psychotic proportions, in order to harness and relate to this pattern in a manner that may lead to some capacity for attachment.

The psychopathically structured person is informed primarily by the impulse to act in the service of survival. Archetypally, the classic goddesses of destruction, the gods of war, figures of villainy, and predatory witches are archetypal energies that possess the psychopath. The fairy-tale villain Bluebeard presents us with an image of the unredeemable psychopath. He must be met on his own terms. In the story, he is killed. However, in the psyche, he will return, for archetypally he is eternal. Our consciousness may gain the upper hand for a time, but this inner figure returns cyclically to be reckoned with.

The predator is a part of nature and is a natural part of the human psyche. Indeed, "the predator within" each of us is indispensable to psychic balance and transformation (Pinkola Estés 1992: 39). Yet, in terms of human character structure, early massive failures of human attachment and a subsequent handicap in developing the neural networks that would lead to the development and regulation of emotion have been arrested. The power of an archetypal predatory identity renders this character structure virtually inaccessible to real change.

Case study: Sue – a beguiling wolf in sheep's clothing

People with high functioning ego development and an underlying psychopathic character structure may not end up in jail, or even in a treatment facility. They live in our neighborhoods, belong to our professional societies, they are our relatives, our patients, and ourselves. These individuals manage to seduce, manipulate, and swindle their way through life, frequently charming their friends, lovers, and helpers and narrowly escaping the law time after time. Yet in the face of all the affective chaos that a psychopathic person generates in others, they themselves exist in a state of affective deadness.

This particular profile could be found in any private practice. This less severe, more subtle diagnostic profile portrays character dynamics that we can all find within ourselves; while they may or may not be our primary underlying structure, their dynamic play within each of our psyches is critical. Those of you in settings where you work with more pronounced psychopathic patients frequently face situations that are more desperate. However, even in these situations you find yourself in the midst of dynamic patterns that are fundamentally similar to the ones we will be discussing.

A colleague who felt that she needed to move a particularly difficult patient out of her practice referred the next patient that we will turn our attention to. This patient, Sue had been a member of the referring therapist's ongoing therapy group and was persistently violating the set boundaries of the group. The colleague reasoned that Sue needed a therapist who was not connected with her community in any way. The referring therapist added, "Sue is a very energetic, beguiling woman." Indeed, she was very dynamic and curiously fascinating. I remember our first session quite well. Sue arrived in a flurry of excitement that she finally got to work with a Jungian, never mind that I was a beginning candidate. When asked how she happened to know all this about me, she responded with an air of triumphant teasing that she was an expert sleuth. She moved quickly to a remarkably intense dream, which she proclaimed would effectively set us off on our journey into the realms of spirit as well as her complicated life circumstances. With that introduction, we did indeed set off into years of a challenging dark dance.

Quite predictably, with hindsight, money became the first territory in which Sue started acting out. When she began seeing me, she agreed to my full fee. Then, as convincing stories of financial strain were introduced, she asked first for a temporary reduction in fee. When her properties were placed under liens and eventually lost, she asked for short extension times on her payments, later for trades, etc. Each move appeared contextually convincing, necessary, and benign. However, within these stories of financial woe, a consistent pattern began to emerge. Her narratives began to reveal numerous plots, which generally involved selling things or brokering deals; not only real estate, but also paintings, "antiques," rugs, etc. She expected enormous and unrealistic profit and was outraged and scornful when the deals fell through. While business is business, and profit is a natural part of it, Sue's predominant emphasis upon "getting away with it," or "pulling it off," should have alerted me to her blatant sense of prerogative and contemptuous delight in victory over others.

The dynamics of an underlying psychopathic character structure were well at play, but I was not tuned into them. Rather, we were busily working on her individuation, very specifically, her creativity. Sue wanted to feel more self-confident, more powerful with the men in her life, freer to do the creative work she dearly loved, her sculpting. She was convinced that all her money struggles were simply a nagging distraction, which kept her from addressing her real issues about her art and the development of her soul. She wanted more than anything just to have time to be in her studio. While she dramatically pledged herself to individuation, she spent every ounce of her creative energy focused on her next investment scam, the one that would be "the jackpot."

Sue only intermittently revealed bits and pieces about her childhood reality. Her mother was highly inconsistent with her feelings as well as in her behavior. She may have been alcoholic. She had frequent unpredictable rage fits, generally directed at Sue, followed by cold withdrawals. Sue was frequently left alone for long unexplained periods of time. She recalled being called names, and then abandoned. Her father was seldom around; he ran a business "of some sort" in the city. Sue remembers him as large and gruff, but also as humorous and "winning" at times. He had little interest in interacting with "the brat," as he called her. Sue overheard numerous fights between her parents, frequently eavesdropping on their heated exchanges of threats and verbal attacks. She recalled finding these conflicts strangely exciting, even sexually exciting.

As mentioned, she recounted these memories only occasionally. I began to notice that after a short story about her parents, Sue would get strangely withdrawn and sometimes appear a bit disorganized. At one point, I mentioned this to her. Her association was to a memory of having read that some tribal people fear when a photographer has taken their picture; the photographer has captured a bit of their soul. When I asked if she felt like I had a piece of her soul whenever she told me a childhood story, she got quite sarcastic, "You don't think I really believe that bullshit, do you? . . . and even if I did, I'd never allow anyone to photograph me until I was really ready – and I was having a good hair day!" When I metaphorically suggested that she had let me photograph her on a bad hair day when she told me stories of her painful childhood, she wryly retorted, "Who finds them painful?"

In the midst of many such dead-ends, we both had the sense for some time that our work was progressing well. She made significant changes in several crisis areas of her life. She ironed out a number of complications in her recent divorce, including forging a creative settlement to a complicated child custody battle. She extracted herself from a potentially dangerous and violent short-term relationship. Most notably, Sue chose to address her frequent use of cocaine. She earnestly wanted to shake this addiction and with a great struggle she finally stopped the cocaine use and stayed abstinent. We celebrated. Meanwhile, she insisted her marginally legal business deals were "off limits" for our process. These were clearly ego-syntonic, even a source of pride.

Over time, Sue's life circumstances began to deteriorate. It was progressively clear to me that our work was not addressing the most critical issues in her life. Indeed, I began to wonder if somehow I was supporting her avoidances and possibly even contributing to her downfall. However, whenever I expressed concern that our work was not progressing well, she would respond with impenetrable declarations of dependency and ideal-ization, as well as a cleverly reasoned case for how our work was saving her life. Her position was not open for discussion; she held her stance and used it cunningly. Any suggestion regarding a shift in our format, e.g. the inclusion of an AA program, a consultation with another therapist, etc., was met with a determined testimony about my brilliance, about how fortunate she was to be seeing me, and about how especially now she needed me and only me. All of these dynamics continued in the midst of bankruptcy, house evictions, and various partners' infidelities, etc.

Eventually, in the face of yet one more lawsuit, she and her partner-of-the-moment abruptly bought an RV and set off to explore Mexico. She did come in for a last session, excited by her new plans for adventure. When I brought up the by now massive debt she owed me, she rather casually and quite triumphantly responded, "Well, maybe someday I'll hit the jackpot and can mail you a fat check!"

It is painfully obvious, in retrospect, that this therapeutic process did not bring her underlying psychopathic character structure into consciousness. My support of her problem-solving procedures, which were in fact scams, was in effect support of her defenses. These defenses left her managing a dead life, without authentic connection to others or to the Self. I can see and feel now that her creative and vital energies were entrapped in her psycho-pathological adaptations. In addition to devoting herself to her numerous disguises, her most engaged attention returned repetitively to one or the other of her plots to succeed: in her relationship, in real estate, with drugs, with life. I now realize that these were not simply plots to succeed; they were plots to dominate. Each new relationship she entered had no more potential than her previous empty couplings. Her dramatic pledges to individuation and the apparent idealized and dependent transference were manipulative strategies used in the service of masking underlying dynamics. Her calculated flattery was in truth disguised attack. I had imagined that I could become the constant object in her life, the one who stood by her. My counter-transference attachment to being her liberator, her Great Mother, blinded me to the reality that I was "being had." Her manipulations of the therapy no doubt served to give her a regular hour of cathartic domination and restore her duplicitous self-esteem.

It is difficult for any therapist to report a case in which they have played an ineffective or collusive role. Many of us have had such experiences, and we can learn deeply from them. In this case, I was clearly naive. I was not prepared at that time to keep a keen focus on the underlying dynamics and consequently I left us both at the mercy of insidious predatory aggression. Her attacks upon our work and me are amply described. However, it is critically important to note also that she was in effect attacking herself. Surviving without sufficient ego strength with which to reflect on the ruthless archetypal core of the predator–prey dynamic, Sue therefore remained possessed by it, preyed upon, and cut off from mutual and satisfying human interactions. Her consciousness remained fundamentally at the beck and call of her aggression and sexuality and she seemed to thrive on these exciting dominations. However, while she consistently fought to get the upper hand and typically experienced triumph, each defeat of our work and me was in truth a simultaneous defeat of her ego and of a step in her own development. We failed to wrest her from the grip of archetypal possession sufficiently to develop a healing attachment.

Therapeutic reflections: a diagnostic imperative

This case emphasizes the critical role of diagnosis when one enters the territory of psychopathy. Naturally, diagnosis is important in all clinical work, but it assumes particular importance when dealing with psychopathy for two primary reasons. First and foremost, the stakes may be high. When the therapist underestimates the level of pathology, it may put the therapist in serious danger and it may leave the patient in serious danger. Serious danger in such a case may involve a person's health and life. In addition, perceptive diagnosis of this dynamic is required in order to enable the therapist to judge whether to and how to initiate effective treatment. The powerful archetypal roots of this dynamic render it highly resistant to transformation. There is wide-ranging consensus that psychopathic individuals are unlikely to benefit from an outpatient treatment approach. The consensus seems to be that some form of residential treatment is needed for even a minimal improvement (Frosch 1983; Gabbard and Coyne 1987; Meloy 1995). "These action-oriented individuals will never get in touch with their affective states as long as they have the outlet of behavior to discharge their impulses. It is only when they are immobilized by an inpatient setting that the treatment staff will see them display emotions such as anxiety and emptiness" (Frosch 1983: 534). Anxiety is short-circuited by impulsive acting out.

On the other hand, there is also a broad consensus that hospitalization in a general psychiatric population will not benefit this patient and will provide an opportunity for exploitation and acting out. Specialized treatment programs that rely heavily on peer confrontation have more success in containing acting out. It is not so easy to con a con.

There are some clinicians who assert that the treatable psychopath can be identified. Structured diagnostic interviews are recommended when initiating treatment with a patient who may be psychopathic.[2] We strongly recommend that a clinician faced with the possibility of assessing a psychopathic patient should conduct a structured interview that tests for psychopathy. Conduct disorder before the age of 15 is one indicator, including, for example, cruelty to others or animals, fire-setting, juvenile delinquency, or truancy. An absence of empathy and anxiety are important signposts in making a diagnosis of psychopathy. The presence of depression or anxiety by definition effectively rules out a psychopathic diagnosis. Depression usually implies some superego development, and some capacity for remorse and anxiety similarly represents some concern about one's behavior and its consequences. Another signal that contraindicates psycho-therapy is sadistic cruelty. It is essential that we are comfortable with the reality that we cannot be all things to all people and that at times it is appropriate, indeed ethical, to make a recommendation for no psychotherapy.

Review of counter-transference challenges

There are numerous counter-transference challenges for the therapist who works with psychopathic patients. As we have mentioned above, counter-transference responses of disbelief, condemnation and collusion all con-tribute to one's capacity to be conned (Symington 1980). Many in the helping professions have a tendency to disbelieve that another can truly be that "bad." Therapists are apt to rationalize behavior as a result of the difficult beginning this person has lived through. A knee-jerk response of condemnation and hopelessness may be the result of a clinician's own difficult past experiences with psychopathy. Collusion is insidious and may be a result of a projective identification of the patient's corruption. We can be seduced, we can be entranced enough to write excuses or falsify records, we can be manipulated by our patients' pseudo affect and suffering into understanding the exceptional nature of their transgressions, we can become inflated enough to think that we can heal when no one else has been able to do the job.

A related observing stance, which nevertheless may be tough-minded and exacting about reality confrontations, introduces an ongoing new experi-ence into the patient's reality. It is this same position of consciousness that enables the therapist to see through the patient's use of the manipulative cycle and be of some help to the patient. Since the very nature of this disorder involves trickery and dissembling, the therapist must be especially perceptive, even an accomplished sleuth herself, in order to see through the deceit. The therapist must perceive the many challenges to enter into this win–lose game. Only a tenacious and determined ability to stay out of this dynamic can free the therapist–patient relationship from this set up and its consequent therapeutic failure.

Working with a person with a psychopathic structure is different from most of the work that we do as therapists. It is ineffective to offer empathic response to the psychopath's expression of rounds of projected blame, cycles of manipulation, artistic conning, and misleading complaints. Here, empathy is an ineffective tool to engender change and is interpreted by the patient as an emotional display of weakness. Undifferentiated empathic relating may serve only to increase the psychopathic patient's devaluation and contempt of the therapist. As we have stated earlier, we cannot talk about a classical transference with a patient with a psychopathic character disorder or an underlying psychopathic character structure. Interpersonally, since the person has experienced massively impaired attachment, there is a consequent lack of internalized objects to transfer on to the therapist. The person is therefore left to the mercy of possession by the archetypes. Enactment at this level provides mere repetition. It could be a grave error to take an idealizing transference too seriously. An authentic idealizing transference would be psychodynamically impossible and the promise of such could lure the clinician into a false complacency and inflation. It is this same position of reflective consciousness that may enable the development of a human relationship and thus facilitate the development of the trans- ference. This development depends on the creation of a consistently firm and constant container. The therapist's determined honesty in confronting the patient with the realistic consequences of her behaviors must be coupled with respect for her as a person.

As stated previously, counter-transference experiences with these patients can be extremely difficult to bear because the therapist must hold all of the affects and images for this patient. Carrying the psychopathic patient's tenaciously disowned vulnerability leaves the therapist in a complicated position. It sets you up to be preyed upon, and unintentionally to become the victim. The patient would need to withdraw the projection of this vulnerability in order to proceed, yet owning these projected contents may be impossible for her to do.

A different counter-transference may occur as well. Like the literary vampire's victim, the therapist may become entranced by the primitive charisma that a psychopathic person may generate. Facing a person in an identity relationship with an archetype can be as captivating and dangerous as facing a Medusa or falling into a trance induced by a vampire. The therapist may be seduced by the patient's daring and may be excited by their ability to dance so close to the fire.[3] She may find herself excited by her patient's aggressive sexuality. The consequences of this counter- transference trap can be so extreme that we want to mention a historical instance where this dynamic reigned. A prominent Detroit academic psychiatrist entered an ongoing ménage-à-trois with a psychopathic patient and his pretty paramour. This doctor ended up writing illegal scripts for the threesome. Ultimately, he was first professionally disgraced, and then, tragically beheaded by his patient.

This story graphically and literally illustrates the possible consequences of an entranced counter-transference. The consequences may be more subtle, but nevertheless treacherous. While writing this book, we met a woman therapist who worked in a prison. Her face was pale, her eyes had very dark circles under them, and her presentation was anxious. She told us that she had the reputation of being "the most easily trusted" by the inmates. She confessed that she felt proud to be so apparently trusted, proud to have her skills so well acknowledged. However, she sometimes questioned whether the expressed trust and the gratifying praise were authentic. She could sense that she was somehow unsettled by it. All of this worried her. She flatly said that she had not been dreaming. She stated that this had been worrying her also, but just recently she had a couple of extremely violent dreams that had no meaning for her. When asked if she cared to tell us about the dreams, she stated, "Oh, like a man doing something violent to a little girl, or one man shooting another." As we continued to talk with her, she could access no feelings or insights about these images. Later we imagined that perhaps she was in denial about the aggression in both her inmates and in herself. We wondered if she had identified with the rescuer, and in doing so had denied her vulnerability. She could sense but not see, except in her "meaningless" dreams, the lurking presence of the attacker. Did her innocence and unconsciousness leave her blind to these pernicious dynamics? Was her denial of her patient's psychopathy and of her own vulnerability entrancing and vampirizing her?

The deadly princess and her wily suitor

Be real, be ethical, beware of entrancement

As Jungians do, we look to fairy-tale themes as symbolic sources of wisdom about relational patterns. Turning now to the tale of "The Sea-Hare" we see rich amplifications of psychopathic dynamics. The actions of the suitor in this tale offer us clues about the specific skills necessary as therapists to how we might proceed in this tricky and challenging work. This tale invites us to consider the useful quicksilver energy of the trickster and the shape-shifter in order to move the patient into the hard-won arena of change. Let's turn again to consider this fairy tale. Here we will focus on the dynamics between the therapist and her psychopathic patient:

> There was once upon a time a princess, who, high under the battle-ments in her castle, had an apartment with twelve windows, which looked out in every possible direction, and when she climbed up to it and looked around her, she could inspect her whole kingdom. . . . As she was haughty, and would be subject to no one, but wished to keep the dominion for herself alone, she caused it to be proclaimed that no one should ever be her husband who could not conceal himself from her so effectively, that it should be quite impossible for her to find him.

He who tried this, however, and was discovered by her, was to have his head struck off and stuck on a post. Ninety-seven posts with the heads of dead men were already standing before the castle, and no one had come forward for a long time. The princess was delighted, and said to herself, "Now I shall be free as long as I live."[4]

As we said above, this is no sweet princess. This is a repeat offender! This is a sadistic murderess, ruthless and brutal, with the keen gaze of the predator who revels in the hunt. The psychopathic person becomes sadistically aroused and excited by the "hunt" and the "kill." Gratification must certainly have played a role as she had 97 heads stuck on poles. In the story, the princess is determined to be "free," that is untouched, unpenetrated. She lives in a fortress built from her characterological defenses, her jail. Archetypal ground is vibrantly alive in this tale; psychopathy as a clinical syndrome is itself an image of this archetype:

> Now three brothers appeared before her desirous of trying their luck. The eldest crept into a lime pit, but she saw him from the first window and had his head cut off. The second hid in the cellar, she saw him from the first window also. His head was mounted on the nine and ninetieth post. The youngest brother approached and asked her for two things. He asked her to give him a day for consideration, and he asked her to overlook it if she discovered him twice, but if he failed a third time his life would be over. She agreed, and was sure he would not succeed.

In a therapist's first encounter with a patient it is essential to begin to set terms, in essence establish a frame. Specific time, date, and fee: each of these establish the boundary conditions, the temenos of the analysis. The youngest brother requests time, thus introducing a potential for reflection. He also asks for three chances. These three chances may symbolize the necessity that a therapist establish the expectation that the patient manage their impulsiveness and tolerate delayed gratification. The next day, the youth meets three animals that are identified with the trickster; the raven, the fish, and then a lame fox:

> The fox cried, "You had much better come here and draw the thorn out of my foot for me." The young man did this, but then wanted to kill the fox. The fox cried, "Don't shoot, and I will reward you." The youth let him go and returned home.

The therapist may initially feel like employing his phallic power, marching into the patient's kingdom, and killing off the raw instincts with which he is confronted. However, he discovers that the instincts have something to offer, something as yet undefined. The animals themselves teach him to respect them. The therapist is learning how to maintain his observing ego and not enact his own impulsiveness in this highly charged field, thereby modeling the containment the patient so desperately needs to discover within himself and develop. The therapist is being schooled to maintain his composure when the patient provokes. The therapist may then learn again the value and the powers of respect:

> The next day he was to hide himself from the princess, but he did not know where to go. He went into the forest and asked the raven whose life he had spared to tell him where to hide. The raven thought for a long time, fetched an egg from his nest, cut it in two, and hid the youth inside. Then the raven made it whole again and sat on the egg.

At this point in the story, we are taken into a radically different realm. Outside the realm of ordinary consciousness lies the residence of the gods, of raven, of the trickster. Raven, mythologically, is a shaman, a messenger who travels into the world of the dead and returns with creative and healing energy and the knowledge of transformation. This trickster hides the youth inside an egg. An expert shapeshifter, he puts the youth into an unborn state, into the unconscious, perhaps back into a time before birth. Encased in the realm of the dead, the young man is safe for a time from the predator's gaze. The therapist must learn to access the energy of the trickster and, like raven, enter into the realm of the dead:

> When the King's Daughter went to the first window, she could not discover the suitor; she was made uneasy. Not until she looked out of the eleventh window could she see the young man hiding in the raven's egg. She ordered the raven shot, the egg broken, and the youth was forced to come out. "For once you are excused, but if you do not do better than this, you are lost!"

When the psychopathic patient is unable to capture the therapist with her usual vigilant, predatory gaze, she is made uneasy. The therapist has entered and activated a realm of the unconscious which makes her anxious. We have discussed that the presence of anxiety is a good prognostic sign in this realm. The therapist is penetrating into an affective deadness in both the archetypal and intersubjective fields, a deadness that is at the heart of her pathology. A primitive possession by the predator leaves a barely nascent ego in the unconscious, unborn. The threat of losing this archetypal identity is cause for panic because she has neither human relatedness nor a differentiated inner object world to sustain her. To enter this deadness would require a descent of psychotic proportions.

In resistance to this threat, the patient may be driven to "the eleventh of her twelve windows," close to the limits of her defenses. From her hypervigilant perspective, the princess can spot the young man inside the egg. The hypervigilant patient, with her characterological armor well mobilized, is able to see into the depths of the unconscious in order to kill off whoever threatens to enter her fortress.

In the story, the young man is discovered encased in the egg, unborn. He has been initiated into the realm of the dead. We would say that the therapist thus entered the "dead space" of the patient. The therapist has entered into a realm of her psyche to which no one else has gained access. From a Jungian perspective, the transformational elements needed in analytic treatment must be activated in the unconscious. The therapist must enter his own unconscious in order to be able to meet the unconscious reality of the patient:

> The next day the suitor went to the lake and asked the fish he had let live on to hide him. The fish thought for a long while, swallowed the young man, and went to the bottom of the lake. Not even from the eleventh window could the alarmed King's daughter see the suitor. At length from the twelfth window she saw him and ordered the fish to be killed. She said to her suitor, "Twice you are forgiven, but be sure that your head will be on the hundredth post."

What might it mean for the therapist of a psychopathic patient that the suitor is swallowed by the fish and taken to the bottom of the lake? This is the theme of the night sea journey in which the hero's descent into the body of the fish is a critical phase in the process of transformation. This suggests that the analyst himself must enter into his own inward, untapped source of instinct. "In the belly of the fish" the therapist is challenged to survive this condition with his observing ego intact. He must contain the impulses to act out and challenge the patient to do the same. In so doing, the therapist offers his own ego functioning to the patient to use in this phase of the process. By maintaining a conscious connection with the deepest reaches of his own physicality, he leads the psychopathic patient towards what is unknown territory for her, a conscious reflection of her impulses to act.

In the story, thus challenged, the princess symbolically resorts to employing her most powerful defenses, her twelfth window from which she exposes him one more time. It is important to note that, even though alarmed, she keeps her agreement with the suitor. She has given him two chances and she will give him one more. Keeping agreements with another person is an enormous achievement for the psychopathic patient. This princess must participate in a contract in order to be a participant in her own process:

> On the last day, the suitor went into the country and asked the fox that
> he had let live on to hide him. Admitting it was a hard task, the
> thoughtful fox came up with a plan. The fox dipped himself into a
> spring, and came out as a stall-keeper and dealer in animals. The suitor
> dipped himself in also, and came out a small sea-hare. The merchant
> went into town, and showed the pretty little animal, and many gathered
> to see it.

The fox, like the raven, is a trickster and a shapeshifter. By now, the stakes
in the story are very high and this trickster realizes that both he and the
suitor must assume a new and inscrutable form. He assumes the form of the
master of animals, that is, an archetypal figure of one who can tame
powerful instinctual energies. With the help of the fox, the suitor assumes
the form of the sea-hare. What are we to make of this paradoxical creature?
Symbolically this creature captures the essence of a hare and of the sea. The
hare, as a skittish and vulnerable animal, is a frequent symbol of prey. The
sea, in its fluidity and depth, is a frequent symbol of the unconscious itself.
When the suitor shifts into this form, he embodies these energies, which
have immense power over the princess for they represent forces that are
uncontrollable, feared aspects of herself from which she is split off.

At this point in the treatment, the therapist must be able to consciously
bear the patient's disowned vulnerability and unconsciousness in such a
manner that they are kept safe from the patient's frontal attack. They must
be held with a degree of profound authenticity. As such, they are held by
the therapist outside of the scope of the patient's predatory vision. From
this point on, the events in the fairy tale and in our treatment analogy
illustrate a transformation that is extremely rare for the psychopathic
patient, and perhaps only a bit more possible with people who are malignant or alpha narcissists. We could speculate that, for the psychopathic
person, their wounding occurred too early and traumatically to be able to
bridge the neurological, psychological and archetypal gaps that were
created for them at that time. In terms of meaning, we might also speculate
that no matter their gains in ego development, such is the nature of fate
or the person's role in the great round of nature to continue to be possessed
by the predator:

> The Princess was in the market; she saw the sea-hare and paid a good
> deal of money for it. Before the merchant sold the creature to her, he
> said to the sea-hare, "When the King's Daughter goes to the window,
> creep quickly under the braids of her hair." And so he does.

In the last part of this fairy tale we gain some clues of what the really rare
occurrence of transformation for the psychopath looks like. We now find
the princess in the marketplace; she is no longer limited to a life in the

fortress. It seems that her defenses are less entrapping; she is venturing into the realm of daily human exchanges. It may be that the sea-hare represents vulnerability and access to her unconscious. It may be that she is drawn to the sea-hare because she cannot see into its paradoxical nature. She takes the sea-hare home with her. Once in the tower, it creeps under the braids of her hair, out of her sight. In this moment, we become keenly aware that although she can see everything outside of her, she cannot see herself. Her vision is limited to a vigilant predatory gaze, which sweeps across the landscape but cannot be turned inward to the self. But something alive and not under her control is alive in her, under her hair, in her unconscious. A potential connection to her own unconscious has quickened.

It is in the recesses of the self where the therapist must now become active. The adept therapist has previously ventured into the unborn, dead spaces of psyche and has suffered the night sea journey. The therapist must now find a shape in which he can evade the predatory gaze and penetrate through the patient's defenses into her most intimate spaces. These spaces are imaged in the tale as behind the walls of her fortress. There, symbolically, the therapist settles between her hair and her skin, on that part of her body, her neck, where one swift move could end her life. It is the end of her life, as she has known it, which must now ensue:

> When it was time to search for the suitor, she went from one window to another without success. When she did not see him from the twelfth, "she was full of such anxiety and anger, she shut it down with such violence that the glass in every window shivered into a thousand pieces, and the whole castle shook."

Pushed to the limits of her defenses, the efficacy of her predatory gaze is finally thwarted. She is seized with anxiety and anger, affects which previously she would not have been able to feel. Instinctively, she violently slams the window. The glass had rendered her impenetrable, left her isolated and was the lens of her gaze. It was the glass which kept her separated from others and herself. Symbolically, the glass is her defense, the essence of her character structure. At this point, it "shivers" into pieces and the castle shakes. It seems clear that the princess is in a state of radical transformation. The disintegration of her defenses is felt as shivers, energetic pulsing through her body which shakes her to her core. Her adaptation, her "mask of sanity," is shattered and her internal disorganization surfaces. This is the regression that may be necessary in the treatment of a psychopathic person:

> She felt the sea-hare under her braids; she seized it and threw it on the ground, exclaiming, "Away with you get out of my sight!" It ran to the merchant. Then they both ran through the spring and returned to their

true forms. The suitor thanked the fox and congratulated him saying, "You know the right tune to play, there's no denying that!"

The youth returned to the palace where the princess who, abandoning herself to her fate, was expecting him. They marry, and the suitor becomes the King and the lord of the entire kingdom. He never tells her where he hid himself or who helped him, so she believes that he did everything by his own skill. She has great respect for him for, "He is able to do more than I."

When the suitor reappears, he finds the princess respectful and willing, now able to enter a mutuality in which relationship is possible. As the patient's defensive structure relaxes, torrents of undifferentiated affect surface which contribute to this phase of her transformation. No longer constricted by her rigid fortress, the patient begins to see within and feel. She now has a differentiated enough ego that she can begin to connect creatively with the Self and others. Integration has taken place, both interpersonally and intrapsychically. With the shattering or dissolution of the psychopathic defense, a more human affective world becomes available for the person, albeit in an initially chaotic form. A person thus released from the grip of raw archetypal possession has greater affective connections and relationship to the Self. The ego has become relativized to the Self. This connection brings with it a new capacity for humility. The person is now merely human, and humility goes hand in hand with being human.

We might imagine that the therapist introduces a new element to the patient, as the sea-hare has done for the princess. The therapist does this by positioning himself relationally outside of the victim, predator, and rescuer triadic field. His observing and related ego stance with the patient over the course of the treatment has helped evoke an enantiodromia in the patient's psyche where an overidentification with the eternal and inhuman qualities of the predator give way to a human experience of vulnerability.

A challenge to action and the trickster within

While success in the treatment of a psychopathic character disorder is indeed rare, the presence of psychopathic complexes in our psyches is not. Inner figures of the robber-raper, the destructive siren, or an evil criminal mind are common in dreams and fantasies. If these images are encountered, experienced, and well held, they can spur us all on to individuation. As stated, intrapsychically, the predator within each of us is indispensable to psychic balance and transformation.

The archetypal image of the trickster in his many guises seems to haunt and inhabit all of us to some degree. He enacts physical vitality, malice, and manipulation. He lives in the unconscious realms with other trickster beings: the coyote, the raven, and the hare, to name a few. The convoluted maneuverings of these tricksters appear in our lives in ways that are painful and shocking, challenging us to recognize them as the divine beings they are, and we are not. Conscious efforts to come to terms with these beings when they appear interpersonally and intrapsychically may indeed secure us our own path.

As paradoxical as it may seem, arising out of their sometimes funny, sometimes deadly, and always tricky manipulations, these archetypal trickster figures may seduce us into admitting our "most secret hopes." In doing so, "an unlit path" towards individuation may open up and lure us out of our resistances to become full and genuine beings. We ask you to imagine that your own trickster or psychopathic complex is narrating this poem by Marjorie Powers.[5]

Dreaming that the M. C. is a Raven

Ladies and Gentlemen, I bring you dusk.
I bring you shadows as large and clumsily shaped
as your most secret hopes. I bring you an unlit path
that winds all night and coils back on itself.
I bring the end of your day.

Strangers and friends,
I bring a silken touch. I bring the caress
of a lilac-scented breeze. I bring a wind
whose direction you cannot place
and which you dare not trust,
so sweet is its draw.

I bring the conclusion
of your resistance, ladies and gentlemen.
One at a time I will swallow you whole
and release your spirits-ghostly lunatics
awhirl in the void. At last without choice,
and you'll begin to love me. You'll begin
to love. You'll begin.
                    (Marjorie Power 1999)

Inner work is not without peril when dealing with the energies of the trickster. Ego consciousness rightfully fears the appearance of these intra-psychic intrusions. Impulsively acting out the urges of these figures can indeed be destructive and dangerous. Yet, unlocking the access to these places within ourselves, mobilizing our capacity to take action, or loosening our sexual and aggressive inhibitions can be exactly what is called for in our individuation process. This is the process we described above in the movie, *Girl Interrupted*. Susanna met the devil herself in Lisa. She did not become possessed by this archetypal power; she resisted the lure of fascination and thus supported the differentiation and strengthening of her ego. From this position, she was able to relate to and dialogue with Lisa's boundless archetypal energy without falling prey to it. These developments enabled Susanna to open up and relate to her own repressed sexuality and aggression, experience yet contain her affective chaos, set realistic goals for, and enter into, her life.

The antagonistic relational pattern manifests in direct action, and in the case of the passive aggressive, indirect action. The dynamics of dominance and submission predictably arise from a state of undifferentiation. Each character style within this pattern tends towards ruthless domination, rigid control, and sly aggression. These forms of oppression and cruelty reign when the defenses in this pattern have the upper hand. However, the "fearful symmetry" of life includes predation and death. Wielded well with impeccable consciousness, this power can be the turning point in transformation. Mobilizing our dynamic potential for agency can bring image and affect into embodiment. When embodiment is archetypally possessed, the consequent action is inhuman and terrifying. However, when embodiment is well held by consciousness, human action can be tantamount to incarnation.

We noted earlier that change is tragically rare for the psychopath. Nevertheless, in the truly exceptional case, we might imagine that regression past the "mask of sanity" into the primal origins of the psyche while accompanied by an important other could regenerate self structures in a free and more creative manner. Spirit is present when one is aligned with the Self. So the resolved addict could become an addiction counselor, the redeemed lawbreaker could become competent in the law and become an advocate for improved prison conditions, and the reorganized abusive mother could teach parent training classes.

Spirituality informed by the trickster is the illumination of power as it is experienced in the body. This is spirit in action. It thrills at the bodily experience of mastery and domination. At its most creative and transformational, this is the same spirit experienced while doing martial arts or other physical activity which is highly disciplined and practiced, from archery to tennis to playing percussion. This expression of spirit can be experienced through competition and victory in athletics, in striving to win for the home team, in the art of social action, and in active work. It is from this wellspring that a hero derives his disciplined capacity to take action.

Notes

1 We'd like to remind the reader that we are alternately using the pronouns he and she in this text. While men are most frequently diagnosed with antisocial character disorder, there are women who also share this disorder.

2 For example, American Medical Association's *DSM4 User's Guide for the Structured Clinical Interview for DSM4 Axis 2, SCID-II*, "Structured Clinical Interview with Antisocial Personality," (1997: 28).
3 For a vivid example of mutual seduction, see *House of Games* (1987) film by David Mamet, Metro-Goldwyn-Mayer.
4 The version of the story is an adaptation of story number 191, "The Sea-Hare" in The *Complete Grimm's Fairytales* (1972: 769–73).
5 "Dreaming that the M. C. is a Raven" by Marjorie Power appeared in the Spring/Summer 1999 issue of *The Atlanta Review*, vol. 11, issue 2. It is reproduced here by kind permission of the author.

Chapter 8

Alpha narcissistic character structure

On top, yet always under siege

In the previous chapter, we described the dynamic and catalyzing effects of the predator, the raw archetypal energy that inspires the antagonistic pattern. In the psychopathic structure, we explored these dynamics while considering the fairy tale "The Sea-Hare." For the alpha structure in the narcissistic phase, this energy is well imaged in the story "King Thrushbeard."[1] As we will explore, this tale echoes several elements of "The Sea-Hare." Both the similarities and the key differences between these tales are apparent in the very first two sentences of this new story:

> A king had a daughter who was beautiful beyond all measure, but so proud and haughty withal that no suitor was good enough for her. She sent away one after another, and ridiculed them as well. . . . She had something to say against each one.

While the Sea-Hare Princess murders her suitors, the Princess in King Thrushbeard maintains her defensive isolation through rejecting and

ridiculing others. Defending herself from the intolerable vulnerability and chaos which relationship would evoke, the princess is haughty and arrogant. Looking at the alpha structure through the lens of the images in this tale, we could see her responses to her suitors as narcissistic devaluation expressed with a cruel edge. She impales her suitors with words. Ridicule is working well for her as this story opens. Scorning and attacking the other, she elevates herself, utilizing her superiority, beauty, and privilege. She hoards her power, withdrawing into splendid isolation. Teetering on the pinnacle of the mountain, she lives in seductive but dangerous perfection. Woe to the person who extends his heart to her and woe to her if that extension disrupts her precarious balance.

Let's imagine into the fairy tale "King Thrushbeard" the developmental history of this princess. The presence of the father in the story suggests that she has had at least enough contact with a parent to facilitate the development of defenses that are relatively less primitive than those of the psychopath. The notable absence of the mother has left this princess painfully impoverished. The contact she did have contributed to her development, while the contact she lacked contributed to her brittleness. Her narcissism works to enable some relationship to the world, but to stay on top she must remain alone. Her narcissistic structure provides her with a protection from psychotic contents, which threaten a psychopath's integration moment to moment. Instead of killing her suitors, cruel rejection does the job.

Restated in clinical metaphor, this is a portrait of a person with an alpha narcissistic character structure. This person depends for her structural integration primarily on the early defenses of idealization as well as devaluation. Historically, her intrapsychic and interpersonal field was marred by a dearth of love and by the presence of commingled sexuality and aggression. Yet, there must have been sufficient attachment, sufficient opportunity for at least a minimal amount of adequate relating, so that a certain amount of subsequent differentiation from the unconscious could occur. Genetic predisposition, impoverished early relationships, early failures of attachment, subsequent lack of capacity to develop emotionally, and a state of continued unconscious identity with a predatory self-object are factors that contribute to this antagonistic form of narcissism.

Narcissism is a developmental acquisition (Edinger 1972: 5). The alpha narcissist is no longer flooded by instinctual sexuality and aggression, no longer completely at the mercy of the archetypal reality of the antagonistic pattern. Increased consciousness allows her to employ some behavioral options in lieu of impulse; she nevertheless remains dominant, determined, and aggressive. These themes appear abundantly in world mythology, in story, and in contemporary media. The aging jealous gods who mete out punishment to those who question their power, the fading but vain diva who demands that she reign unrivaled, the leader of the gang who demands exaltation and subservience, all symbolically amplify this antagonistic form of narcissism: perfection honed for the sake of triumph. This triumph is not triumph for the sake of honor, love or mastery. It is for domination.

The dynamics of envy and destruction of that which is perceived to be good

While destructive envy is not unique to this character structure, it is a major force behind the aggressive competition that feeds an alpha narcissistic person's determination to win. Another fairy-tale figure that comes to our minds when we think of envy is the wicked stepmother in "Little Snow White" (Grimm 1972).[2] The dark queen asks her challenging question relentlessly: "Mirror, mirror on the wall, who is the fairest one of all?" If the mirror answers that another is more beautiful, the queen is sent into a rage and is driven to kill off the other. When the dark queen burns with this painful affect, she acts it out. When the mirror informs her she is no longer the "fairest of them all," she sets out to kill Snow White. Driven by her propensity for action, her inability to suffer, and her narcissistically required perfection, the alpha narcissist may drive herself and those around her into pressured extremes. While envy is a dynamic issue in all patterns of narcissism, the alpha character structure bares an especially lethal variant.

Envy emerged as a theoretical cornerstone in the work of Melanie Klein (1957). Klein describes envy as an infant's first expression of aggression. Specifically, she defines envy as the tendency to establish hostile relations with a good object, not with a feared bad persecutor. Attacking and spoiling the contents of a good object because it is good is a very different dynamic than aggression expressed towards the frustrating object that withholds, or the feelings of violence towards a rival that has occupied the good object for itself (Hinshelwood 1991: 167). Klein stresses that the envious phantasy of entering a good object and spoiling its contents is more primary than a vengeful response to persecution.

One distinguishing feature of alpha narcissism is a structural preoccupation with envy. "Envy is an attack on object relations in order to preserve omnipotence and self-idealization" (Kernberg: 1984: 174). Narcissistic envy is an attack on the good object to preserve omnipotence and grandiosity essential to cohesion of a narcissistic personality structure. While winning competitions, the alpha narcissist might be found subtly snubbing her envied sister, darkly gossiping about her friends, and generally creating malicious trouble. The dependent narcissist tends to agonize over her envious feelings and then explode in tears or anger or unconsciously compensate for these feelings and be ingratiatingly solicitous towards the envied other; the counter-dependent narcissist denies her envy and expresses it in her aloofness and superiority. Meanwhile the alpha narcissistic person acts it out antagonistically.

People with alpha narcissistic character structures lead lives characterized by an internally pressured need to triumph. With a focus on competition, they are determined to succeed. In fact, they enjoy and value their keen competitiveness. But even more critically, destructive spoiling is the ingredient that maintains their delicate intrapsychic balance. It is a defense against the experience of failure and unbearable shame. Thus, success itself carries a defensive merit in their lives. This constant, pressured need to win is accompanied by a frequent use of the strategy of contempt. Aggressive envy that works to devalue or spoil anything that is experienced as good serves to defend against disappointment and rage which subsequently threatens to disrupt their tenuous intrapsychic balance. However, this strategy also interferes with the development of normal attachments and dependency.

Narcissistic injury for the alpha narcissistic person is experienced as nearly intolerable. The malignant quality of regression after injury will be considered at length later in this chapter. Suffice it to say here, that when this drive to prevail is defeated, vulnerability to vengefully act out becomes imperative. The same aggressiveness used in service of competition and contempt can be turned against others or the self. When this aggression is turned against others, a person with an alpha narcissistic structure can become provocative and cruel. Turned against himself, he is inclined to view himself with contempt and redouble his efforts to succeed. In addition, the risk of suicide often hovers in the background.

While the quest for, and even multiple experiences of, success may be amply evident in the life stories of people with an alpha narcissistic character pattern, upon deeper examination it becomes apparent that many of the basic pleasures and comforts of life are absent in day-to-day existence. Unable to tolerate intimate relationships, a meaningful personal life is absent. Perhaps they are sexually active, yet the quality of their sexuality is often impersonal, aggressive, and tinged with tangled violence. While their internal life can be driven and demanding, it holds little personal meaning. Their serial experiences of success never satisfy.

Case vignette: CEO out of work

Let us turn to a brief case in order to further acquaint ourselves with these challenging dynamics. I worked with a man for several months who had been the CEO of an engineering firm. He had abruptly lost his position in an aggressive buy-out. For the last year, he and his family had been supported by his wife's secretarial position. This was the first time in his marriage that his domination and superiority was not evident. It was his first experience with depression and he managed it antagonistically. He came to therapy at the urgent request of his wife. She objected to his emotional attacks upon her and her friends, and she was frustrated that he was not out looking for a job. She had grown tired of supporting him and taking his abuse and she was feeling more and more empowered by being the sole support of her family. It was not incidental that her husband was spending his days working out at the gym, perfecting his physique. It was not incidental that he came to our sessions in his brief work-out shorts.

He arrogantly objected to the entire process of job hunting and interviewing because he was highly over-qualified for the positions that he saw on the open market. Meanwhile he had two frauds on the back burner that he hoped would come through: one involved selling information he had stolen from his previous position, the other involved getting money together with a new partner to start up a business that would rival his previous firm. It seemed to me that he came into therapy to placate his wife and keep her from leaving him while he bought some time.

During our sessions, he repeatedly attempted to use our time for superficialities, such as spiritualized intellectual discussions about articles and books on marriage and relationship that he was reading to appease his wife. This patient's use of superficiality as a defense served several functions. First, it was an attempt to distract us from addressing the desperate status of his career and marriage that would have been overwhelming and wounding for him to discuss with another person. Second, it worked to conceal a negative transference. The alpha narcissistic person's omnipresent defenses of competitiveness and contempt work to create a negative transference that is inadmissible for strategic reasons. Such transference is pervasive in this structure and can be extremely difficult to catch, interpret, and transform. The negative transference never became an identified issue in our sessions because money came through for his second business scam. With the achievement of this success, he abruptly left therapy, his bill unpaid. He was able to avert any subsequent efforts to contact him to collect.

In this brief case, we can see evidence of many characteristics of a person with an alpha narcissistic character structure. He was a person who had an entitled sense of grandiosity that was expressed by utilizing an interpersonal strategy of omnipotent control. His intense competitive drive was infiltrated with aggression. He had an undeveloped capacity for empathy and attachment, along with a paradoxical, well-denied dependency upon his wife. In addition, his affective range, as is true for this character structure, was severely impaired and primarily limited to experiences of rage and contemptuous delight.

Theoretical antecedents

There are several relevant historical antecedents in analytic literature for delineating a specific form of narcissism characterized by an instinctual vitality, colored by a commingling of sexuality and aggression, and marked by difficult attachment dynamics, an underdeveloped superego, and a manipulative interpersonal strategy.[3] Theodore Reich describes a specific form of aggressive narcissism in the metaphor of libidinal theory, which was prevalent at the time he wrote *Character-Analysis* (1949). Using the term "phallic narcissism," he observed that people with this character structure are highly competitive men; most frequently athletes, pilots, military men, and engineers. While Reich's examples were stereotypically male-dominated professions, particularly in his time, we can now add other examples such as female athletes, corporate and world leaders, military personnel, fashion models, etc. These well-paid professions are competitive and have high visibility. As described by Reich, the phallic narcissistic character is one who is physically robust, athletic, emotionally vain, arrogant, and aggressive. Routine attitude towards others is described either as being coldly reserved or contemptuously aggressive. "Their attitude towards the object, including the love object, is always infused with more or less concealed sadistic characteristics" (Reich 1949: 218). In gaining the attention of others, a phallic narcissist can be charismatic and a high achiever. "The most pronounced types tend to achieve leading positions in life, and are ill-suited to subordinate positions in the rank and file." Indeed, aggressive courage is one of their strengths. Reich feels that "their enormous self-confidence is based on their physical vigor and beauty." However, when they do not succeed and are not sought after, they are inclined to either downgrade themselves, or become exhibitionistic, provocative, and aggressive. Reich emphasizes that for the phallic narcissist the phallus is an instrument of aggression, not of love; the focus is on his erective potency, not orgiastic potency. Sexuality is unconsciously experienced as a piercing or a destroying of the other. When erective potency is disturbed, there can be sudden and violent vacillations in self-confidence and mood.

Our conceptualization of the alpha narcissist incorporates these key pieces of Reich's formulations: the cold reserve, the aggressivity, the concealed sadism, the devaluation of others and themselves, the lack of capacity for authentic love, the phallic power drive. We would add from here, however, that these dynamics partake in the commingling of sexuality and aggression, which is rooted in the lack of differentiation in the archetypal realms, along with a concomitant lack of differentiation of the ego from the unconscious. This differs from Reich's general formulations, which suggest these dynamics are based on the developmental vicissitudes of aggressive and sexual drives alone.

Otto Kernberg articulated the concept of "malignant narcissism." He suggests that the malignant narcissistic character structure is a pathological narcissistic variant (Kernberg 1984). In this variant, Kernberg describes how a premature condensation of the grandiose self and sadistic strivings short-circuits the subsequent development of a normal ego and superego. "In contrast to ordinary narcissistic character structures, these patients experience increased self-esteem and confirmations of their grandiosity when they can express aggression towards themselves or others" (Kernberg 1984: 257). Encountering feelings of grandiosity is a part of normal development, but when a child prematurely links these grandiose strivings to a defensive identification with the stranger-self object, the stage is set for the development of a grandiose self-structure.

The term: alpha narcissistic character structure

As discussed above, there are several analytic theoretical antecedents for delineating a specific form of narcissism. After much deliberation, we have chosen to use the term alpha narcissism over Reich's phallic narcissism or Kernberg's malignant narcissism. Neither malignant nor phallic narcissism are terms that can be easily identified with, nor are they psychological terms which accurately fit the alpha person's experience of self. It is for these last two reasons that we ultimately decided not to use them. It is our intention in this book to write a work where therapists and individuals can learn about themselves and how they function; where people can identify their character structure and learn about both its restrictions and its potentials. It seems to us that to refer to an individual character structure as malignant is unnecessarily punitive and inaccurate. In addition, the term malignant in our culture is associated with an incurable disease. Phallic narcissism carries along with it associations to a gendered sexuality, instinctual drive theory, and a sexualized access to power which highly complicate its use for us. Using either of these terms to describe this phenomenon seems to interfere with comprehending the alpha narcissistic person's intense daily struggle with maintaining their precarious intra-psychic balance as well as their real fears of a dangerous regression. The terms malignant and phallic may also interfere with the development of a therapist's compassion for their patient. A colleague of ours intuitively understood this when he said, "No one wants to be a malignant narcissist, but everyone would like to be an alpha!"

The experience of self for an alpha narcissistic person closely follows the description of the behavior of an alpha animal in a pack. The alpha narcissistic person experiences himself as able to make decisions and act on them. He feels able to take charge and frequently "win over" others that he feels he is stronger than and he often identifies himself as a leader. He is acutely aware of his position in relationships to others, in groups, and is inclined to move to the head of the pack. He is not infrequently surprised when others describe him as aggressive. Establishing himself at the top of any pecking order serves to relieve anxiety and create an internal experience of safety.

It is our clinical experience that the diagnosis of alpha narcissism is frequently missed, or underdiagnosed by well-meaning clinicians.

Unfortunately, the result of not realizing the antagonistic foundations of this character pattern contributes to analytic work remaining at a superficial level. This miscalculation may delay or render impossible establishing an analytic frame that would support the development of a negative transference and subsequent paranoid regression that is necessary to work effectively with this challenging character structure. While both dependent and counter-dependent narcissistic patients show some capacity for idealization that is not linked to self-idealization and evidence a more consistently functioning superego, the alpha narcissistic patient does not. Inadequately diagnosed and treated, there can be no progress in these important areas. These therapeutic gains are impossible unless a regression occurs in which the negative transference can be worked through.

Alpha narcissism in the antagonistic relational pattern

Throughout this relational pattern, major similarities exist which result in the antagonistic defense and work against the development of individual consciousness. When confronted with their antisocial behaviors, an individual with a psychopathic structure exhibits a lack of effort to morally justify or rationalize behavior, or react with self-righteousness or lie to avoid responsibility for the behavior (Meloy 1988). In contrast, people with an alpha structure would be keenly aware of a need to appear more socially appropriate, and perhaps more cunning and charming.

While the psychopathic person is freer to act out a violent condensation of sexuality and aggression without regard of status, the alpha narcissistic person must maintain their place in the pack. Antagonistic negation of desire and longing is a defense that attempts to protect this person from interpersonal exposure that can be quite lethal. With a more developed ego consciousness, the alpha person has more impulse control than the psychopathic person. The alpha narcissistic person's predatory archetypal identification manifests in a determination to win, to spoil or humiliate the other, to put one over on. He cannot psychically afford to overtly indulge in antisocial behaviors that would socially make him the target of shame. While unconsciously remaining identified with the aggressor, socially these individuals do the right thing in order to avoid narcissistic wounding. Unlike a psychopathic person, the competitive alpha person's position in society is paramount, highly guarded and valued. For example, while a psychopathic person may engage in random acts of sexual perversion, the alpha narcissistic individual's more subtle expression of aggressive sexuality may appear in the form of manipulative teasing or seductively enacted revenge. Sexuality and aggression may continue to color each other, but for a person with an alpha structure actions are tempered by the acquisition of some degree of ego consciousness and social awareness.

However primitive and highly charged sexual encounters may be, they are enacted with an affective lifelessness and absence of relatedness. While a sexual experience of the body may be vital, affect is underdeveloped and undifferentiated in this relational pattern[4]. This absence of responsive affective expressions and the presence of identification with the aggressor also reflect their childhood attachment challenges. Underdeveloped super-ego functioning likewise is evident in the alpha narcissist's strategies of omnipotent control and specifically while using deception and manipulation to attempt to maintain a "one-up" position in relation to others. In this person's chronic manipulations, we can see the workings of an undeveloped moral conscience that is endemic in this relational pattern. The psycho-pathic personality, the alpha narcissist, and the passive-aggressive person-ality all systematically use a manipulative defense to maintain intrapsychic as well as interpersonal balance.

Bursten's work on the manipulative cycle (1972) outlines how crucial manipulative cycling is to the equilibrium of the psyche of individuals in the antagonistic relational pattern. Bursten breaks down the cycle into four components. First, there must be an initial conflict of goals; the manipu-lator must want something from the other person that the other person does not want to give. Next, the manipulator must intend to influence or manipulate the other. Accidental influence is not a manipulation. The third component is deception or insincerity. This introduces the act of fraud most often initiated by "artful, unfair, insidious means." Finally, there is the affective payoff if the deception is successful. The person concludes the manipulation with an agreeable feeling of having put something over on the other person. When victory over the other is perceived, contemptuous delight is experienced. One intrapsychic function of this manipulative cycling is to ward off envy by mobilizing aggression and deception against the other. The affective consequences for the manipulator are feelings of exhilaration and contempt. This sequence restores an unstable intrapsychic balance. The subsequent experience of exploitative gratification underscores how interpersonal motivations are based on the dynamics of power and control, rather than attachment and bonding. The manipulative cycle achieves two goals simultaneously: it allows expression of sexual and aggressive energy and maintains a position of power and dominance over the other.

The manipulative cycle is used differently within each phase of the antagonistic pattern. The psychopathic personality enacts this cycle with the least conflict and in accord with their archetypal identity state. With some increased ego development, the alpha person has more consciousness with which to be manipulative, and more control about delaying enactments for strategic reasons, aiming for the appearance of social appropriateness. The passive-aggressive person is likely to have more consciousness, more object needs and employs more indirect ways of obtaining release using this cycle.

Jungian theory: developmental dynamics

As we have explored, at birth, a human infant's nascent consciousness is immersed in archetypal reality. As consciousness develops through the process of good-enough relating, the child becomes progressively able to differentiate self and other. Affect and imaginal resources facilitate these progressive differentiations. However, a child in the antagonistic pattern has less of these resources to draw upon. Undifferentiated opposites in the unconscious continue to exist in a chaotic state; a commingling of love and hate, dependence and independence, animal and human, etc. Kernberg considers a similar paradigm when he observes that in malignant narcissism, oral, anal and genital fantasies are condensed into a de-differentiated libidinal aim based on a fusion of sexuality and aggression (Kernberg 1993).

The dynamics of envy and the paranoid regression

Often in analysis, we need to go into dark and primitive places in order to find authentic contact with the Self. In a well-held therapeutic regression, one can experience the reality of those primal realms. All regression into the earliest layers of the psyche are fearful and challenging. Because of the real dependency needs of an infant, survival issues are paramount in the first year of life. Subsequently, anxiety abounds. As a result of the predominance of impulse towards action and an extreme sensitivity to his place in society, analytic regression is especially threatening for an alpha narcissistic person.

A person with an alpha narcissistic character structure is faced with the challenge of regression into either a paranoid or a psychopathic state.[5] In the pre-differentiated realm of the psychopathic patient, the impulse to action is primary. Therefore, impulsive violence, directed towards self or others, becomes a terrifying real possibility. Instead of re-experiencing the intolerable threat and shame of being powerless in the face of childhood persecutors, or of acting out the homicidal aggression of the archetypal predator, suicide is a real risk for the alpha narcissistic person. In a regressive state, the poverty of inner objects and absence of supportive social connections supply little consolation. Considering the presence of undifferentiated aggression characteristic in the antagonistic relational pattern, after a serious narcissistic injury the danger of suicide deserves serious attention and management.

The therapist must find a way of bringing the patient into a confrontation with her projected despised powerless devalued part. She must face it, be humbled by it, and eventually step into relationship with it. The tricky thing here is that the therapist may well have to carry this projected devaluation, while carefully remaining separate from it, both in her own and in the patient's mind. What do we mean by carry the projection? The therapist might say, "You seem to see me as inferior in the academic world. . . . Tell me more." Again, the trick here is for the therapist to identify the projection, keep her boundaries firm, and differentiate herself from the patient's reality. It is necessary for the therapist to remember establishing and holding the therapeutic frame.

Case study: Elizabeth – pain, superiority, pain

Rejecting while in a desperate state of solitude

Elizabeth sought treatment after a six-year psychotherapy relationship with another psychologist in our town. She felt like she had gotten all she could from their supportive relationship and sought me out because I was a Jungian. She hoped that an analytic approach might be useful at this point in her life. Her initial complaints included both her experience of loneliness and isolation, as well as an inability to produce as much as she would like in her work. Elizabeth, a medical doctor, with a specialty in pathology and a subspecialty in oncology, works at a university medical center. Her career in academic research has flourished and she has an international reputation in her field. She has not practiced clinically and is aware that she has problems in relating to others. At different points in her career she has considered doing clinical work and has rejected the idea of interacting with patients as it seems too boring and taxing to her. In addition to being professionally accomplished, she is a talented painter who has exhibited widely.

Elizabeth was raised on the East Coast by parents who were well-known intellectuals. She was the eldest of three siblings. All of the siblings were strictly encouraged to succeed and compete. Her father was described as cold and ruthless in pursuit of power in his profession and in pursuit of respect at home. He was prone to bouts of rage. Her mother worked as a researcher and was often overwhelmed by the demands of work and family, and was depressed. The youngest sibling, a son, often bore the brunt of the father's rage. The mother was unable to protect her son from these attacks, and was unable to protect her other children from her husband's demands for success. All three siblings have completed a Ph.D. level education and have developed subsequent successful careers. As adults, none of the siblings are close. It was clear to me that Elizabeth and her family had generations of failures in attachment. She lacked primary reciprocal attachments to her parents, as well as to her siblings.

Elizabeth had a commanding presence, a serious bearing, and she was starkly beautiful. Dressed in severe and sophisticated black, she emanated an elegant sexuality, which fascinated more than invited contact. Indeed, she shamed anyone who responded to her provocative presentation and approached her. It seemed to me that she emanated a sense of authority. At age 50 as she entered treatment, she admitted that her work had been her life. As she approached midlife, she was more and more concerned that she had created no family or circle of friends. She had never been married or been in a long-term relationship. She realized there was a void in her personal life and felt at a loss regarding what to do about it. She was aware of her lack of skills interpersonally and felt that this was a handicap to her politically at work as well.

From the first session, her presentation fit Theodore Reich's classic description of the phallic narcissist, "athletic type, hearty, self-assured, arrogant, energetic, impressive in her bearing, solidly reserved or contemptuously aggressive, with a flagrant display of superiority and dignity" (Reich 1949: 217). Her attitude towards others was infused more or less with aggression and covert sexuality. She anticipated any impending attack with an attack of her own. She was especially threatening to those who are not in control of their own aggression. She was ill suited to subordinate positions and easily dominated those beneath her. I sensed that she was close to burning out on her power strategy. At midlife, her fading youth was narcissistically wounding. Pain and a sense of futility were her most frequent inner companions; rather than the pride and triumph that she had depended upon earlier in her life. Meanwhile, she took great pains to insure that no one around her knew her suffering. Although no one in her immediate family had ever committed suicide, the reality of suicide had appeared in her extended family on both sides several times. The father's brother and the mother's great aunt had killed themselves. The rigidity of her defenses alerted me to the real potential for a suicide attempt in her treatment. Over time, I may have let this observation restrain my calling her into account for a number of dynamics that cropped up in the transference.

As we worked, I could see how Elizabeth prevented any reciprocal relationships from forming. I could see it in her relationship with me, as well as in her reports about other people in her life. I and others experienced her as aloof and uninvolved. With the least slight or injury, which she frequently discovered in even the most passing interaction, she could be quite punishing in her response. More clinically stated, she suffered attacks of rage and depression when her pathological grandiosity was challenged. She defensively reverted to omnipotent control of her inner reality, as well as controlling her interaction with the person who hurt her. At these times, she experienced a traumatic sense of humiliation and defeat, which when not fended off with immediate retribution cast her into intense suffering and rage. Being at the mercy of these intense feelings was in turn another humiliation because she associated them with weakness and vulnerability. Because she associated emotion with weakness and vulnerability, her affective range overall was poorly developed. She did not recognize or articulate ordinary emotions. This meant that, even if all went well, we would need to take quite a long time to develop reflectivity and affective depth of experience.

Therapeutic reflections

The times in our work together, when Elizabeth was available to do some real work were the same times when she was in her deepest pain. There was an opening in her defenses, which allowed some internal energetic movement. But these times were fleeting and at the next injury quickly seemed to be forgotten. While transference for the psychopath is the projection of internal predator or prey, transference manifests in time in an alpha character structure in the dynamics of envy.

When Elizabeth did move towards relating to me, her envy would arise, she would feel vulnerable, and then attack. To keep her distance, she was often condescending, at first with derogatory smiles, and finally angry accusations. After a brief initial honeymoon period, the work heated up quickly. After a few months, it became apparent to me that she was suspicious and unnerved by any comments from me that she perceived as kind. Primitive envy is an active devaluation and depreciation of the more tender parts of life. We might surmise that she had no experience with love and empathy, "so the antisocial patient has no way to understand a therapist's interest, and will try to figure out the practitioner's angle" (McWilliams 1994: 159).

Returning for a moment to the image of the evil stepmother in "Snow White," we can imagine an instructive and daunting image of the process of regression for an alpha narcissist. When faced with an undefeatable challenge to her supremacy, the dark queen becomes green with envy and she is driven into a regressive, psychopathic murderous rage. Similarly, a person with an alpha narcissistic structure could be driven to primitive emotional or even literal attacks upon the other.[6]

With Elizabeth, we easily fell into a vicious cycle that seemed to feed her and was exhausting for me. It occurred like this: I'd stay related; I'd make or she would find an error; she would blame me for my error, my callous slight of her, or for my general coldness. She would then triumphantly announce my error or flaw and its meaning with some bitter woundedness and would end the interaction with an expression of haughty contempt. Throughout, I would attempt to stay related, mirror her affect and work on reality testing her perceptions. In response, she accurately pointed out that my attempts to help her are weak and ineffective and that her life continues in great pain and suffering. She complains that she is becoming a workaholic, working late into the night to complete the analyses of one more experiment, to complete one more publication. She directs her sadistic grandiose intense aggression inwardly. In this case, the inner attack manifested as masochistic workaholism.

In the face of her attacks upon me, however, in Winnicottian terms, I survive them and attempt to stay in relationship with her (Winnicott 1971: 91). Yet this holding environment did not resolve in desire and connection.

Instead, we were very stuck in a process where she seemingly feels victim-ized by me, expresses her rage, and leaves feeling contempt for me. At the same time, no progress is made on any of her treatment goals.

Over time, she increasingly accused me of having no empathy for her, accused me of just sitting there while she suffered, accused me of being stiff and silent in the face of her pain. She felt that my inadequate responses to her discouraged her from being angry with me, anger that would be healing for her to get in touch with and express. She felt my interventions and interpretations were an attack, an attempt to hurt and demean her. She felt that any empathic errors on my part were due to my lack of investment in her. As if to underscore her isolation, she would scatter phrases like these with contempt, "I have no where else to express myself but here," or "At least I can come here and say what's on my mind." Meanwhile, her symptoms flared; both the frequency and intensity of her sexual acting out increased and her workaholism was magnified.

I often felt exhausted, frustrated and angry. Yet I also sometimes won-dered if her terrible suffering was somehow my fault. Nancy McWilliams observes that the clinician's experience of this kind of hostility is "shock and a resistance to the sense that one's essential identity as a helper is being eradicated" (McWilliams 1994: 159). She further warns that we are tempted to prove that our intent is to be helpful, which supplies more material for the patient to attack and devalue. I did fall into this trap, and we became deeply entangled in a therapeutic stalemate.

In retrospect, I see that I was afraid to confront Elizabeth. I was afraid to contribute more to her sense of internal devastation, afraid of the hatred she directed towards me, afraid of her intelligent rationalizations, afraid of her acting out. I was filled with fear, felt that my hands were tied, and she wasn't getting the help she needed. As I was doing worse, she seemed to be doing somewhat better. She put some effort into making social contacts and brought her experiences into the sessions. She made some attempts at ordinary dating. These contacts were short-lived. She expressed pain and anger at their rapid dissolution. It became evident to me that whenever she could express gratitude or pleasure to someone, it was quickly followed by a critique. She would get or give something good, then destroy it. Her need for omnipotent control seemed to destroy relatedness at every turn.

She became more controlling in the sessions: she did not want to discuss her dreams; she did not want to discuss her work life; she did not want to sit in silence. It was her preference to process my shortcomings. It came to me in a dream that I needed supervision, and I got it.

The therapeutic approach that I learned about at that point is most succinctly described by Otto Kernberg, in *Severe Personality Disorders* (1993: 244). In working with a malignant narcissistic patient, chronic thera-peutic stalemate is to be expected and is defined as the first transference resistance. I had to stop hoping that a "facilitating environment" would help this woman and confront the stalemate itself. At first she was nonchalant about the fact that she was getting nowhere. As I pointed out her lack of concern about the stalemate, she objected fiercely, as I imagined she would. Yet these interventions caught her interest. In confronting the stalemate, the long work of uncovering her efforts to defeat me began to slowly emerge. These efforts were a result of her envious narcissistic need to destroy what is valuable. "It's better to risk becoming a bull in a china shop than to remain paralyzed . . . lulled into passive collusion with the patient's destruction of time. This approach reconfirms the therapist's concern for the patient and determined intolerance of impossible situations and confidence in the possibility of change" (Kernberg 1993: 235). The patient's determined attacks upon any constructive intervention create a stalemate that suspends the therapeutic interactions in an eternal moment. This timelessness obliterates any possibility of change and leaves the person with the experience of being triumphant in their destruction. This stalemate and destruction of time is a characteristic dynamic in all of the interactions of the alpha narcissist.

As I continued to bring the stalemate into focus, previously unconscious contents regarding her mother's passivity, depression, and inability to protect her children from the father's rage began to emerge. In addition, I consistently reflected to her the moments of concern and repose that we had shared together, pointing out how she dissociated them.

I became increasingly aware of her aggressive sense of entitlement. She had many ingrained habits that expressed this entitlement, in addition to her unrelatedness. Mid-session, she would go through all the many steps to polish her glasses, make a check notation, look into her date book about another matter she wanted to confirm while she thought about it. She attempted to bring her cell phone into session. She would look outside the window and notice things, make comments on the weather. There were so many of these incidents that I felt that I had to choose my battle, since my attempts to reflect them were experienced by her as incredibly wounding. She would respond with righteous indignation and very intelligent counterpoints.

As her efforts to defeat me became more conscious, a paranoid transference emerged, and the degree of the capacity that I had to wound her increased. She became increasingly suspect about my motives. She would accuse me of being gratified by how often I wounded her. She wondered where I heard things about her; how I knew things that she had not told me? She wondered if I had been talking to people in the community about her? Her affect when wounded seemed to change from contemptuous triumph to fear and sometimes terror. At this time, after a developing friendship with a colleague blew up, she fell into a serious reactive depression accompanied by depressed mood, lethargy, sudden weight gain, inability to sleep, and difficulties with concentration that interfered with her doing her work, and active suicidal thoughts.

After some time, in addition to working with the manifest material, I recommended that she see a psychiatrist to be evaluated for antidepressant medication. This threw her into a rageful tailspin. She did go and receive a prescription for an antidepressant. She reported that after taking one half-strength dose of the medication she had a gross reaction – fearful hyper-activity, panic attacks, tachycardia. She came into her next session enraged and accusatory. She felt the psychiatrist and I were in a conspiracy to harm her. She stated a political concern that the medical establishment wanted to drug and sedate women and further debilitate them by the numbing sexual side effects of antidepressant medication. She accused me of not wanting to relate to her pain and trying to medicate her symptoms so I would not have to work so hard. She stopped taking this medication immediately, and after several weeks the severity of the depression seemed to lift. In retrospect, I think that her rage at me and the psychiatrist restored her grandiose self and served to keep her depression and vulner-ability at bay.

As the paranoid transference developed further, Elizabeth's efforts to defeat me emerged in two different fields. First, whatever she experienced as most helpful coming from me, she would strike down and obliterate with the most velocity. When I could accurately reflect these power dynamics to her, she seemed to calm down, and she would leave in a thoughtful, reflective state of mind that sometimes gave way to deep grief for the bind that she was in. With the realization that these self-defeating responses were true for her, material about her explosive and sadistic father came into the picture through her dreams. Her unconscious identification with the aggressor then became available to work with.

Second, as I attended to the details of her life and our interactions, a pattern of chronic dishonesty in the transference, mostly in the form of withholding vital information, emerged. Within the painful negative trans-ference that developed, she became selective and manipulative about what she shared, withholding or manipulating facts in order to have the upper hand. As these distortions and justifications were processed, again I caught her interest in a new way. She would smile at being caught, but then really look at me as though for the first time. I felt like I was beginning to be recognized as another real person who was sitting in the room. Her grandiose self was finally being challenged and held in relationship.

The dishonesty and lying in the transference culminated in another inci-dent around antidepressant medication. Her sister's husband committed suicide and she returned home to New England for the funeral. She was able to express a good deal of concern and relatedness to her sister, her parents and her extended family at the time of the funeral and in the subsequent weeks. These interactions evoked lots of new material from the unconscious, and the intimacy involved with her family evoked a retaliatory aggression that, at this point, she was able to reflect upon in our work. We were also able to process her renewed grief at her isolation upon returning home from New England to her empty apartment. However, the velocity of her aggression was too intense for her ego to contain and soon it became directed inwards, and another severe episode of depression ensued. One session several weeks later, she triumphantly announced that she had returned to the psychiatrist that I had referred her to, and that they had decided together to put her on antidepression medicine that she had already started one week prior. I interpreted this autonomous action as withholding important information from our relationship, as well as another attempt to triumph over and defeat me.

She slowly continued to be able to hang in there with such interpretations, contain a retaliatory response and begin to acquire some insight. Her growing capacity to contain her overpowering acting out spilled over to her work at the university, where she made a friend. Her analysis continued from this point. Her drive and commitment to her own individuation process seemed to support the work, even when both she and I faltered.

Treatment issues: transference, counter-transference

Kernberg summarizes a greater part of my experience with this patient in this statement:

> The most salient characteristic of the activation of the aggressively infiltrated grandiose self is the need to destroy the analyst psychologically: his interpretations, his creativity, his values as an autonomous good object . . . The unconscious motivations for such relentlessly destructive ends include envy of the analyst as a nurturing object . . . and, beyond that, envy of the analyst for not being victim of the same pathology as the patient. The acute awareness that the analyst may be able to enjoy his own life becomes intolerable to the patient imprisoned by his sadistic, grandiose self.
>
> (Kernberg 1993: 303)

As in all three forms of narcissism that we outline, what is transferred on to the therapist is not a historical caregiver, but rather unintegrated aspects of the patient's self. While the alpha narcissist may superficially idealize the analyst, given her dependence upon dominance, she doesn't easily surrender and project the grandiose idealized aspect of herself. It is defensively used as an internal source of superiority. Before too long, the patient transfers a devalued and radically disowned aspect of herself on to the therapist and then attacks it. The patient is defending herself from these affects and images that she therefore belittles. The warmth inherent in affective mirroring or the clarity that images and interpretations may provide are repetitively rejected, even used as evidence of the therapist's inadequacy.

The patient's aggression may be disguised to herself as a very well rationalized defense. She may be consciously identified with a victim while unconsciously identified with the persecutor. Consciously identified with the victim, she is then shamelessly free to act like a tyrant. While unconsciously identified with the aggressor, she may insist that she rightfully acts in order to be safe. It is therefore critical in the treatment not to avoid the analyses of identification with the aggressor and observed manifest sadistic behaviors. One goal for long-range treatment of the alpha narcissist is the development of an affective depth of experience through the acknowledgment of ordinary emotions and acceptance of weakness and vulnerability.

In the face of either collusive idealization or the repetitive onslaught of rejection and ridicule, the analyst may have difficulty holding her balance. Counter-transference feelings may vary wildly. At one moment, the idealized therapist may feel inflated, special, brilliant and powerful, seduced and initiated into a secret society. On the other hand, the devalued therapist may feel the full load of the vulnerability that the patient has disowned. In this case, the therapist may feel defeated and preyed upon and so threatened that she becomes tempted to strike back to defend herself. In the counter-transference pull, she may feel the seductive induction into the role of the sadistic tyrant.

In summary, the psychological dynamics and the treatment of the alpha narcissist are tremendously complex and demanding; and the risk of suicide is real. As we worked with this material on the alpha narcissist, it became apparent to us how undiagnosed this character structure has been in both of our training experiences and our practices. When diagnosed as a "generic narcissist," therapists would be inclined to adopt treatment strategies which include empathy, mirroring, interpretation of the idealizations, etc. All of these strategies fail to address the impulse to destructively act out envy, the consistent devaluing of the therapist and attacks against the good object, and the identity with an archetypal predator which is at the very root of alpha narcissistic dynamics.

The mythic dimension: the darkest side of the human soul

The mythic stories which parallel the power dynamics of alpha narcissistic characters tend to dramatize the darkest side of the human soul. We see these shadowy potentials startlingly portrayed in the archetypal stories of mothers who spitefully murder their own young children in retaliation to their husbands' betrayal. Their archetypal quest for conquest and triumph is never satisfied and can drive them to incomprehensible extremes. Psychologically, we might conclude that to suffer loss without adequate reprisal could dissolve the fragile structure of an alpha narcissist. As with Medea, it would then become possible to fall into a murderous frenzy. The Greek tragedy of *Medea*, written by Euripedes, leads us through these dynamics in excruciating detail (Euripides 1998). Losing was never an option for Medea. She betrays her grandfather in order to assist Jason in obtaining the Golden Fleece. She kills the giant serpent that guards the fleece and then kills and dismembers her own younger brother to buy time so that she and Jason can escape by sea. She tosses pieces of her brother's corpse behind the Argo as they sail for Greece.

They return to Jason's kingdom where his uncle now rules. In order to secure the throne for themselves, Medea tricks the uncle's unwitting daughters into believing that their father's youth can be restored by her magic, after he is killed and cut into pieces. Rather than win Jason the throne, this gruesome treachery forces Jason, Medea, and their children into exile. Once in exile, Jason secretly takes a new bride. Medea discovers his betrayal and kills Jason's new bride and father-in-law with the aid of poisoned gifts. To make her revenge complete, she kills her own children to wound Jason. She speaks lovingly to her children, in a scene that is both moving and chilling, even as she steels herself so that she can kill them. She has a moment of hesitation, but she overcomes it. There is no room for compromise.

At the end of the play, Medea appears above the palace in a chariot drawn by dragons. She has her children's corpses with her. She mocks Jason pitilessly, foretelling an embarrassing death for him. For a person with an alpha narcissistic structure, mocking and triumphant victories can repeatedly be had at the cost of everything held dear. Riding a chariot pulled by the force of her own primitivity, she can make a dramatic exit into the night sky, completely alone.

While Medea portrays these dynamics in classical Greek form, they appear in folk tales as well. Perhaps the most frequently told tale in the American Southwest is La Llorona, the wailing woman. La Llorona was seduced by a handsome stranger, bore him two beautiful children, and was then betrayed. In a fit of desperate rage and shame, she threw her children into the fast flowing river to drown. Her wailing is heard as the evening winds along the rivers (Beatty and Kraul 2004).

This archetypal story is also tragically acted out in present time. Several years ago in North Carolina, there was the haunting story of Susan Smith who drove her two young children into the lake to drown while she stood by, possibly in an attempt to make herself more appealing to a rejecting lover. Both Medea and La Llorona teach us about power dynamics taken to extremes. These stories symbolically amplify the pressure that an alpha narcissistic person faces when in the face of narcissistic injury, she regresses into a murderous psychopathic state. In that state, she can commit even the most repellant of crimes. She strikes out at what is good, reasoning that the cruelest attack upon her man would be to kill off his children, even more cruel than killing him. In doing so she kills off her own children. We might interpret this as killing off herself: parts of herself, her own creativity, her own potential. However, in a state of psychopathic consciousness, this is not experienced as self-sacrifice, this is experienced with satisfaction, perhaps as retaliatory triumph.

Why might these tales, symbolically analogous to alpha narcissistic dynamics, conclude tragically, without an image of redemption? It is our conclusion that this scenario may indeed be "clinically" accurate. The alpha narcissistic person sits on a precarious intrapsychic pinnacle indeed. A narcissistic injury may lead to an entrenchment of the narcissism; but if this fails, a psychopathic eruption may ensue. Dominated by the impulse towards action, when turmoil strikes the alpha narcissistic person is propelled into unreflective action. Given the propensity for action in the antagonistic relational pattern, deeds may be committed which are irrevocable, unredeemable. These tales compellingly teach us, and in no uncertain terms warn us, about these possibilities.

Above, in the case of Elizabeth, we have illustrated that for an alpha narcissistic person what is needed for healing is a paranoid regression in the transference and in the analysis. Regression into paranoia puts a person with an alpha character structure into a position to experience and integrate a human potential for vulnerability and anxiety. With these experiences integrated, a subsequent progression and potential for wholeness may become possible. Yet in the archetypal stories of Medea and La Llorona, we do not see healing. We do not see animus or Self figures who arrive and transform the pattern. In human terms, we can imagine these stories having a different outcome. We can imagine an alpha narcissistic person choosing a lover strong enough to wield trickster energy, but who was not identified with or conflated with the trickster. This presence in her life might help to loosen the character grip. Yet, when we stay close to the story, we have to come to terms with the symbolic reality that both Medea and La Llorona chose dashing romantic lovers who unambiguously betrayed them. In a clinical metaphor, they chose men like themselves, men who were also motivated by power dynamics. These men were unswervingly out for themselves, for their personal gain. They did not embody generative energy that could contribute to the protagonists' transformation. This reflects, once again, how tenaciously entrenched these dynamics tend to be.

Trickster in the antagonistic relational pattern

While the archetypal trickster can be an agent of transformation, his transformative nature is not included in the facet of the archetype with which the psychopathic person or the alpha narcissist forms an identity.

The psychopathic person is possessed by the archetypal predator. The alpha person is entwined in a conflation with the trickster. We might imagine that the alpha narcissistic person swings between devaluing and idealizing. The alpha powerfully performs the black magic of devaluation destructively directed towards others. In doing so, they spread disorder among the lives of the people they relate to, as well as indulging in the dehumanizing effects of idealizing themselves.

Because of the early wounding and consequent archetypal conflation of the ego, a dialogic relationship between the ego and the Self is impossible. With an archetypal identity with a dark aspect of the unconscious, like the witch or the black magician, the alpha uses whatever magic she can conjure up in service of herself. As the stepmother in "Little Snow White" does, the alpha uses the energy of the trickster to play tricks for her own selfish purposes. In psychotherapy, if a person can allow enough disintegration and then walk out to the edge of chaos, it is possible that she will become guided by the self-organizing principle of the psyche. With that integration, the alpha narcissist learns to use her tricks in the service of the Self.

We have mentioned above that an alpha narcissistic person may serve to be a catalyst in others' lives, charismatic use of tricks and cons sets many a myth, fairy tale, and human story in motion. Writer P. L. Travers says that the wicked witch in fairy tales is the "goddess in the machine" (Travers 1989). She is frequently the one who provides the energy for the action in a story and propels the hero and heroine on the way to their destiny.

Embodied and integrated, archetypal trickster energy can work his magic and make surprising contributions

The particular gifts that an alpha narcissistic or psychopathic character structure offer are related to their adventurous spirits and aggressive courage. These expressions of spirit can be unconstrained by fear and anxiety. If the grip of this character structure gives way to the development of a functioning ego–Self axis, a dialogue between the personal and transpersonal layers of the psyche becomes possible. It is at this point that the whole archetype of the trickster is able to function in the life of the alpha narcissistic person and work its healing/confounding/regenerative magic. Instead of being conflated with one portion of the trickster, the person is free to use charisma, power, and magic in service of the Self.

The alpha narcissistic person has often developed enormous access to resources and knowledge about the use of power in the world. When the trickster spirit is working in concert with the Self, this power can be used to empower, tricks can be employed to move others out of their defenses into relationship, with each other or with spirit itself. If this character structure becomes "resolved enough," generative, transformative, and creative aspects of the trickster archetype are able to constellate more creatively.

A constructive use of this power to empower must be free of personal gain. A faith healer conflated by the trickster can be a thief, a manipulator, and a con. But in service to the Self, the shaman can use magic to heal the sick, a mentor can empower others with uncanny insights, a corporate businessman can make use of his connections in the world in dialogue with the greater whole.

The convoluted power of the trickster is not always nice. Used consciously within a grounded human spiritual practice, the sacred trickster archetype can be activated in the "magic" realm of effectiveness of healing and devotion, as we see, for example, in the profound healing power of a shaman. Trickster magic is the boon with which the alpha narcissistic person can return from his journey. This embodied spirit is the pearl of great price that he has to offer the world.

Searching for meaning in alpha dynamics in all of our lives

The presence of alpha narcissistic dynamics in our lives, in our psyches, and in our culture is pervasive. In the antagonistic relational pattern on a grand scale, this dark energy serves a role in the great round. We might ask, on a day-to-day basis, how might the unredeemed alpha narcissistic person be serving the purposes of the Self? As we have seen, the agent in many fairy tales who initiates the journey towards wholeness is an image of the same archetype that informs the alpha narcissistic character structure. In this way, what might look like sheer brutality may be a critical or necessary wounding; we recognize the value of this act in a Zen-like strike on the head, or a proverbial kick in the butt. The appearance of trickster clothed in his cape of liminality may deliver magic and spark transformation when least expected. He may spur growth and individuation. Things "happen" when the trickster is around. An unsavory affair, a mean-spirited challenge, or an insult issued by an alpha narcissistic person can be the last straw needed in order to break up an attitude of repressed sexuality or aggression, childlike passivity, or an attachment to being compliant. These encounters can force us to relinquish outworn adaptations. In an alpha narcissist's conscious, well-held wielding of trickster energy, he may embody trickster's capacity to lure us in, quickly cross boundaries, and break taboos, only to widen our consciousness about how rigid or undeveloped we are.

Needless to say, we may encounter trickster energy that embodies alpha dynamics intrapsychically as well. The combined nature of animal and divine being, inherent in the archetypal trickster, is neither this nor that; he easily carries the "third thing" nature of the transcendent function. Trickster is the god of humor, deceit, lawlessness, and sexuality. He is also the god of boundaries, healing magic, and divine messages. In his adventures, what begins as quest to satisfy his desires can magically result in our enlightenment. His antics in our dreams and fantasies can lead to a manifestation of the transcendent function in our lives in surprising and even shocking ways.

Notes

1 Our version of this story is an adaptation of story number 52, "King Thrushbeard," in *The Complete Grimm's Fairytales* (1972: 244–8).
2 This version of the story is an adaptation of story number 53, "Little Snow White," in *The Complete Grimm's Fairytales* (1972: 249–59).
3 In his work on "The Manipulative Personality" (1972) and in *The Manipulator* (1973), Bursten outlines several distinct forms of narcissistic personality. He differentiates craving, paranoid, manipulative, and phallic narcissistic variants. The detailed differences that Bursten suggests do not relate directly to our interests here. However, this work is useful to note because it does introduce the idea of delineating variants of narcissism.
4 Only by differentiating from and working through the dynamics of idealization can the dynamics of sadism be neutralized. When the child identifies with the stranger self-object, the balancing potential of idealization is compromised and the dynamics of sadism dominate the psyche and lead to the inhibition of the development of the superego (Kernberg 1984: 300).
5 Given that the alpha narcissist and the passive-aggressive may each regress into a paranoid position, it seems essential that we briefly describe these dynamics even though we have chosen not to consider a separate category of paranoid character structure. "The essence of paranoid personality organization is the habit of dealing with one's felt negative qualities by projecting them; the disowned attributes then feel like external threats" (McWilliams 1994: 205). This character style certainly fits well within the antagonistic relational pattern. In a person who is paranoid, the aggression that would move "against" the other is transferred into protecting oneself from the other's malevolence. Evidence that the person with a paranoid character structure is developmentally in the primal phase is evidenced in: (a) an orientation toward issues of power and tendency to act out; (b) powerful use of primitive denial and projection; (c) inability to access a sense of shame within the self. As a child, this person may have felt repeatedly overpowered and humiliated.
6 In order to appreciate an alpha narcissistic person's fear of regression, let's contrast this experience of regression with that of the dependent narcissistic person and then the counter-dependent person's experience of regression. A dependent narcissistic person regresses into the intrapsychic reality of borderline consciousness. Borderline reality is dominated by powerful archetypal affect. The person with a borderline character structure has little access to idea or action. His is an affective struggle in the primal field of "kill or be killed," in which he is most apt to be overwhelmed by fears and rage. Since borderline reality is primarily affective, access to the ability to take action, physically defend themselves or attack, is limited. Comparatively, this minimizes the threat of acting out an ultimate, literal death.
   Similarly, the counter-dependent narcissist person fears regression into the schizoid position, into the experience of dissolution, into the gut-wrenching familiarity of falling into nothingness, into the experience of dissolving into a void, into depersonalization. Easy access to mind and the imagination amplify these fears. Remaining conscious of oneself while in a terrified state of non-being

is the experience of psychic death. The person, for example, might experience himself suspended in deep space, in millions of particles, surrounded by threat, but having no way to organize to protect himself. Although the counter-dependent narcissist is fearful of this experience, he also is most often not in danger of actual death. The struggle in schizoid reality is a psychic one. There is limited access to affect and impulse to action.

Chapter 9

Passive-aggressive character structure

The Tar-Baby beckons

A sticky mess

Every parent facing an adolescent child who passively procrastinates picking up his room on Saturday morning and then wants to run off to the movies has experienced the frustrating presence of passive-aggressive behavior. This parent faces a teenager who most certainly did not want to pick up his room, but he never directly refused to do it. He simply delayed. As time went by he got distracted and "forgot" his agreement. We might imagine that he began with a vague intent to comply, but that as he became interested in whatever was distracting him, he easily rationalized that he could do the room later. When it was time for him to set off for the movies, he acted like there was no real issue and left without a word. He thought, after all, he could pick up his room tonight. When he returned from the movies, it was left to his parents to mention the broken contract, ask him

why the job wasn't done, call him in to account for his irresponsibility, and stand over him angrily to make sure the job got done. At that point, the resistant child who just wanted to go to sleep then got bullied by a furious tyrant – and in his own bedroom! He crawled into bed feeling powerless, defeated, and depressed. His parents crawled into their bed feeling manipulated, enraged, and powerless to prevent the scene from being repeated the next morning.

While this adolescent may be experimenting with these behaviors, a person who has this pattern entrenched in his character presents these resistant, obstructionistic, and self-defeating dynamics pervasively. The fact that these behaviors are associated with a phase which most people outgrow accounts for why "these personalities are referred to in adulthood as emotionally immature" (Millon 1981: 245).

We begin with a few notes, which we will expand later, about the classic Uncle Remus folk tale "The Tar-Baby" (Lester 1987; Harris and Chase 2002). This tale so succinctly and cleverly portrays passive-aggressive maneuvers that it works well as an introduction into these confounding dynamics. In this tale, very briefly, Brer Fox resents Brer Rabbit's power and authority, his being "the boss of the whole gang." Does he voice this directly? No, he lays bait. He constructs Tar-Baby and leaves her in the road while he "lay off in the bushes" to see what would happen. Removing himself from the scene, he plants the bait, this sticky mess, in the middle of the rabbit's path. Rabbit comes along, greets the Tar-Baby and gets no response. Provoked by the Tar-Baby's silence, Rabbit begins to ask one question after another until he eventually strikes the Tar-Baby and gets hopelessly stuck in her sticky tar.

Haven't we all happened upon someone else's sticky mess in the middle of our path? Haven't we often missed the reality that the person is "laying off in the bushes" waiting to see how stuck we get in his tease. We are no longer in the field of a predator lying in wait to kill his prey; but nevertheless, entrapment and conquest remain the goal. More subtle than the psychopath or the alpha narcissist, passive-aggressive entrapment is sticky, provoking, and enraging, though clearly not lethal. Like the rabbit, at first one might be simply astonished. The struggle begins when we feel provoked and get engaged.

The story of the Tar-Baby does not end here; it trickily turns itself upside down. The fox begins to gloat and brag about how he will cook and eat the rabbit. But the rabbit craftily convinces the fox that the very cruelest act would be to throw him into the briar patch. The fox is convinced and hurls him into the thorns. However, the briar patch is, of course, the rabbit's natural home. So he scampers off, free and trickily victorious. Yet freedom in this case is merely a ticket to enter the next round of trickery. Although this story ends here, Brer Fox and Brer Rabbit continue their capers indefinitely, without real release or transformation.

We may be enticed to respond to a passive-aggressive maneuver with a tricky retort, as Rabbit did, but this offers only a transient release. Playing tricks on a trickster may end one round, or a chapter, but the dynamic simply reasserts itself. The Tar-Baby story captures the tricky, sticky quality of passive-aggressive behaviors and how difficult it is to extract oneself from them. How might we handle these provocations in our personal lives and as therapists? As we proceed to examine passive-aggressive dynamics, we will approach this question from various perspectives.

The clinical profile

A patient with a passive-aggressive character structure is sufficiently developed to want a relationship and to move towards it. However, his capacity for intimacy is limited by several factors. Clinical experience suggests that the passive-aggressive child experienced his caretakers as overpowering and contradictory and himself as defeated and unseen. This leads to vague but deep fears of inadequacy and inferiority. As we have explored in the last two chapters, the developing ego of a child in the antagonistic relational pattern remains entangled with the archetype of the trickster who has thrown a shroud of unconsciousness over emerging consciousness. As an adult, the passive-aggressive person consciously experiences only a very vague sense of this defeat; it remains mostly unconscious. These unconscious fears of inadequacy and defeat then undermine an ability to express a fundamental predisposition towards attaining power and dominance, which as we have described is inherent in the archetypal configuration of this relational pattern. The interaction between fears and this predisposition towards power creates an internal double bind. The passive-aggressive person not only experiences others as powerful and himself as weak; he also deeply resents and envies the powerful other.

Again, it is important to emphasize that these experiences reside primarily in the unconscious. Without access to painful memories of his early defeats, and confounded by ongoing power struggles, he repeats the behaviors that frustrate and alienate those around him. Defensively and unconsciously, he mobilizes covert maneuvers, becoming obstructionistic, irritable, and blaming. He expresses his aggression in such a slippery manner it is virtually impossible to catch and confront him. All the while, he effectively denies this aggression to himself as well as to others. Gratification consequent to the passive-aggressive maneuver, though clearly a key element in the dynamic, also tends to remain in the unconscious and thereby generally eludes the person himself. Thus covert and denied, this aggression is usually not only unsatisfying but also extremely tricky for anyone else to identify and name.

Living in this shifty mixture of consciousness and unconsciousness, the person with a passive-aggressive character structure has particular difficulty with acquiring a sense of self. His relative lack of ego strength makes it difficult for him to entertain and work with even the mildest, most responsibly delivered negative feedback. Every external statement is heard and responded to as if it were a true and incriminating statement about his being. For example, a woman might say to her husband, "You hurt my feelings when you forgot my birthday." What he would hear is that he is a lousy husband. He gets angry and defensive and withdraws. He may proceed internally by fueling his righteous anger with examples of how he is a good husband. He might mobilize a counter-attack, blaming his work for being too demanding, etc. Or he may proceed by sinking into fatalistic defeat. In the middle of all of this, the wife's feelings are not addressed. Birthdays go unacknowledged, relationships are endangered, and the passive-aggressive spouse is likely to fall into a manipulative self-serving pout remaining tenaciously unconscious of this cycle. While psychopathic and alpha narcissistically structured people act out their frustration directly on others and the world, the person with a passive-aggressive character structure is more apt to go on a sit-down strike and not act; procrastinate, forget, or be obstructionistic.

Three perspectives on one story

The tricky, unconscious maneuvers of the passive-aggressive person render him unable to track himself and they also erase footprints that others might follow. Yet, it is essential to identify the internal experience of these dynamics in order to be able to consider whether this particular pattern is our own underlying character structure, as well as to have insight into and compassion for a person with this structure. At best, a therapist would be able to access each character structure with well-developed empathy so that the dynamics of this landscape do not remain experienced as other. Thus, while it may be tempting to focus on the sly and sticky passive-aggressive maneuvers, it is essential to convey this individual's intrapsychic experience. For example, let's take a look at how a sequence of passive-aggressive behaviors looks from different perspectives.

The day at work, the night at home

John has a project that he has long put off which is scheduled for completion today at work. In addition, he agrees to help his eight-year-old son with a big science project that comes due tomorrow. At work, he calls his suppliers demanding last-minute information that he needs for his report. When he discovers that one of the faxes is missing, he becomes enraged at his secretary, writes her up, and puts a letter of rebuke into her file. He returns home, wanting to unwind from this stressful experience, but his wife asks him about the status of his son's report. He tells his wife that he had a terrible day at work, and that furthermore the son never reminded him of the due date. He decides to go to the gym.

Now let's consider this sequence from John's perspective

When John comes into work, his secretary reminds him that a major report that determines his department's budget is due today. John experiences her tone as bossy and critical. This report reflects a change in procedure instituted a month ago by his new boss whom he finds overbearing and obnoxious. John feels cornered and overwhelmed. He anticipates that his boss will use this as an excuse to criticize and humiliate him. He spends all morning on the phone, calling his suppliers in order to get the information needed to complete the report. He spends a harried afternoon compiling the data, only to find out that a crucial fax is missing. Frustrated and furious, he concludes that his inefficient secretary has once more misplaced files. This time he is determined to get back at her for making him look like a fool in front of his new boss. He writes her up for a third time and places the letter in her employment file. He leaves the incomplete report on his desk. He drives home from work repetitively going over in his mind how inadequate she is and simultaneously feeling vaguely that he has failed.

John goes home hoping to withdraw and regroup. Instead, he is met by what he experiences as his wife's demands to help his son with his homework. He immediately latches on to the fact that his son had not reminded him of the project. He feels that this is more than he should be expected to deal with in one day. With tenuous self-justification, he sets out for the gym to work off some steam. When he gets home, he wants to avoid it all. He puts on a video and never again mentions the topic of his son's report to his wife or to his boy. As he falls asleep, he summarizes the day as one of those when people asked far too much and obviously don't appreciate him enough.

Reflections about this sequence of behaviors

We might imagine that John was a child who experienced himself as defeated in the face of an over-involved mother and a father who was not involved enough to help him negotiate or separate from his intrusive mother. In response to these dynamics, John grew up feeling that he was unlovable and he defensively turned towards an identity with the trickster. Denial and unconsciousness became essential defenses, as he was not able to tolerate knowing how rejecting and unrelated his parents were and how defeated he felt. These defenses evolved into a passive-aggressive character pattern. Now, as an adult, with little experience at being effective and powerful, John projects his unintegrated power and authority on to others. In the face of demands from these perceived-as-powerful others, he feels defeated and paralyzed. Through the lens of his character structure, he experiences every agreement that he makes as a submission and every contract as a set up for more failure. John attempts to cover his internal experience of paralysis by utilizing a variety of defensive maneuvers that enable him to sidestep the perceived demand and the dreaded failure: he forgets, procrastinates, hedges his bets. He may also say yes even though he really means no; he may say yes and fulfill the request poorly or not at all. Most importantly, he denies any or all of these maneuvers to himself and to others.

Above we have presented three different perspectives describing a sequence of passive aggressive behaviors. We looked first at how the sequence might appear to an outsider, then at John's perspective, and finally we considered his psychological history and dynamics. These different perspectives illuminate the complexity of these tangled dynamics. In the midst of these infuriating double-binds and sticky conflicts, it is easy to miss that what underlies a passive-aggressive character formation is a sense of isolation, rejection, and an intense unmet need for contact and reassurance. The childhood origins of this struggle reflect a deep disappointment in love. From a systems perspective, as paradoxical as it may seem, the relational intention of passive-aggressive behavior is to provoke contact. Yet, because this intention is enacted with such unrelatedness, unconsciousness, and covert aggression, the interpersonal result of the passive-aggressive defense is most often self-defeating. It does not elicit sustainable contact and reassurance; it most often works in the long run to preclude relating and evoke rejection. This interactive sequence confirms for the passive-aggressive person his unlovability, his discontented self-image, and his conviction that he is misunderstood and unappreciated by others.

As with the psychopath and the alpha narcissist, an early archetypal possession by the trickster significantly interferes with development in the passive-aggressive person. The continued immersion of the ego in the unconscious limits the person's development of a sense of self and undermines his ability to actualize initiative. Unable to mobilize direct action, the person resorts to forgetting or trying. His early experiences of defeat kindle his insistent projection of blame and a revenge-seeking that become outlets for unconscious aggression. In the pre-neurotic phase, normally we find the emergence of an internalized sense of morality and subsequent experience of guilt. However, for the passive-aggressive person, while pervasive guilt feelings do evidence a developing superego, it appears that these feelings are both proclaimed and denied. For example, failure in keeping contracts with others does not seem to be a source of suffering. He employs denial, expressed as evasion, collapsing, or self-pity, along with projecting blame, to distance himself from not following through on agreements. Like the trickster who is fond of inhabiting the territory of this pattern, we might say that the passive-aggressive person "gets into one ridiculous scrape after another. Although he is not really evil, he does the most atrocious things from sheer unconsciousness and unrelatedness" (Jung 1956b: para. 473). Just as the trickster moves from one disaster to the next, the person with a passive-aggressive character structure refines the art of self-sabotage to sheer perfection. He thinks he is tricking his enemy, the authority, but he ends up defeating himself. Life for the passive-aggressive is full of weak attempts at using power that backfire.

Identifying the passive-aggressive character structure

The theoretical background

The use of the diagnostic term passive-aggressive personality disorder is relatively recent in the history of psychological thought. The term "passive-aggressive" arose in the U.S. military during World War II, when officers noted that some soldiers shirked duties by adopting passive-aggressive type behaviors. Subsequently, it was adopted by the first version of the *DSM* in 1952 (Millon 1981: 247). Yet the patterns of this personality disorder had been considered from a number of perspectives for many years. In the psychoanalytic tradition, infantile sexuality plays a major role in development that passes through three stages: oral, anal, and phallic. The dynamics associated with the oral-sadistic and anal phases of development are directly associated with passive-aggressive behaviors. These dynamics become manifest as hostility, envy, an ambivalence towards others, an inclination to blame the world for one's pain, a tendency to be cantankerous, petulant, and discontented, and as a propensity to obstruct the goals of others and then be overwhelmed by unconscious guilt (Millon and Radovanov 1995: 313).

Wilhelm Reich proposed that the tendency to obstruct others through passively provocative behaviors arises from a deep disappointment in love. The person, caught in an infantile spite reaction aimed at getting back at and torturing his rejecting parents, in effect resorts to "demands for love in the form of provocation and spite" (Reich 1949: 224–6). This attitude of "You treat me horribly, and I am right in hating you" expresses the antagonistic quality of the relational pattern that we see underlying this character structure.

When guilt prevails over dependency needs, passive-aggressive behaviors reflect a compromise solution. Whitman, Trosman, and Koenig offer a clear psychodynamic interpretation of passive-aggressive behaviors. When aggression is inhibited by internal guilt or fear of external retaliation, a regression to a dependent position occurs. Shame experienced as a result of assuming a culturally unacceptable passive role leads to hostility which is expressed behaviorally by the passive-aggressive person's pseudo-aggression (cited by Millon 1981: 251).

Passive-aggressive personality in the form that we understand it today is most fully presented as an Axis II personality disorder in the *DSM-IIIR* "in which there is passive resistance to demands for adequate performance in both occupational and social functioning." This diagnostic category was moved in the *DSM-IV* to Appendix B ("Criteria Sets and Axes Provided for Further Study"). The diagnosis as it was defined in *DSM-IIIR* raised several issues. The *DSM-III* definition of passive-aggressive personality focused specifically on one trait, that is of resistance to external demands. The other issue was a research problem. In psychometic testing of the diagnostic criteria, the diagnosis as defined produced the poorest diagnostic agreement of all the personality disorders (Fossati et al. 2000: 72–83).

Millon succinctly captures the dynamic of the passive-aggressive, "The passive-aggressive's strategy of negativism, of being discontent and unpredictable, of being both seductive and reflecting, of being demanding and then dissatisfied, is an effective weapon not only with an intimidated or pliant partner, but with people in general." Switching among roles such as the martyr, the guilt-ridden, the overworked, etc., the passive-aggressive gains the attention and reassurance he craves, while he also vents his anger and hostility (Millon 1981: 258).

In our experience, denial is the bedrock defense of this character structure. The persistent unconsciousness about aggression that is covertly expressed through evasion, collapsing, self-pity, or projecting blame takes on an insistent quality. It almost seems as if the passive-aggressive person practices unconsciousness, becoming an expert in intentional inefficiencies and unheroic evasions. Yet his experience remains one of being-done-to. In the sense that the ego has not been wrested from the grip of the trickster, this is to some extent true. However, it is not another person who has caused his suffering, but rather the archetypal possession.

Victoria: in denial of defeat and dependence

Victoria arrived at her session with nothing but complaints about her husband, her children, and our society. She was an accomplished graphic artist but had recently lost her job. She described her husband with hostility and scorn, while minimizing her financial and emotional dependence on him. She often wondered about a divorce, but dreaded not being able to make it on her own, especially since she knew she could not replicate the life style she now enjoyed. It took only a few sessions for her complaints to be turned towards me. I simply was not appreciating what she was up against. Not only that, my office was too hot, too bright, and too hard to get to. Meanwhile, she had been a few minutes late for each session; once she forgot her checkbook, the next her check bounced. We were off to quite a start. As our work proceeded, her negativism took center stage for much of our time while her inner experience remained staunchly unavailable for examination. While Victoria was aware that she resented her husband, she was tenaciously blind to how she expressed her resentments aggressively through her blaming negativism. She expressed her aggression passively and vehemently renounced it as it was expressed.

Issues that passive-aggressive people have with others whom they perceive as powerful, authoritative, or valuable to them in any way, grow directly out of their conflicted issues of dependence. Paradoxically, passive-aggressive acts are often an attempt at separation leading to independence. However, in their undifferentiated state they lead to a perseveration that impedes further development of separation. It was apparent that Victoria's passive-aggressive acts left her trapped in her denied dependency while her hostile assertion wreaked havoc in her life. Unable to explore her early experiences of loss, Victoria's experiences of defeat drove her to defeat others.

As is prevalent in the antagonistic relational pattern, one way that passive-aggressive people manage the conundrum of their dependence is by making use of the manipulative cycle. They engage in a manipulative series of interactions where they attempt to "put something over on someone." Reflecting a pre-neurotic development, their motivations are more subtle than predatory aggression, theft, or acts of dominance. Strategy for passive-aggressive people aims towards a sneaky come-uppance against someone they view as powerful.

The passive-aggressive character structure

While there is some debate in the clinical literature about retaining passive-aggressive as a diagnostic category, we find that the archetypal images that inform these dynamics convincingly identify it as a character structure within the antagonistic relational pattern, at a pre-neurotic level. Quite dramatically, the trickster inserts its twists and turns throughout passive-aggressive dynamics. In the last two chapters, we have described how the trickster impacts the development of the character structures within this relational pattern from the earliest primal phase. While it manifests itself in psychopathic dynamics as the predator and in alpha narcissistic dynamics as the powerful magician, it finds its incarnation in passive-aggressive dynamics as the frequently humorous, self-defeating figure that obstructs, inverts, undoes and "plays with" reality. Unprepared to face the imminent responsibilities of three-person, Oedipal dynamics, the passive-aggressive child resorts to tricky, defeated, resentful attacks upon those he experiences as presenting any challenge.

Eric Neumann's work in *The Great Mother* offers a perspective that helps to elucidate how the trickster archetype impacts development in this relational pattern. He proposes: "The process of the differentiation of archetypal phenomena [by the ego] . . . leads to the emergence of individual archetypes from a great complex mass, and to the formation of coherent archetypal groups" (Neumann 1954: 7). Generally, the ego differentiates itself initially from the Great Mother and is then presented with a procession of the archetypes. The Great Mother in effect stands at the gateway to the activation of the innumerable archetypes of the unconscious. Neumann, like Jung, was inspired by heroic myth and story and imagined that consciousness is first embedded in the unconscious which is considered to be a manifestation of the Great Mother archetype. Individual consciousness then heroically frees itself from the unconscious. Symbolically, we are accustomed to imagining this as the hero's quest to free the village from the threat of the dragon/mother and win the anima. This heroic quest motif is an accurate image of development for people whose character structures evolve within the seeking and withdrawing relational patterns. However, in the antagonistic relational pattern, partaking archetypally as it does of the trickster cycle of myths and legends, development out of the unconscious is less an adequate metaphor than a co-existence of consciousness within the unconscious. Heroic conquering and winning is a less adequate description of the dynamics of the antagonistic lineage, than an anti-hero's adventuring and maneuvering.

This radically different archetypal landscape dominated by the trickster emerges when a child attempts to minimize the power of the personal and archetypal mother by forming an identity with "that which is not mother," the trickster.[1] Attempting to obliterate the importance of the mother, the child stakes out territory in a landscape independent of the mother. In effect, the very ground of the child's being becomes rooted in the nature of the trickster, not the mother. The child's psyche then remains firmly held in the grip of the trickster, with limited access to the Great Mother and to the progressive differentiation of the archetypes. The identity with the trickster creates the illusion of independence for a child who is unable to differentiate from a mother who seems threatening and dangerous and thus assists the child in defending against the reality that he is inextricably dependent on his mother. Nevertheless, the reality of his denied dependence looms large and is a constant source of conflict.

Possession by the elemental trickster works to trap consciousness in the unconscious. It is as if the trickster has cast a pall over the never-free-to-fully-develop ego. Extrication from the domination of the trickster would require a fundamental restructuring of the ego and would be a considerable challenge. This alternative would necessarily entail a regression to the archetypal ground of the Great Mother in order to readdress the moment when a confrontation with the Great Mother was avoided and the psyche turned to the trickster. Facing the Great Mother through such a regression would then require the patient to engage in the heroic battle for emergence from her and thus activate the differentiation of the innumerable archetypes. This challenging sequence of events could release the singular grip of the trickster.

Case vignette: Dan

This archetypal landscape was pervasive in the treatment of a man named Dan. A professor at a local university, he entered therapy because he was upset that his wife was threatening to leave him. He had always experienced her as demanding, even a nag, while he saw himself as generous, reliable, hardworking and taken advantage of. At work he had shied away from administrative responsibilities, choosing what he honored as dedication to teaching. He excelled in the large lecture halls, where his dry, sniping humor was impersonally at play.

In our sessions, as his domestic and professional stories unfolded, I could see how he defended against real contact. His wife, wanting more connection, was constantly knocking on his door, rattling his cage. I could sense Brer Fox and Brer Rabbit romping in Dan's life – and in my treatment room. However, it took quite a long time for him to see the contours of the mess that he repetitively created. Hour by hour we began to identify these messes. It seemed that the moments when he felt threatened by her or by me were the moments when he subtly attacked. At first, when I asked him to reflect on these attacks, he would retreat into a glum silence that seemed to vibrate with resentfulness. His sulky resentfulness was bait that I found virtually impossible not to react to. Similarly, the passivity of his gloomy silences created invisible obstructions that deadened the hour while they slyly beckoned for an intervention from me that he could reject. Passive-aggressive maneuvers aim to place the locus of aggression into the other, through projective identification, so that the other begins to nag, get angry, and in effect carry the person's disowned aggression.

Work with a person with a passive-aggressive character structure so often conjures up images of Brer Fox and Brer Rabbit romping around the room that it will serve us well to return to the tale.

Brer Fox and Brer Rabbit: endless rounds of trickery

One form of the Tar-Baby motif arises out of the American South at the time of slavery. Yet this tale has interesting historical layers. African Americans brought with them their tales of the spider trickster Anasazi from Ashanti myth. Once here, these stories shapeshifted into the tales of Brer Fox and Brer Rabbit. Important cultural references to both defiance and defeat dance to the surface of this enormously popular tale. Clever defiance in the face of defeat works to sustain a people through the tensions of impossible social oppression. Such defiance is also an essential element of the passive-aggressive character defense. Let's turn to the tale to see how this story of the trickster and the Tar-Baby illuminates passive-aggressive dynamics.

"The wonderful Tar-Baby story"[2]

> One day after Brer Rabbit had cleverly fooled Brer Fox once again and
> was acting fat and sassy and like the boss of the whole gang, Brer Fox
> plotted how to set a trap for the uppity rabbit.

As we observed at the beginning of this chapter, this fox clearly resents the
rabbit's power, authority, and narcissistic delight in being the boss of the
whole gang. Rather than express his resentment directly, he sets a trap:

> Brer Fox went to work and got himself some tar, mixed it with some
> turpentine, and fixed up a contraption that he named Tar-Baby. Brer
> Fox then plunked this here Tar-Baby, all dressed up with a fancy straw
> hat, square in the middle of the big road and then he lay off in the
> bushes to see what the news was goin' be.

Soon:

> Brer Rabbit came strutting down the road – lippity-clipity, clipity-
> lippity – just as sassy as a jay bird. Brer Fox, he lay low. Brer Rabbit
> came prancing along until he spied the Tar-Baby and then he raised up
> on his hind legs like he was astonished. The Tar-Baby she just sat there,
> she did, and Brer Fox, he lay low.

Passive-aggressive entrapment is sticky and provoking, and the problem is,
we tend to get engaged:

> "Morning!" says Brer Rabbit, says he. "Nice weather this morning,"
> says he. Tar-Baby don't say a word, and Brer Fox, he lay low.

Rabbit is precariously close to getting stuck; he engages, gets no response,
yet does he go on his way? No, he stays engaged. We may think this is
extreme. However, we all know the moment when we initiate contact, we
meet resistance, and something in us moves to ask for more. Tar-Baby's
inert, dark, still mass and the way Brer Fox lays low express the way in
which the passive-aggressive person provokes engagement:

> "How ya feeling this morning?" says Brer Rabbit, to the Tar-Baby,
> says he.

How many times do we ask the unresponsive passive-aggressive other how
they are feeling? It's a dangerous move, because then we have moved into
the trap. Why do we do it? It must be that our own dynamics are engaged.
Possibly, because of our own early wounds we cannot bear the silence, the

lack of a response to our overture. It could be our own need to be seen or be dominant, our own arrogant impulse to serve or to save. In the story, Brer Rabbit insists on being met, being mirrored, and he gets royally stuck:

> Brer Fox, real slow he winked his eye and just lay low and the Tar-Baby she ain't saying nothing.

The slow wink lets us know that Brer Fox is quietly thrilled and gratified by Brer Rabbit's powerlessness in the face of Brer Fox's trap. The gratification is so quiet that it may remain unconscious. Tar-Baby didn't say a thing, she didn't have to. The passive-aggressive maneuvers of taunting and withholding drive Brer Rabbit into an ever-increased frenzy:

> "What's going on with you then? Are you deaf?" says Brer Rabbit, says he. "Cause if you is, I can holler louder," says he.
> The Tar-Baby stayed still and Brer Fox, he lay low.
> "You're stuck up, that's what you are! You're just too good to talk to me," says Brer Rabbit, says he. "I'm gonna cure you, that's what I'm gonna do!" says he.

Rabbit's increased frenzy finally turns into an inflated resolution to diagnose and cure the Tar-Baby. In the face of the traps set by the passive-aggressive person, the person who wants a relationship, perhaps the therapist, concludes, "I'm going to cure you!" With that grandiose intention, we become stuck in the tar, and at the mercy of the trickster:

> Brer Fox started to chuckle in his stomach, he did, but Tar Baby wasn't sayin' a word.

This is the moment when the passive-aggressive person becomes more deeply gratified by his aggression, though there's not a clue on his face that reveals his aggression or gratification. The chuckle in his stomach is deep within the body, lost to even his own awareness. The anger of the passive-aggressive person is unconscious, and will remain staunchly denied, even as it is being expressed. Indeed his aggression is egodystonic, and consciously he denies the inward chuckle:

> Brer Rabbit kept on asking Tar-Baby why she wouldn't talk and the Tar-Baby kept on saying nothin' until Brer Rabbit finally drew back his fist, he did, and hit the Tar-Baby square on the jaw. When his fist hit that thick tar, it got bad stuck and he couldn't pull it loose. Tar-Baby, she just stayed still, and Brer Fox, he lay low.

Brer Rabbit's frenzy escalates into physical aggression. Brer Rabbit hit again with his other fist, then both feet, and then with his head, until he was good and stuck.

As we saw above, even though Brer Rabbit gets caught, he then tricks the tricky fox into throwing him into the briar patch and he's thus trickily released – and Brer Fox is defeated, once again. Here we see how a passive-aggressive person gets caught in his own destructive dynamic. He thinks he is tricking the other but his weak attempts at power backfire and he ends up in humiliation.

The trickster at work in the passive-aggressive character structure

Symbolically akin to the tale just told, coyote, rabbit, and raven are recurrent animal forms that the trickster assumes. Coyote prowls on the plains; the Great Hare romps in the woodlands; and Raven soars along the Pacific Northwest Coast. We recognize these colorful characters in cartoon form in the characters of Wylie Coyote, Bugs Bunny, and Heckle and Jeckle. Being possessed by these critters is no small possession. The dark aspects of the trickster can be mean, humiliating, and manipulative. Their cunning tricks are enacted by means of preying on human fears, naivete, and ignorance. However, coyote, rabbit, and raven also represent a unique divine connection. They cavort in the realm of the holy fool and the divine messenger. When this archetypal energy is held in dialogic relationship with the ego, it can be the wellspring of the spiritual energy that is used by a healer, a shaman, or an inspired teacher. The humor inherent in coyote's shenanigans can bring medicine into the most difficult situation, it can lighten up whatever is weighing heavily and restore balance. Rabbit's elusiveness and agile tricks can entertain, amuse, and even turn us on. He can charm us into opening up to our own instinctual life. Raven delivers messages from the Otherworld, manifests magic, and is shapeshifter par excellence. Trickster brings us the possibility of breaking out of restrictive patterns, whether they've been imposed by ourselves, our families, or our culture. Like the nature of divinity itself, his is the power of creation and transformation.[3] "As the trickster flounders toward a sacred life rooted more in carnate being than in divine being, ambiguity, irony, change, and humor fill the emptiness caused by the kenosis of immortality" (Sullivan 1987: 46).

The antics of this ever so powerful archetypal being rule the lives of people with a passive-aggressive character structure. We see the cunning in their interpersonal manipulations and the devious defiance of truth in their persistent evasions. We also often find a numinosity in their physical vitality, a vigor that seems given by the gods. If we are fortunate, we experience the magic of their humor, transforming a profane moment into a sacred drama. Throughout their lives, for better and for worse, we feel the pulsating presence of the trickster.

The treatment of passive-aggressive dynamics

In the treatment of a passive-aggressive patient, the task of maintaining an engaged but boundaried relatedness while the course of a person's individuation process emerges is particularly demanding. The cases that follow illustrate two quite different scenarios, both in the landscape of the trickster.

Paul: obstinate obstruction

Paul was in his early fifties when he entered analysis. He owned a property management company that served numerous wealthy clients in the city. His second wife had become deeply frustrated with their interactions and had insisted that he enter therapy. He recognized that when his relationship with his first wife had reached this same moment, he had become paralyzed and had done nothing. That marriage had ended in divorce. However, he did not have the temperament to remain single for long and when he met his prospective new wife he became quickly involved. She was serious, competent, and direct, while he was charismatic, funny, carefree, and to all appearances emotionally available.

He was tall and attractive, yet he stooped a bit, as if he were carrying the burdens of the world on his back. He held his head slightly down and from this angle his eyes flashed seductively. His thick dark hair made him look years younger than his actual age. He was not a person who attended to or easily talked about personal business. He appeared shy and somewhat awkward in my office. While he seemed uncomfortable with silence, he made no attempt to fill in the quiet moments. I restrained the impulse he evoked in me to carry our interaction.

After his wife's ultimatum regarding therapy, he admitted that he was dragging his feet about calling my office until he had the following dream, which provided him with a topic for the first session. It was essentially the first thing he said when he arrived. This was the dream:

> There is a small boy, hungry, alone in an empty room. In the adjacent room, people are enjoying a sumptuous meal. At the head of the table is the boy's mother surrounded by a number of men whom she has entranced and is holding at bay. His father is absent. This single scene seems to go on forever. Suddenly a little girl from next door appears. The boy baits her into wrestling with him; they tussle, and after he hits her hard, she is bloodied.

Paul awoke puzzled. He had a terrible headache and felt discouraged. He attributed these feelings to the bottle of wine that he had at dinner the night before the dream. When he finished telling me the dream, we sat in silence. Eventually I said, "I wonder if your headache had anything to do with your dream?" He said, "Oh no. I just thought you'd find the dream interesting."

With this response, I knew we were at the beginning of a very long dance. Paul's mother was manipulative and intense. She could be by turns demanding, praising, and seductive. His mother was unable to see Paul for himself, allowing no room for his individuality. His father was a lawyer, always full of deals and out of the house for long hours. When he was at home, he was submissive to his bossy, nagging wife. He would shame Paul to control him and he afforded Paul no protection or relief from his powerful mother.

Our first sessions consisted of his various attempts to get me to do the work. He not only expected me to interpret his dream, but also wanted me to help him understand how to figure out and handle his wife. He had severely limited access to his psyche and it quickly became apparent that he wanted me not to embarrass or expose him by asking him to be reflective. While he first presented with a charismatic flourish, this quickly gave way to a deep-seated attitude of defeat and martyrdom. He had no idea what his wife wanted of him, nor did he understand that his dream was asking anything from him. This put me in a double-bind, facing long hours of stagnant obstruction. This was just as it must have been with his first and now his second wife. Our interactions were all the more frustrating because he had no clue he was obstructing anything. The transference was well under way.

Every once in a while, Paul would mention the first dream. He'd say something like, "You know, I've been thinking about that first dream . . ." and then we'd sit. When I did ask what he'd been thinking, or if he'd had any associations to it, he'd say, "No, not really." Yet in these long, silent stretches of time, when he seemed to have nowhere else to go, he would return to the dream, over and over. Then one day he said, "You know, I realize now that when I think of that dream, I am in that room with that small boy." After exploring the details of that experience with him, I said, "Do you think it's possible that the hungry boy is you?" His immediate response was, "God forbid, no! I just think I'm standing in the room." A number of sessions later, he asked me why I wondered if he was the hungry boy, adding, "But that would suggest that I hurt the little girl in the room." I responded, "Let's consider that possibility." He immediately denied ever having any aggressive feelings like that. He quickly concluded that he was not the small, hungry boy.

In the next phase of the work, he had a series of dreams with recurring themes. In one, he is not ready to take an exam. In another, he is with a couple of buddies out on the town. His buddies keep stumbling at every turn, saying the wrong things, generally being unprepared for everything they take on. They go into a Seven-Eleven and while one of them flirts with the night attendant, the others walk out with a six-pack without paying. They then encounter some girls, and the best they can do is whistle and duck. Paul brought each of these dreams to our sessions with a beckoning and challenging attitude, as if to say, "Here's another meaningless dream. What can you of make of it?"

When he brought in the dream about being unprepared for an exam, I thought he might be able to recognize this as himself. So I said, "Look Paul, one way that analysts look at dreams is to consider each of the characters within the dream as an expression of a part of yourself. Would you like to do that with this dream?" He responded, "Oh sure, you bet I felt unprepared for those exams at business school! So did all of my friends. Those exams were killers! It's a good thing that my friends kept an 'Old Test File.' Those answers saved me a number of times!"

From there, we began to explore how he felt in this situation and how he might identify with the other guys in this dream series; how he has felt unprepared and inadequate, as well as tricky and a thief. Eventually Paul could see that the dream series was quite accurately detailing his own daily behaviors. He began to realize how often he did resort to "whistling and ducking." While this challenged his ego ideal, it confirmed a deeply hidden certainty that he had vaguely sensed about himself.

Eventually, Paul began to speak with me about his ongoing stalemates at work. As we talked about his dilemmas, I begin to see how he undermined his employees with double-binds and tried to shortchange his customers. He constantly experienced his customers as too demanding, and he dug in his heels with resistance. He rationalized that each petty overcharge was inconsequential; his resentment of his clients' wealth justified these choices. It took months for Paul to imagine that he himself contributed to the disturbances in his work. He began to consider how his behaviors were self-defeating. In the face of these realizations, he began to make some choices and take some responsibility for his behaviors. As this ability to make choices developed, he felt somewhat more empowered in his life.

At the point when Paul began to work with admitting his contribution to the stalemates with others, I thought he now might be ready to turn towards developing insight into the origins of these behaviors in his child-hood. Intuitively, I imagined that Paul chronically experienced being defeated. I surmised that he experienced himself, in his life, as at the mercy of a sadistic overpowering bully. Projecting aggression, power, and authority on to others, he defended against all perceived demands for per-formance. In this state, every agreement that he made was experienced as a submission, every contract felt like a set-up. His fear and anger at being dominated internally by his experience of defeat and powerlessness were enacted passively in his daily interactions with others. For example, he frequently evaded commitments by employing his favorite mantra, "I'm trying," which served to obfuscate his accountability. I wove these various insights into numerous responses and interventions, yet these well-developed intuitions of mine were neither appreciated by nor useful to Paul. I became increasingly convinced that interventions based on these intuitions led us nowhere and that insight into his historical and intra-psychic dynamics was not to be the source of Paul's transformation.

Given that this conclusion contradicted not only my training but my familiarity with my own process, it was with quiet reserve that I sat with my frustration. Over time as I experienced Paul's growing empowerment, I became increasingly aware that his treatment needs were different than mine and from those which I had been trained to address. Nevertheless I remained saddened in our sessions when I could not find in Paul a capacity to consciously engage in the direct exploration and confrontation of his intrapsychic dynamics. I realized that this simply was not going to happen. We were not going to achieve the ultimate analytic goal, the differentiation of consciousness from unconsciousness and the development of a dialogue between the two. I then took it upon myself to live with this sadness and leave Paul to his individual form of development.

For a person whose character structure is in the antagonistic relational pattern, the ultimate analytic goal must sometimes be relinquished in order to acknowledge and respect the person's authenticity and connection to archetypal reality. Therapeutic naivete in this regard will only serve to leave the therapist enmeshed and the patient's individuation process stalled. We need not presuppose that this person must develop conscious insight and effective integration of affect. In this situation, we need to set aside these analytic assumptions. It may well be that with certain passive-aggressive people, treatment directed towards the containment and creative expression of aggression, regardless of conscious insight, is the most viable and effective path.

Indeed, as my work with Paul proceeded, it was not conscious insight that developed. However, he did develop a capacity to take responsibility for his part in passively provoking stalemates, and he continued to strengthen his ability to make choices in his life. Furthermore, something else opened up. He had always enjoyed rafting as a young man but had given it up when he first got married. At this point, he reentered this world and established himself as quite an accomplished river guide. Paul recog-nized that he enjoyed being valued and appreciated by the guys he rafted with. Through the Big Brothers Association, he began to lead river excur-sions for adolescent boys and he hit it off with these kids right away. He found that the kids appreciated his silly sense of humor and the playful trickiness in his teaching style.

Engaging in this physical and community endeavor brought Paul a new sense of well-being. He also learned to appreciate his wife's serious competence and she learned to play with his progressively less aggressive humor. Their relationship became more satisfying to both of them. Not irrelevantly, Paul left analysis stooping far less than when he began; the weight of his obstinate need to obstruct had been lightened. It is essential to note that Paul's growth happened without insight, reminding us that this is one way that growth can occur for a person with this character structure.

Sheila: releasing the mantle of the martyr

While treatment for Paul led him into refining the strength and flexibility of his ego within the realm of the trickster, an alternative process of transformation for a person with this character structure sometimes appears. In this process, the person is called into a regression that, as described earlier, requires an encounter with the dynamics that initially led to a possession by the trickster. This regression leads to the moment when a confrontation with the Great Mother was circumvented and the psyche turned to the trickster. Regression to this moment allows the patient to readdress their possession by the trickster and face the archetype of the Great Mother. Effectively handled, this confrontation can then lead to the activation of the progression of the innumerable archetypes from the unconscious. It is important to note that not all patients in this character structure are called and can meet the call to this descent which requires a disintegrative surrender of egohood and a deep and challenging confrontation in the archetypal realms. While Paul moved towards refining his ego, the woman in the brief case vignette that follows was summoned into a descent.

Sheila was a rebellious, defiant woman who arrived in treatment blaming everyone and everything in her world for her suffering, yet she ultimately developed a capacity for emotional honesty. She worked with me at least twice a week, for more than five years. In the first half of this process, she presented one crisis after another. She robustly defended against considering the prospective meaning of these crises by repetitively insisting that the world was against her. She aggressively clung to the mantle of the martyr, vociferously proclaiming her recurrent defeats. Any attempt to dig for the dynamics or meaning in these crises was vehemently resisted. As she steadily remained in the container of analysis, a regression slowly began to take place. We began to notice that she was intermittently disorganized, disorientated, and agitated. Over the next couple of years, we sat in the middle of her terrifying states of disintegration even as her anxiety level increased almost intolerably. Facing the overwhelming intensity of her disowned vulnerability, she learned to tolerate the felt experience of her inner, defeated child. Very slowly she developed a capacity to sit with and reflect upon her pain and suffering.

During these tumultuous years, Sheila's curiosity began to break through her defenses. She wondered if her life could be less conflict ridden and burdened. As her capacity to stay with her feelings deepened, she began to make decisions about her life that she could not have imagined herself making. Turning her focus from her intense embattlement and disappointment with others, she began to pursue her own development. She had worked as an interior decorator for a prominent upscale firm that was filled with competition for accounts, shifty billing practices, and relentless power dynamics. Following clues from her dreams, she realized that her job had suited the trickster archetype that she no longer wanted to serve. Wresting herself from this impersonal force, surprising images arrived inspiring her to take her creativity seriously. She decided to leave her job and return to graduate school for a Masters in Fine Arts.

The discipline of graduate school and the humility required to be a student again challenged Sheila's arrogance and provided a container within which she could start to set aside her defenses and experiment with some new ways of being. She began to explore her own autonomy, initiative, and desire for mutuality with others. Facing her fears of being overpowered and overwhelmed, she was able to develop conscious connection to her aggression and learn to employ it as assertion. In her last years of treatment, she chose to include group work along with her individual sessions. She entered the group context with an intent to confront and transform her emotional dishonesty. Over the course of these sessions, I observed her struggle to enter into a vulnerable space while expressing her authentic feelings. In this context, she was able to explore just how stubbornly she had employed rebelliousness as a defense against any feeling of dependency. In the midst of all this, she developed a fulfilling creative process from which she managed to earn a substantial livelihood.

Transference and counter-transference challenges

The patient with a passive-aggressive character structure, armed with an extreme ambivalence about relationship, may well experience the therapist as a dangerously powerful force to be distanced and controlled. Experienced as a probable source of rejection and defeat, you may be criticized, attacked, blamed, discounted, or simply minimized. Along with projections of unfathomable power, you may also be seen as the intolerable authority or the predator/perpetrator. The grip that the trickster has upon the person's ego reveals itself in his persistent, sly maneuvers to defeat you. While denying any feeling of dependency upon you, this patient tends to be demanding and belligerently engaged, or hostile and distant and quiet.

The counter-transference experience with a patient who has a passive-aggressive character structure is extraordinarily demanding. Like with the alpha narcissist, the therapist must carry most of the emotional and imaginal energy in the relationship, staying very present and not overly involved. Meanwhile, the patient's sulky, resentful, and blaming engagements are powerful emotional lures that are not only difficult to handle well but are also felt as extremely demoralizing. As we noted above, it is ever so easy to get stuck in the Tar-Baby. In these moments, it is essential that we ask ourselves whether our own dynamics are constellated. The therapist may have to wrestle diligently with her own early wounds in order not to get entrapped by the patient's myriad obstructions, swipes, silences, etc. Effectively receiving and metabolizing thoroughly denied aggression is without doubt a sophisticated art.

Final reflections

When people with this character structure find themselves developing sufficient ego strength to forge a relationship with the archetypal trickster, rather than remain possessed by it, they have the opportunity to bring this dynamic, potentially creative spirit into human life, their own and others'. They can then move from passivity and evasiveness towards creative assertion and intentional, responsible action. Their wit, employed creatively rather than aggressively, can brighten and deepen life. Rather than being caught in endless rounds of power struggles and tricks imbued with defeat, they can use their power for themselves, as well as for the empowerment of others. Consciously held, the brilliance and charisma of the trickster can transform reality: now you see it, now you don't, the world is turned upside down, and truths are dispassionately revealed. Bringing vibrant energy into their activities and relationships, people with a passive-aggressive character structure can make vigorous and transformative contributions to life.

Summary of the antagonistic relational pattern

Each of the character structures within the antagonistic pattern has a common feel to it, just as the character structures within the other two relational patterns did. The predatory Sea-Hare Princess will go to any lengths to maintain her domination. The arrogant and cold-hearted Medea will ruthlessly murder to obtain her self-serving goals and to exact a triumphant retaliation. The sneaky Brer Fox has infinite patience to entrap the rabbit in his sticky mess. In this relational pattern, the source of survival, integration, and meaning is maintained by acts of violence, seduction, domination, manipulation, control, and trickery; aggressive attacks upon the object pervade. Inspired by the trickster, the individual employs this archetypal power defensively to ensure her victory at any cost. The predator can never be prey-like for one moment. Interpersonally, protecting herself from being touched, she becomes untouchable. Her merciless domination of others leaves her trapped in her own manipulative entrapments. Often bestowed with an unusual physical vitality, fueled by sexuality and aggression, with limited access to the clarity and inspiration of mind and image, as well as limited development of the emotional wealth and glue of archetypal affects, the antagonistic person remains isolated in her world of actions.

It is an exceedingly rare person that can face a descent through these particular developmental phases and disconnect their possession by the archetype of the trickster. However, when this does occur, the person can emerge with a capacity for conscious expression of the trickster archetype. When this archetype possesses the person, she may appear much like the paradigmatic fairy-tale stepmother who serves to initiate the transformation of the protagonist but remains untouched herself. In this case, the person is used ruthlessly by the trickster archetype; from a human perspective this is a cruel fate indeed. Yet, if she can work through her defensive possession by this archetype and emerge with a conscious and active dialogue with it, she can consciously bring transformation to others, as well as possibly to herself. We have seen how someone in this relational pattern can spark individuation, create challenge, and move lives along their paths. Freed from the defensive grip of the trickster, this person may also be able to lead a lusty and energetic life, living her physical vitality to its fullest, with a developed capacity for responsibility. When we speak of "the laws of nature," we are wandering in the archetypal landscape inhabited by the trickster and the person who is rooted in these realms participates in the great rounds of life and death, unconsciously – or consciously. The dynamics in this relational pattern can be seen as archetypal expressions of the Self revealing a perspective that is larger-than-human, including the light and darkened aspects of the divine.

Spirituality informed by this archetypal landscape is the illumination of power. When embodiment is well held by consciousness, human action can be tantamount to incarnation. This is spirit in action. It thrills at the bodily experience of mastery. At its most creative and transformational, it is also the spirit experienced while doing martial arts or other physical activity which is highly disciplined and practiced, from archery to tennis to playing percussion. It is from this archetypal wellspring that one derives his capacity to take action. This form of spirituality can be experienced through competition and victory in athletics, in working to win for the home team, in the art of social action, and in active physical work.

Notes

1 When the child's psyche forms an identity between the nascent ego and the trickster for protection from an overwhelming personal and/or archetypal mother, we see the dynamism of the Self at work. We might wonder if the self-organizing principle of the psyche is seeking a position that will ensure survival. We also might speculate, in theological terms, on the intentions of the Self. In this vein, we might conclude that possession by the trickster must serve the purposes of the Great Round, the greater whole. We have identified how the workings of this

archetype can inspire radical transformation. Yet, the conundrum of this relational pattern is that it leads to such severe suffering in the human lives that embody it. The seeming unfairness of this extreme suffering reminds one of Job. Job rails at God for the suffering and unfairness of his divine plan. He does not understand God's purpose until he is granted the vision to see the world from God's perspective. He returns from that vision sober and humbled.

2 We have adapted this story from both Harris and Chase (2002) *The Complete Tales of Uncle Remus* and Lester (1987) *The Tales of Uncle Remus: The Adventures of Brer Rabbit.*

3 The trickster figure in Native American myths has two major variants. In one, his prodigious animal nature is featured. His body is often the source of his tricks and magic; his organs and orifices are enormous, his appetite and sexual hyperactivity are astonishing. He embodies instinctual desire of cosmic proportion. We meet him frequently in humorous stories that teach us about our humanity and our limitations.

Trickster is often represented as a male, but shows up as a female as it suits his or her purposes. In another variant of the trickster mythic cycle, he harnesses his divine nature as creator and transforms mythic reality into form. Moving easily from this world to the Otherworld, he facilitates life on earth by creating the necessities of human life: land, animals, and fire. Not infrequently, these acts of creation are accomplished by stealing from the gods. They may involve surprises and twists that create an outcome different than expected. Capable of tricking us, tricking the gods, and tricking himself, he is nevertheless a divine creator.

Conclusion

Character structures, consciousness and spirituality

> Our vessel must be such that in it matter can be influenced by the heavenly bodies. For the invisible celestial bodies and the impressions of the stars are necessary to the work.
>
> (Dorn, as quoted by Jung 1968b: para. 338n)

We cannot roam with abandon in the precincts of the spirit. Our vessel "must be such" that we can receive and hold these enormous influences. Soul takes up its residence on earth in our bodies, affects, and imagination – and in human wisdom and logic.[1] It is to the quality of our vessels that we have attended in these last chapters, exploring our character structures, as the residence of soul, so that we can be "influenced," and not overwhelmed, by the archetypal realms.

As character structures emerge during the first years of life, they create a pattern that reflects interplay between experiences that may be called archetypal and those that are identifiably more personal. Character structures, informed by archetypal wellsprings, are a defensive development, as well as an adaptive and prospective profile. We have considered how different character structures are associated with identifiably different archetypal landscapes. Defining and differentiating these experiences, we have explored how our spirituality may be seen as an emergent dynamic informed by the various attributes that underlie each character structure.

The different archetypal landscapes that underlie our character structures can lead us into spiritual dialogue or can become consolidated defensively. A schizoid character structure may lead a person, for example, towards the experience of an inspiring image of an ordered universe, or it may become defensively consolidated into the haunting experience of the icy grip of the Snow Queen. Meanwhile, a borderline character structure may lead a person towards an experience of an ecstatic union with the divine or it may become defensively consolidated into a lifetime of being battered by archetypal affects. A psychopathic character structure may lead a person towards a realization of having a meaningful place in the great rounds of life and death or it may become defensively consolidated into an unconscious seductive and manipulative use of others, fueled by the harsh demands of the archetypal predator.

Demons that appear to be only persecutory and pathological can become important guides to our connection with sacred realms. Individual suffering is connected to universal or larger themes. It is not individual pathology versus divine drama; it is individual pathology as a manifestation of and interaction with divine drama, appearing in our character structures through the underlying archetypes. There is a cultural and a clinical tendency to miss the divine spark in madness, to miss the sacred in suffering. When we address the "pathological" embodied in the rigidity and inflexibility of our character structures, we encourage the emergence of an unobstructed dialogue between the ego and the Self. We invite our humble human being, as vessel, to hold the Self.

In the Introduction, and throughout this work, we have talked about the Self as the holy of holies, the unnamable creator, our psychic core, although we have also noted that it is not definable, not nameable, certainly not a "thing." Schenk captures this poetically when he writes that Self "is the revealing and concealing of imaginal presence giving space its visibility and time its voice. Self becomes a moment of encounter, the self-awareness of a world opening itself as event living us and receding from us at once" (2001: 146). Self, as a "moment of encounter," finds its way, as sparks of madness, into our lives through our character structures.

As we have considered each character structure, our intent has been to "call out the names" so as to enable us all to strengthen our capacity for dialogue – dialogue between the ego and the Self, as well as dialogues between each other, individually and in community. Holding the image of "calling out the names," we are reminded of *Tehanu*, Ursula Le Guinn's tale of redemption that informs us about the gifts from the "Otherworld" (LeGuin 1990). In this metaphorical tale, we learn about a mystic or prophet's potential to contribute to the evolution of culture.

Tehanu is an orphan, partially blinded and crippled, who is taunted and shunned by many. She is an abandoned, wounded, and withdrawn child who eventually, with much struggle and courage, is able to form a healing bond with a shamaness. The state of her country has reached a precarious balance between the forces of life and death; nothing is growing, no new life is born. No heads of state, no religious leaders, no one can be found who can tap into a greater source of wisdom. There seems no hope for survival; no show of force, no ideas, no inspirations, no inventions, no prayers or appeals, seem sufficient to avert this crisis. Something other is needed. Someone "Other" is needed.

Tehanu has endured her sufferings and isolation, and has traveled into the depths that were hers to travel. While she was in this place of mystery, she learned how to call the ancient ones, "the great winged ones," the dragons. At a time when no hope or future seems possible for the world, she goes to the edge of a high cliff that hovers over a great abyss. Using the connections she has formed in the deepest wellsprings of her soul, she calls into the winds and evokes the spirits of the world's elders. Speaking in the dragon's own tongue, she calls him, by name; "Kalessin!" The ancient one arrives amidst "a roaring fire, the rattle of mail and the hiss of wind upraised in great wings, the clash of his talons like scythe blades on the rock." With the mystical powers of the primitive and the elders, Kalessin delivers the balm into her hands, new information and inspiration, which restores life's balance. How and when this balm is used is a human task.

As we become able to consciously meet, relate to, and dialogue with the immense void and chaos of the archetypal realms, we may emerge with the pearl of great price. When no longer possessed by the unconscious, we can come into dialogue with the Self and bring the fruits of these realms into life on earth. Like Tehanu, we can learn a new language, discover a new paradigm, become a source of inspiration or evolution that can be a treasure for the culture at large. The true gifts of the unconscious are hard won; revelations of the *mysterium tremendem* are more than most can bear. Yet a person who has come into an integration of mind, body, and heart may be blessed with inspiration that infuses her own creative work with an energetic mystery and brings a necessary vision to the world.

We'd like to conclude this work with "The Northumbrian Sequence," written by British mystic poet Kathleen Raine in the early 1950s.[2] Raine is an artist whose work is said to be reminiscent of early William Blake. She was deeply influenced by Yeats and Jung. Writing in the same period as T.S. Eliot, she takes a stand against The Waste Land by asking us to enter into it. She explores harrowing landscapes of psychic pain as a springboard to the universal.

Northumbrian Sequence, 4

Let in the wind
Let in the rain
Let in the moors tonight.

The storm beats on my window-pane,
Night stands at my bed-foot,
Let in the fear, Let in the pain, Let in the trees that toss and groan,
Let in the north tonight.

Let in the nameless formless power
That beats upon my door,
Let in the ice, let in the snow,
The banshee howling on the moor,
The bracken-bush on the bleak hillside,
Let in the dead tonight.

The whistling ghost behind the dyke,
The dead that rot in mire,
Let in the thronging ancestors
The unfulfilled desire,
Let in the wraith of the dead earl,
Let in the unborn tonight.

Let in the cold,
Let in the wet,
Let in the loneliness,
Let in the quick,
Let in the dead,
Let in the unpeopled skies.

Oh how can virgin fingers weave a covering for the void,
How can my fearful heart conceive
Gigantic solitude?
How can a house so small contain
A company so great?
Let in the dark,
Let in the dead,
Let in your love tonight.

Let in the snow that numbs the grave,
Let in the acorn tree,
The mountain stream and mountain stone,
Let in the bitter sea.

Fearful is my virgin heart
And frail my human form,
And must I then take pity on
The raging of the storm

That rose up from the great abyss
Before the earth was made,
That pours the stars in cataracts
And shakes this violent world?

Let in the fire,
Let in the power,
Let in the invading might.

Gentle must my fingers be
And pitiful my heart
Since I must bind in human form
A living power so great,
A living impulse great and wild
That cries about my house
With all the violence of desire
Desiring this my peace.

Pitiful my heart must hold
The lonely stars at rest,
Have pity on the raven's cry
The torrent and the eagle's wing,
The icy water of the tarn
And on the biting blast,

Let in the wound,
Let in the pain,
Let in your child tonight.
            (Kathleen Raine, *The Collected Poems of Kathleen Raine* 2000)

It is our desire for this work that by increasing our ability to enter into the realms of each character structure, we ourselves and each of you may be more able to be deeply present, to call out the names – and then enter the nameless.

Notes

1 Soul may be image, but soul is not *only* image. In addition to its residence in our bodies, affects and imagination, the soul is inherent in reason and logic. Jungian analyst Wolfgang Giegerich articulates this important, and for some of us, central point in our individuation, in his work *The Soul's Logical Life: Towards a Rigorous Notion of Psychology* (2005, New Orleans LA: Spring Journal Books).
2 "Northumbrian Sequence, 4" is printed by permission of the Estate of Kathleen Raine from *The Collected Poems of Kathleen Raine* (2000, Ipswich: Golgonooza Press).

Bibliography

Akhtar, S. (1992) *Broken Structures: Severe Personality Disorders and their Treatment*, Northvale, NJ: Jason Aronson.

American Medical Association (1997) 'Structured Clinical Interview with Antisocial Personality,' in *DSM4 User's Guide for the Structured Clinical Interview for DSM4 Axis 2, SCID-II*, Washington, DC: American Psychiatric Press, p. 28.

American Medical Association (2003) *Physician ICD-9 CM2003: International Classification of Diseases*, Hyattsville, MD: NCHS.

American Psychiatric Association (1968) *Diagnostic and Statistical Manual of Mental Disorders*, 2nd edition (*DSM-II*), Washington, DC: American Psychiatric Press.

American Psychiatric Association (1980) *Diagnostic and Statistical Manual of Mental Disorders*, 3rd edition (*DSM III*), Washington, DC: American Psychiatric Press.

American Psychiatric Association (1994) *Diagnostic and Statistical Manual of Mental Disorders*, 4th edition (*DSM IV*), Washington, DC: American Psychiatric Press.

American Psychiatric Association (2000) *Diagnostic and Statistical Manual of Mental Disorders*, 4th edition, *Text Revision* (*DSM IV-TR*), Washington, DC: American Psychiatric Press.

Andersen, H.C. (1976) *Hans Christian Andersen: Eighty Fairy Tales*, New York: Pantheon.

Balint, M. (1968) *The Basic Fault: The Therapeutic Aspects of Regression*, Evanston, IL: Northwestern University Press.

Baring, A. and Cashford, J. (1991) *The Myth of the Goddess: Evolution of an Image*, London: Viking Arkana.

Barrie, J.M. (1991) *Peter Pan*, New York: Viking.

Beatty, J.S. and Kraul, E.G. (eds) (2004) *La Llorona: Encounters With the Weeping Woman*, Santa Fe, NM: Sunstone Press.

Beck, A.T., Freeman, A. and Davis, D. (2003) *Cognitive Therapy of Personality Disorders*, 2nd edn, New York: Guilford Press.

Benjamin, L.S. (1993) *Interpersonal Diagnosis and Treatment of Personality Disorders*, New York: Guilford Press. Second edition 1996.

Benjamin, L.S. (1996) 'An interpersonal theory of personality disorders,' in J.F.

Clarkin and J.F. Lenzenweger (eds) *Major Theories of Personality Disorder*, New York: Guilford Press.

Bernstein, J. (2005) *Living in the Borderland: The Evolution of Consciousness and the Challenge of Healing Trauma*, London: Routledge.

Bion, W. (1950) 'Attacks on Linking,' W. Bion, *Second Thoughts*, New York: Jason Aronson, 1967.

Bion, W. (1967) *Bion, Second Thoughts*, New York: Jason Aronson.

Bleuler, E. (1922) 'Die probleme der Schizoidie und der Syntonie,' Zeitschrift fuer die gesamte *Neurologie und Psychiatrie* 78: 373–88.

Bleuler, E. (1929) 'Syntonie-schizoidie-schizophrenie,' *Neurologie und Psychopathologie* 38: 47–64.

Boer, C. (trans.) (1970) *The Homeric Hymns*, Dallas, TX: Spring Publications.

Bolen, J. (1984) *Goddesses in Everywoman: A New Psychology of Women*, New York: Harper & Row.

Bolen, J. (1990) *Gods in Everyman Reissue: Archetypes That Shape Men's Lives*, New York: Harper.

Bollas, C. (2000) *Hysteria*, London: Routledge.

Borossa, J. (2001) *Hysteria*, Cambridge: Icon Books.

Bowlby, J. (1969) *Attachment and Loss: Vol. 1. Attachment*, New York: Basic Books.

Bowlby, J. (1973) *Attachment and Loss: Vol. 2. Separation: Anxiety and Anger*, New York: Basic Books.

Bowlby, J. (1988) *A Secure Base: Clinical Applications of Attachment Theory*, London: Routledge.

Briggs, K. (1970) *A Dictionary of British Folk Tales*, Bloomington: Indiana University Press.

Bursten, B. (1972) 'The Manipulative Personality,' *Archives of General Psychiatry* 26: 318–21.

Bursten, B. (1973) *The Manipulator*, New Haven: Yale University Press.

Cahill, T. (2004) *Sailing the Wine-Dark Sea: Why the Greeks Matter*, New York: Anchor Books.

Calasso, R. (1993) *The Marriage of Cadmus and Harmony*, New York: Vintage.

Carroll, L. (1907) *Alice's Adventures in Wonderland*, New York: Gramercy Press, 1995.

Cleckly, H. (1976) *The Mask of Sanity: An Attempt to Clarify Some Issues About the So-Called Psychopathic Personality*, St. Louis, MS: Mosby.

Corbin, H. (1972) *Mundus Imaginalis, or the Imaginary and the Imaginal*, Dallas, TX: Spring Books.

Donahue, B. (Speaker) (September 1995) 'Why didn't she knock on the door?,' New York: National Meeting of Jungian Analysts, cited with permission of the author.

Dougherty, N. and West, J. (2005) 'Dismemberment and anxiety: anxieties at the edge,' paper presented at the North American Conference of Jungian Analysts, *At the Edge Between Hope and Despair: Confronting Cultural, Political, and Clinical Dilemmas through Analytical Psychology*, Chicago, 22–25 September.

Downing, C. (1987) *The Goddess: Mythological Images of the Feminine*, New York: Crossroads.

Downing, C. (1993) *Gods in Our Midst: Mythological Images of the Masculine, A Woman's View*, New Orleans: Spring Journal Books.

D'Silva, K., Duggan, C. and McCarthy, L. (2004) 'Does treatment really make psychopaths worse? A review of the evidence,' *Journal of Personality Disorders* 18: 163–77.

Edelman, S. (1998) *Turning the Gorgon: A Meditation on Shame*, Putnam, CT: Spring Publications.

Edinger, E. (1972) *Ego and Archetype*, New York: Putnam.

Eigen, M. (1986) *The Psychotic Core*, Northvale, NJ: Jason Aronson.

Euripides (1998) *Medea, Hippolytus, Electra, Helen*, Oxford: Oxford University Press.

Euripides (1999) "The Bacchae," in D. Grene and R. Lattimore (eds), W. Arrowsmith (trans.) *The Complete Greek Tragedies*, Chicago: University of Chicago Press.

Fairbairn, W.R.D. (1954) *An Object Relations Theory of the Personality*, New York: Basic Books.

Faulkner, R. (trans.) (1969) *The Ancient Egyptian Pyramid Texts, translated into English*, Oxford: Oxford University Press.

Fenichel, O. (1945) *The Psychoanalytic Theory of Neurosis*, New York: Norton.

Ferenczi, S. (1925) 'Character and anal eroticism,' *Psychoanalysis of Sexual Habits*, New York: Brunner/Mazel, 1980.

Fonagy, P. (2001) *Attachment Theory and Psychoanalysis*, New York: Other Press.

Fontenrose, J. (1959) *Python: A Study in Delphic Myth and its Origins*, Berkeley: University of California Press. Republished as *The Delphic Oracle*, Berkeley and Los Angeles: University of California Press, 1978.

Fordham, M. (1957) *New Developments in Analytical Psychology*, London: Routledge, Kegan & Paul.

Fordham, M. (1974) 'Defenses of the self,' *Journal of Analytical Psychology* 19, 2: 192–99.

Fossati, A., Maffei, C., Bagnato, M., Donati, D., Donini, M., Fiorilli, M. and Novella, L. (2000) 'A psychometric study of DSM-IV passive-aggressive (negativistic) personality disorder criteria,' *Journal of Personality Disorder* 14, 1: 72–83.

Freud, S. (1914) 'On narcissism: an introduction,' *Collected Papers*, English translation, vol. 4, London: Hogarth Press, 1935.

Frosch, J.P. (1983) 'The treatment of antisocial and borderline personality disorders,' *Hospital Community Psychiatry* 34: 243–8.

Gabbard, G.O. (2005) *Psychodynamic Psychiatry in Clinical Practice*, Arlington, VA: American Psychiatric Publishing.

Gabbard, G.O. and Coyne, L. (1987) 'Predictors of response of antisocial patients to hospital treatment,' *Hospital Community Psychiatry* 38: 1181–5.

Gabbard, G.O. and Menninger, R.W. (1988) 'The psychology of the physician,' in G.O. Gabbard and R.W. Menninger (eds) *Medical Marriages*, Washington, DC: American Psychiatric Press.

Gabbard, G.O. and Wilkinson, S.M. (1994) *Management of Countertransference with Borderline Patients*, Northvale, NJ: Jason Aronson.

Gell-Mann, M. (1994) 'Complex adaptive systems,' in G.A. Cowan, D. Pines and D. Meltzer (eds) *Complexity, Models, Metaphors, and Reality*, Reading, MA: Addison-Wesley.

Gibbon, M.B., Spitzer, R.L., Williams, J.B.W. and Benjamin, L.S. (1997) *DSM IV*

User's Guide for the Structured Clinical Interview for DSM IV Axis II Personality Disorders (SCID-II), Washington, DC: American Psychiatric Press.

Giegerich, W. (2005) *The Soul's Logical Life: Towards a Rigorous Notion of Psychology*, New Orleans: Spring Journal Books.

Girl Interrupted (1999) film by James Mangold, Columbia Pictures.

Glickauf-Hughes, C. and Wells, M. (1998) *Object Relations Psychotherapy: An Individualized and Interactive Approach to Diagnosis and Treatment*, Northvale, NJ: Jason Aronson.

Goldstein, W. (1996) *Dynamic Psychotherapy with the Borderline Patient*, Northvale, NJ: Jason Aronson.

Grand, S. (2000) *The Reproduction of Evil: A Clinical and Cultural Perspective*, Hillsdale, NJ and London: Analytic Press.

Grant, B.F., Hasin, D.S., Stinson, F.S., Dawson, D.A., Chon, S.P., Ruan, W.J. and Pickering, R.P. (2004) 'Prevalence, correlates and disability of personality disorders in the United States: results from the national epidemiologic survey on alcohol and related conditions,' *Journal of Clinical Psychiatry* 65, 7: 948–58.

Graves, R. (1955) *The Greek Myths*, vols 1 and 2, Harmondsworth: Penguin.

Greenwald, H. (1974) 'Treatment of the psychopath,' in H. Greenwald (ed.) *Active Psychotherapy*, New York: Jason Aronson.

Grimm, J. and W. (1972) *The Complete Grimm's Fairy Tales*, New York: Random House.

Grotstein, J. (1982) 'Newer perspectives in object relations theory,' *Journal of Contemporary Psychoanalysis* 18: 43–91.

Gunderson, J.G. (1984) *Borderline Personality Disorder*, Washington, DC: American Psychiatric Press.

Guntrip, H. (1969) *Schizoid Phenomena, Object Relations, and the Self*, New York: International Universities Press.

Guntrip, H. (1971) *Psychoanalytic Theory, Therapy, and the Self: A Basic Guide to the Human Personality in Freud, Erikson, Klein, Sullivan, Fairbarn, Hartmann, Jacobson, and Winnicott*, New York: Basic Books.

Guthrie, W.K.C. (1980) *The Greeks and Their Gods*, Boston: Beacon Press.

Halleck, S.L. (1981) 'Sociopathy: ethical aspects of diagnosis and treatment,' *Current Psychiatric Therapy* 20: 167.

Hamilton, E. (1940) *Mythology: Timeless Tales of Gods and Heroes*, New York: New American Library.

Hare, R. (1986) 'Twenty years of experience with the Cleckley psychopath,' in W. Reid, D. Dorr, J. Walker and J. Bonner (eds) *Unmasking the Psychopath: Antisocial Personality and Related Syndromes*, New York: Norton.

Hare, R.D. and Hart, S.D. (1998) 'Association between psychopathy and narcissism: theoretical views and empirical evidence,' in E. Ronningham (ed.) *Disorders of Narcissism: Diagnosis, Clinical, and Empirical Implications*, Washington, DC: American Psychiatric Press.

Harris, A. (2005) *Gender as Soft Assembly*, Hillsdale, NJ: Analytic Press.

Harris, J.C. and Chase, R. (2002) *The Complete Tales of Uncle Remus*, New York: Houghton Mifflin.

Hart, D.L. (2001) *The Water of Life: Spiritual Renewal in the Fairy Tale*, Lanham, MD: University Press of America.

Heylighen, F., Joslyn, C. and Turchin, V. (eds) *Principia Cybernetica*. Online.

Brussels: Principia Cybernetica Project. Available HTTP: http://pespmc1.vu-b.ac.be/ (accessed: 21 October 2005).

Hillman, J. (1972) *The Myth of Analysis*, Evanston, IL: Northwestern University Press.

Hillman, J. (1979) *Puer Papers*, Dallas, TX: Spring Publications.

Hillman, J. (1983) *Interviews*, New York: Harper & Row.

Hillman, J. (1999) *The Force of Character and the Lasting Life*, New York: Random House.

Hinshelwood, R. (1991) *A Dictionary of Kleinian Thought*, London: Free Association Books.

Hoch, A. (1910) 'Constitutional factors in the dementia praecox group,' *Review of Neurology and Psychiatry* 8: 463–75.

Hogenson, G. (2004) 'Archetypes: emergence and the psyche's deep structure,' in J. Cambray and L. Carter (eds) *Contemporary Perspectives in Jungian Analysis*, London: Brunner Routledge.

Horner, A. (1991) *Psychoanalytic Object Relations Therapy*, Northvale, NJ: Jason Aronson.

Horney, K. (1939) *Neurosis and Human Growth*, New York: Norton.

Horney, K. (1945) *Our Inner Conflicts*, New York: Norton.

Horowitz, M.J. (1991) *Hysterical Personality Style and the Hystrionic Personality Disorder*, Northvale, NJ: Jason Aronson.

House of Games (1987) film by David Mamet, Metro-Goldwyn-Mayer.

The Jerusalem Bible (1966) Garden City, NY: Doubleday.

The Jerusalem Bible (King James Version, 1611) Philadelphia: National Publishing Company, 2000.

Johnson, S. (1985) *Characterological Transformation: The Hard Work Miracle*, New York: Norton.

Josephs, L. (1995) *Character and Self Experience*, Northvale, NJ: Jason Aronson.

Jung, C.G. (1909) *The Psychology of Dementia Praecox, Collected Works 3*.

Jung, C.G. (1919) *Instinct and the Unconscious, Collected Works 8*.

Jung, C.G. (1926) *Spirit and Life, Collected Works 8*.

Jung, C.G. (1928) *Analytical Psychology and 'Weltanschauung,' Collected Works 8*.

Jung, C.G. (1933) *The Spiritual Problem of Modern Man, Collected Works 10*.

Jung, C.G. (1935) *The Relations Between the Ego and the Unconscious, Collected Works 7*.

Jung, C.G. (1943) *Psychology and Alchemy, Collected Works 12*.

Jung, C.G. (1945) *The Relations Between the Ego and the Unconscious, Collected Works 7*.

Jung, C.G. (1947) *Epilogue To Essays on Contemporary Events, Collected Works 10*.

Jung, C.G. (1953) *The Collected Works* (Bollingen Series XX). Trans. R.F.C. Hull, H. Read, M. Fordham and G. Adler (eds) Princeton, NJ: Princeton University Press, 20 vols.

Jung, C.G. (1955) *The Conjunction, Collected Works 14*.

Jung, C.G. (1956a) *Symbols of Transformation, Collected Works 5*.

Jung, C.G. (1956b) *On the Psychology of the Trickster-Figure, Collected Works 9 I*.

Jung, C.G. (1958) *The Psychogenesis of Mental Disease, Collected Works 3*.

Jung, C.G. (1960) *The Structure and Dynamics of the Psyche, Collected Works 8*.

Jung, C.G. (1963a) *Memories, Dreams, and Reflections*, London: Collins, Routledge, Kegan & Paul.

Jung, C.G. (1963b) *Mysterium Coniunctionis, Collected Works 10*.

Jung, C.G. (1968a) *Psychology and Alchemy, Second Edition, Collected Works 12*.

Jung, C.G (1968b) *The Tavistock Lectures, Collected Works 18*.

Kalsched, D. (1980) 'Narcissism and the search for interiority,' *Quadrant* 13, 2: 46–74.

Kalsched, D. (1996) *The Inner World of Trauma: Archetypal Defenses of the Personal Spirit*, London and New York: Routledge.

Kalsched, D. (2003) 'Daimonic elements in early trauma,' *Journal of Analytical Psychology* 48, 2: 145–69.

Kerényi, K. (1962) *The Heroes of the Greeks*, New York: Thames and Hudson.

Kerényi, K. (1972) 'Commentary on the trickster,' in P. Radin *The Trickster: A Study in American Indian Mythology*, New York: Schocken.

Kerényi, K. (1976) *Dionysus: Archetypal Image of the Indestructible Life*, Princeton, NJ: Princeton University Press.

Kerényi, K. (1978) *Athene: Virgin and Mother in Greek Religion*, Putnam, CT: Spring Publications.

Kerényi, K. (1983) *Apollo: The Wind, the Spirit, and the God, Four Studies*, Dallas, TX: Spring Publications.

Kerényi, K. (1996) *Hermes: Guide of Souls*, Putnam, CT: Spring Publications.

Kernberg, O. (1970) 'Factors in the treatment of narcissistic personalities,' *Journal of the American Psychoanalytic Association* 18: 51–85.

Kernberg, O. (1975) *Borderline Conditions and Pathological Narcissism*, Northvale, NJ: Jason Aronson.

Kernberg, O. (1984) *Severe Personality Disorders: Psychotherapeutic Strategies*, New Haven: Yale University Press. (Reprint edition 1993.)

Klein, M. (1946) 'Notes on some schizoid mechanisms,' *International Journal of Psychoanalysis* 27: 99–110. Republished in *Melanie Klein, Paula Heimann, Susan Issacs, and Joan Riviere: Developments in psychoanalysis*, New York: Hogarth, 1952.

Klein, M. (1957) *Envy and Gratitude and Other Works 1946–1963*, New York: Free Press.

Knox, J. (2004) *Archetypes, Analysis, Attachment*, London: Routledge.

Kohut, H. (1971) *The Analysis of the Self: Systematic Approach to Treatment of Narcissistic Personality Disorders*, New York: International Universities Press.

Kohut, H. (1977) *The Restoration of the Self*, New York: International Universities Press.

Kohut, H. (1984) *How Does Analysis Cure?*, A. Goldberg (ed.), Chicago: University of Chicago Press.

Komor, C. (2000) *OCD and Other Gods*, Grand Rapids, MI: Self Help Books.

Kraepelin, E. (1913) *Psychiatrie: Ein Lehr*, Leipzig: Barth, 8th edn, as cited in Millon 1981.

Lasch, C. (1978) *The Culture of Narcissism: American Life in an Age of Diminishing Expectations*, New York: Norton.

LeGuin, U. (1990) *Tehanu: The Last Book of Earthsea*, New York: Atheneum.

Leonard, L.S. (1985) *The Wounded Woman, Healing the Father–Daughter Relationship*, Boston: Shambala Press.

Leonard, L.S. (1993) *Meeting the Madwoman: Empowering the Feminine Spirit*, New York: Bantam.

Lester, J. (1987) *The Tales of Uncle Remus: The Adventures of Brer Rabbit*, New York: Puffin.

Lewis, C.S. (1980) *Till We Have Faces: A Myth Retold*, San Diego: Harcourt Brace Jovanovich.

Likierman, M. (2001) *Melanie Klein: Her Work in Context*, London and New York: Continuum.

McCullough, P.K. and Maltsberger, J.T. (2001) 'Obsessive-compulsive personality disorder,' in G.O. Gabbard (ed.) *Treatments of Psychiatric Disorders*, vol. 2, 3rd edn, Washington, DC: American Psychiatric Publishing.

McDowell, M. (2001) 'Principles of organization: a dynamic systems view of the archetype-as-such,' *Journal of Analytical Psychology* 46, 4: 637–54.

McGrew, L. (1988) 'Shame: the paralysis of feminine initiative, an analysis of the Athene/Persephone woman,' unpublished thesis, C.G. Jung Institute of Chicago, cited with the kind permission of the author.

McWilliams, N. (1994) *Psychoanalytic Diagnosis: Understanding Personality Structure in the Clinical Process*, New York: Guilford Press.

Mahler, M., Pine, F. and Bergman, A. (1975) *The Psychological Birth of the Human Infant: Symbiosis and Individuation*, New York: Basic Books.

Marlan, S. (2005) *The Black Sun: The Alchemy and Art of Darkness*, College Station: Texas A & M University Press.

Masterson, J.F. (1976) *Psychotherapy of the Borderline Adult: A Developmental Approach*, New York: Brunner/Mazel.

Masterson, J. (1981) *The Narcissistic and Borderline Disorders: An Integrated Developmental Perspective*, New York: Brunner/Mazel.

Masterson, J. (1988) *The Search for the Real Self: Unmasking the Personality Disorders of Our Age*, New York: Free Press.

Maturana, H. and Varela, F. (1991) *Autopoiesis and Cognition: The Realization of the Living*, Dordecht: Reidel.

Meloy, J.R. (1988) *The Psychopathic Mind: Origins, Dynamics, and Treatment*, Northvale, NJ: Jason Aronson.

Meloy, J.R. (1995) 'Antisocial personality disorder,' in G.O. Gabbard (ed.) *Treatments of Psychiatric Disorders*, vol. 2, 2nd edn, Washington, DC: American Psychiatric Press.

Meloy, J.R. (ed.) (2001) *The Mark of Cain: Psychoanalytic Insight and the Psychopath*, Hillsdale, NJ: Analytic Press.

Meltzer, D., Bremner, J., Hoxter, S., Weddell, D. and Wittenberg, I. (1975) *Explorations in Autism*, Perthshire, Scotland: Clunie Press.

Merkur, D. (1991) *Powers Which We Do Not Know: The Gods and Spirits of the Inuit*, Moskow: University of Idaho Press.

Miller, A. (1975) *Prisoners of Childhood: The Drama of the Gifted Child and the Search for the True Self*, New York: Basic Books.

Millon, T. (1981) *Disorders of Personality: DSM-III: Axis II*, New York: Wiley.

Millon, T. (1998) *Psychopathy: Antisocial, Criminal, and Violent Behavior*, New York: Guilford Press.

Millon, T. (2000) *Personality Disorders in Modern Life*, Hoboken, NJ: Wiley, 2nd edn 2004.

Millon, T. and Davis, R.D. (eds) (1996) *Disorders of Personality: DSM-IV and Beyond*, 2nd edn, New York: Wiley.

Millon, T. and Radovanov, J. (1995) 'Passive-aggressive (negativistic) personality disorder,' in W.J. Livesley *The DSM-IV Personality Disorders*, New York: Guilford Press.

Mitrani, J. (2001) *Ordinary People and Extra-Ordinary Protections: A Post Kleinian Approach to the Treatment of Primitive Mental States*, London: Brunner-Routledge.

Moctezuma, E.M. (1992) *The Great Temple: Official Guide*, Mexico City: Inah-Salvat.

Modlin, L.C. (1983) 'The antisocial personality,' *Bulletin Menninger Clinic* 47: 129–44.

Mogenson, G. (2003) *The Dove in the Consulting Room*, London: Routledge.

Neumann, E. (1954) *The Origins and History of Consciousness*, Princeton: Princeton University Press.

Neumann, E. (1963) *The Great Mother: An Analysis of the Archetype*, Princeton, NJ: Bollingen.

Ogden, T. (1986) *The Matrix of the Mind: Object Relations and the Psychoanalytic Dialogue*, Northvale, NJ: Jason Aronson.

Ogden, T. (1994) *The Primitive Edge of Experience*, Northvale, NJ: Jason Asonson.

Oldham, J.M. and Morris, L.B. (1990) *The Personality Self Portrait*, New York: Bantam.

Otto, R. (1923) *The Idea of the Holy: An Inquiry into the Non Rational Factor in the Idea of the Divine and its Relation to the Rational*, Oxford: Oxford University Press.

Otto, W. (1964) *The Homeric Gods*, Boston: Beacon Press.

Otto, W. (1981) *Dionysus: Myth and Cult*, Dallas, TX: Spring Publications.

Paris, G. (1986) *Pagan Meditations: The Worlds of Aphrodite, Artemis, and Hestia*, Dallas, TX: Spring Publications.

Perry, J. and Christopher, M. (1996) 'Dependent Personality Disorder,' in G.O. Gabbard and S. Atkinson (eds) *Synopsis of Treatment of Psychiatric Disorders*, 2nd edn, Washington, DC: American Psychiatric Press.

Pinkola Estés, C. (1992) *Women Who Run With the Wolves: Myths and Stories of the Wild Woman Archetype*, New York: Ballantine.

Pipher, M. (1994) *Reviving Ophelia: Saving the Selves of Adolescent Girls*, New York: G.P. Putnam's Sons.

Power, M. (1999) 'Dreaming the M.C. is a Raven,' *Atlantic Review* 11, 2. With the kind permission of the author.

Pratt, A. (1994) *Dancing With Goddesses: Archetypes, Poetry, and Empowerment*, Bloomington, IN: Indiana University Press.

Radin, P. (1972) *The Trickster: A Study in American Indian Mythology, with Commentaries by Karl Kerenyi and C.G. Jung*, New York: Schocken.

Raine, K. (2000) *The Collected Poems of Kathleen Raine*, Ipswich: Golgonooza Press.

Reich, W. (1933, 1949) *Character-Analysis*, New York: Farrar, Strauss, Giroux. Third edition 1980.

Reid, W.H., Dorr, D., Walker, J. and Bonner, J. (1986) *Unmasking the Psychopath*, New York: Norton.

Rodgers, P. (2005) 'Book review of G. Mogenson (2003) *The Dove in the Consulting Room: Hysteria and the Anima in Bollas and Jung*, Hove, UK: Brunner-Routledge,' in *Journal of Analytical Psychology* 50: 107–9.

Salman, S. (1999) 'Dissociation and the self in the magical pre-Oedipal field,' *Journal of Analytical Psychology* 44: 69–85.

Samuels, A. (ed.) (1991) *Psychopathology: Contemporary Jungian Perspectives*, New York: Guilford Press.

Satinover, J. (1980) 'Puer aeternus: the narcissistic relation to the self,' *Quadrant* 13, 2: 75–108.

Schapira, L.L. (1988) *The Cassandra Complex: Living With Disbelief, a Modern Perspective on Hysteria*, Toronto: Inner City Books.

Schenk, R. (2001) *The Sunken Fish, the Wasted Fisher, the Pregnant Fish: Postmodern Reflections on Depth Psychology*, Wilmette, IL: Chiron.

Schore, A.N. (1994) *Affect Regulation and the Origin of the Self: The Neurobiology of Emotional Development*, Hillsdale, NJ: Lawrence Erlbaum Associates, Inc.

Schore, A.N. (1997) 'Early organization of the nonlinear right brain and development of a predisposition to psychiatric disorders,' *Development and Psychopathology* 9: 595–631.

Schore, A.N. (2003a) *Affect Dysregulation and Disorders of the Self*, New York: Norton.

Schore, A.N. (2003b) *Affect Regulation and Repair of the Self*, New York: Norton.

Schore, A.N (2003c) 'Early relational trauma, disorganized attachment, and the development of a predisposition to violence,' in M.F. Solomon and D.J. Siegal (eds) *Healing Trauma: Attachment, Mind, Body, and Brain*, New York: Norton.

Schwartz-Salant, N. (1982) *Narcissism and Character Transformation: The Psychology of Narcissistic Character Disorders*, Toronto: Inner City Books.

Schwartz-Salant, N. (1989) *The Borderline Personality: Vision and Healing*, Chicago: Chiron.

Searles, H. (1986) *My Work With Borderline Patients*, Northvale, NJ: Jason Aronson.

Seinfeld, J. (1990) *The Bad Object*: Handling the Negative Therapeutic Reaction in Psychotherapy, Northvale, NJ: Jason Aronson.

Seinfeld, J. (1996) *Containing Rage, Terror, and Despair: An Object Relations Approach to Psychotherapy*, Northvale, NJ: Jason Aronson.

Showalter, E. (1998) *Hystories: Hysterical Epidemics and Modern Media*, New York: Columbia University Press.

Shulman, H. (1997) *Living at the Edge of Chaos: Complex Systems in Culture and Psyche*, Einsiedlen: Daimon.

Siegel, D.J. (1999) *The Developing Mind: Towards a Neurobiology of Interpersonal Experience*, New York: Guilford Press.

Siegel, D.J. (2003) 'An interpersonal neurobiology of psychotherapy: the developing mind and the resolution of trauma,' In M.F. Solomon and D.J. Siegal (eds) *Healing Trauma: Attachment, Mind, Body, and Brain*, New York: Norton.

Solomon, M.F and Siegel, D.J. (eds) (2003) *Healing Trauma: Attachment, Mind, Body, and Brain*, New York: Norton.

Spensley, S. (1995) *Frances Tustin*, London: Routledge.

Sperry, L. (1995) *Handbook of Diagnosis and Treatment of the DSM-IV Personality Disorders*, New York: Brunner/Mazel.

Sperry, L. and Carlson, J. (1993) *Psychopathology and Psychotherapy: From Diagnosis to Treatment*, Muncie, IN: Accelerated Development.

Steel, F. (1994) 'The Three Little Pigs,' in *Goldilocks and the Three Bears and Other Classic English Fairy Tales*, New York: Children's Classics.

Stein, L. (1967) 'Introducing not-self,' *Journal of Analytical Psychology* 12, 2: 97–113.

Stein, M. (1998) *Jung's Map of the Soul: An Introduction*, Chicago and La Salle, IL: Open Court.

Stern, D. (1985) *The Interpersonal World of the Infant: A View from Psychoanalysis and Developmental Psychology*, New York: Basic Books.

Stolorow, R.D., Atwood, G.E. and Brandschaft, B. (eds) (1994) *The Intersubjective Perspective*, Northvale, NJ: Jason Aronson.

Sullivan, L.E. (1987) 'Tricksters: an overview,' in M. Eliade (ed.) *Encyclopedia of Religion*, New York: Macmillan.

Symington, N. (1980) 'The response aroused by the psychopath,' *International Review of Psychoanalysis* 7: 291–8.

Travers, P.L. (1989) *What the Bee Knows: Reflections on Myth, Symbol and Story*, London and New York: Arkana.

Tuckett, D. (1993) 'Some thoughts on the presentation and discussion of the clinical material of psychoanalysis,' *International Journal of Psychoanalysis* 74: 1175–89.

Tustin, F. (1990) *The Protective Shell in Children and Adults*, London: Karnac.

Van der Kolk, B., McFarlane, A. and Weisaeth, L. (1996) *Traumatic Stress: The Effects of Overwhelming Experience on Mind, Body, and Society*, New York: Guilford Press.

Van Sweden, R.C. (1995) *Regression to Dependence: A Second Opportunity for Ego Integration and Developmental Progression*, Northvale, NJ: Jason Aronson.

Von Franz, M.L. (1981) *Puer Aeternus*, 2nd edn. Santa Monica, CA: Sigo Press.

Von Franz, M.L. (2000) *The Problems of the Puer Aeturnus*, Toronto: Inner City Books.

Webster's New Universal Unabridged Dictionary (1983) New York: Simon and Schuster.

Widiger, T. and Lynam, D. (1998) 'Psychopathy and the five-factor model of personality,' in T. Millon, E. Somonsen, M. Birket-Smith and R. Davis (eds) *Psychopathy: Antisocial, Criminal, and Violent Behavior*, New York: Guilford Press.

Wilkinson, M. (2003) 'Undoing trauma: contemporary neuroscience: a Jungian clinical perspective,' *Journal of Analytical Psychology* 48: 235–53.

Wilkinson, M. (2005) 'Undoing dissociation: affective neuroscience: a contemporary Jungian clinical perspective, *Journal of Analytical Psychology* 50: 483–501.

Winnicott, D.W. (1958) *Through Paediatrics to Psychoanalysis*, London: Tavistock.

Winnicott, D.W. (1960) 'Ego distortion in terms of the true and false self,' in D.W. Winnicott (1965) *The Maturational Processes and the Facilitating Environment*, London: Hogarth Press.

Winnicott, D.W. (1965) *The Maturational Processes and the Facilitating Environment*, London: Hogarth Press.

Winnicott, D.W. (1971) *Playing and Reality*, London: Tavistock.

Withers, R. (ed.) (2003) *Controversies in Analytical Psychology*, New York: Brunner-Routledge.

Young-Eisendrath, P. and Weideman, F. (1987) *Female Authority: Empowering Women Through Psychotherapy*, New York: Guilford Press.

Zhang, L., Xing, G.Q., Levine, S., Post, R.M. and Smith, M.A. (1997) 'Maternal deprivation induces neuronal death,' *Society for Neuroscience Abstracts* 23: 1112.

Author index

Subject index

Note: page numbers in **bold** refer to diagrams.

dreams
  archetypal 25, 27
  borderline 122, 124–5
  of counter-dependent narcissists 63,
    64
  of dependent narcissists 141–2, 145,
    146, 148
  hysteric 159–60
  living in 24, 25
  obsessive-compulsive 90, 97, 98, 99
  passive-aggressive 249–51
  schizoid 24–5, 27, 29, 33–5, 44, 48
  sexually violent 141–2
  symbolic 25, 29
drug use 195–6
dyadic to triadic relating 10, 81–3, 159,
  161, 165

earth goddess n6 78
  see also Gaia
earth mother 75
eccentricity 24
ego
  and Aphrodite 175, 176, 177
  archetypal possession/invasion of
    11–12, 18, 27–8, 130–1, 197,
    231
  borderline 108, 111, 112, 114, 117,
    130
  as centre of consciousness 7
  of the counter-dependent narcissist
    62, 65
  creation 67
  defenses of 13, 165, 166
  of the dependent narcissist 136–7,
    138, 139, 148, 153–4
  developed psychopathic 187, 188,
    193–4, 206
  differentiation from the unconscious
    4, 81, 216, 244
    failure 40, 186–7, 190, 237, 240
  domination by the animus 167
  emergence 4
  hysteric 161
  inflated 10, 136
  obsessive-compulsive 79, 82, 90, 93–5,
    101–2
  passive-aggressive 237–8, 255
  of the primal phase 8–9
  psychopathic 186–7, 188, 190, 193–4,
    206
  rigid/weak 18, 41

schizoid 25, 28–30, 34, 36–7, 40–1,
  43–4, 46, 48–9
and the Self 5–6, 7–9, 11, 64
  conflation 13, 136–7, 138, 140, 149,
    152
  differentiation from the 7, 9, 10,
    165
  isolation from the 8, 11
  realignment 14, 15, 18
  in the schizoid personality 28
  strength 36, 37, 161, 237–8, 255
  underdeveloped 28–30, 34, 82, 93–4,
    101, 186–7, 190
ego Self dialogue 148, 153–4, 231–2,
  260–1
ego–Self axis 5–8, 71, 138
  of the alpha narcissist 231
  break along the 11
  of the counter-dependent narcissist
    62
  defensive 10, 11, 13
  of the dependent narcissist 135,
    140
  hysteric 163, 165
  of the obsessive-compulsive 80, 82,
    95
  rigidification 8
  schizoid 28, 41
Egyptian mythology 1, 17, 18
embodiment 37, 44, 47, 49, 81, 208
"emergence" n2 51
empathy 135, 154, 193, 199
  absence of 69, 198
  breakdown of 119
  capacity for 67–8, 70
  parental 66, 67
  therapeutic 67–8
emptiness
  of the counter-dependent narcissist
    53, 55, 58, 65, 68
  obsessive-compulsive 90
  schizoid 24, 25, 33, 34, 38
encapsulation 11, n7 19, 150
  of the counter-dependent narcissist
    54, 57–60, 62–6, 69, 71, 76, 102
  functions of 91
  hysterics and 166
  obsessive-compulsive 79–80, 83, 90–1,
    102
  opening of 30
  schizoid 25, 28, 29, 30, 32–9, 41–2,
    45–9, 102